THE WORLD RECORD

POETRY PARNASSUS

Taking inspiration from Mount Parnassus in Greece, one of poetry's spiritual and mythical heartlands, **Poetry Parnassus** echoes the Epinicians – poetry commissioned as part of the ancient Olympic Games. It also builds on Southbank Centre's biannual Poetry International Festival, inaugurated in 1967 by Ted Hughes. Part of Festival of the World with MasterCard, Poetry Parnassus is one of the projects made possible with additional support from Southbank Centre's key funder Arts Council England. It is part of the London 2012 Festival, a spectacular 12-week nationwide celebration running from 21 June until 9 September 2012 bringing together leading artists from across the world with the very best from the UK. The London 2012 Festival is the finale of the Cultural Olympiad, a four-year programme of cultural events which began in 2008.

Poetry Parnassus was developed by Southbank Centre's Artistic Director Jude Kelly with curator Simon Armitage, and organised by Literature and Spoken Word Coordinator Anna Selby supported by Southbank Centre's literature team.

THE WORLD RECORD

INTERNATIONAL VOICES FROM SOUTHBANK CENTRE'S POETRY PARNASSUS

EDITED BY
NEIL ASTLEY & ANNA SELBY

BLOODAXE BOOKS

ISBN: 978 1 85224 938 0

First published 2012 by
Bloodaxe Books Ltd,
Highgreen,
Tarset,
Northumberland NE48 1RP
in association with
Southbank Centre,
Belvedere Road,
London SE1 8XX.

www.bloodaxebooks.com
For further information about Bloodaxe titles
please visit our website or write to
the above address for a catalogue.

Supported by
ARTS COUNCIL
ENGLAND

Cover design: Neil Astley & Pamela Robertson-Pearce.

Printed in Great Britain by
Bell & Bain Limited, Glasgow, Scotland.

CONTENTS

INTRODUCTION

For the three years leading up to the summer of 2012 I worked as a visiting Artist in Residence at London's Southbank Centre, quite possibly the world's largest arts complex, whose characterless, concrete exterior hides classic design features from the 50s and 60s and innumerable artistic endeavours. Conceived at the time of the Festival of Britain as a kind of people's palace, the Southbank Centre was said by some to have lost its identity and direction over subsequent decades. But following a recent physical remodelling and a reappraisal of its outlook under Artistic Director Jude Kelly, the Southbank Centre feels to have recommitted to ideals of participation, celebration and integration, and its dizzying daily programming – incorporating everything from classical music to graffiti art – bears witness to the scope and ambition of its creative thinking. Most importantly there's an open door policy, a democratic feel to the place, as if its cafés, bars, dance-floors, workstations, thoroughfares and public spaces had evolved into an informal hub for the wider artistic community. I once described poets as the tramps of literature, something I feel more keenly when I'm in London than anywhere else in Britain. But at the Southbank Centre a poet can sit, think and compose while enjoying uninterrupted views of Eliot's Thames and Wordsworth's Westminster Bridge and Blake's 'charter'd streets' without attracting the attention of security personnel. It's also home to the Saison Poetry Library, a national treasure house of books and other poetic resources, open to all and free of charge.

Responding to this environment and atmosphere, and with the monolith of the Olympic Stadium being slowly assembled just a few miles downstream, I proposed the idea, two years ago, of a global gathering of poets to coincide with Olympic year – a poet from every Olympic country, under one roof. Mount Parnassus would be our inspiration, sacred haunt of the god Apollo, spiritual home of the muses and "first poet" Orpheus, and for a week we would aim to re-create the footslopes of that mountain along the shore of the river and among the many rooms, foyers and auditoria belonging to the Centre.

Last year, boosted by a public appeal for suggestions, we started to identify poets from 204 Olympic countries (the number seemed to vary week by week as nations emerged, merged, disappeared, boycotted the Games etc) whose work excited us and whose presence we hoped would bring energy and integrity to this curated project, some decidedly literary, others from storytelling, oral or performing traditions, some world famous, others barely known outside their own borders (and some hardly known within them either). It probably goes without saying that this proved to be a colossal administrative and organisational task. Obtaining visa status for so many visitors was a particular headache at a time when factions within Britain's insecure coalition government were making loud and not particularly welcoming noises about immigration and refugees. In some senses, that kind of negativity and obstruction made it all the more important to press ahead and succeed. In more anxious moments I did worry that we were creating an utterly unmanageable nightmare scenario, an amalgamation of the Tower of Babel and the Eurovision Song Contest. But I also clung to the idea that Poetry Parnassus could be unique, not just in its size and ambition, but in its attitude and ideology. In its daring, in fact. Building on the Southbank Centre's Poetry International Festival, inaugurated in the 60s by Ted Hughes amongst others, and with a nod in the direction the landmark and legendary 1965 Albert Hall event which went down in history as 'the Poetry Olympics', Parnassus developed into a week of readings, translation, conferencing, workshops, discussion, argument, and all things poetic.

As well as spectacular headline-grabbing events such as the Rain of Poems (100,000 poems dropped from a helicopter onto Jubilee Gardens) and gala readings involving Nobel Laureates, the programme includes more intimate or specialised events, reflecting the range of poetic voices at work in the world today and recognising the varying forms and approaches that poetry might take. And this anthology will be available in two other formats: *The World Record*, a single handmade book consisting of handwritten poems by poets of every nation to be kept in the Saison Poetry Library, and a multilingual e-book including the handwritten pages with the English texts or translations.

London, it seemed to me, was always going to be the perfect city for such an unprecedented coming together, being home to communities of people from every corner of the globe, offering the possibility of connecting those communities with poets of their own tongue and background, and generating new readerships and audiences beyond the usual literary crowd. The timing also seemed especially apt. It's possible that every generation since the beginning of time feels to have lived through momentous historical circumstances, and if that is the case, then our own age has been no less momentous, with conflicts raging across Africa and the Middle East, religions at loggerheads, economic recession in the west, the prospect of nuclear proliferation, the continuing devastation of the natural world and the spectre of climate change overshadowing the entire planet. A good time, as ever, for poetry to maintain its bearings, assert its validity, and to speak its mind. In an era of so much fragmentation and delineation, Poetry Parnassus seeks to overcome barriers, ignore borders, and promote the convergence of peoples of every nationality through a shared interest and a common thread.

Poetry, we're told, was part of the original Olympics, and quite possibly an actual event. But in contrast with the great political and financial behemoth into which the modern Olympics has morphed, Parnassus was conceived as non-commercial, non-corporate and decidedly (at least in terms of medals or "winning") non-competitive happening. Possibly even something of an anti-Olympics; if we were to have found a line of poetry to summarise Parnassus and draped it around the inside of the Royal Festival Hall, I'm sure it would have been quite different in tone and spirit to Tennyson's, 'To strive, to seek, to find, and not to yield', the phrase engraved at the heart of the Olympic village as an inspiration to athletes. Poets have always been signed up members of the awkward squad, dissenters from the norm and the expected, and poetry has always been a practice under pressure. Its intensity of language and thought has made it the art form of concentration, which on some very elemental level means it isn't for everybody, especially when other modes of mental stimulation are so readily and casually available. In terms of popularity it cannot and would not seek to compete with the immediacy of prose, or the ubiquity of the visual image, or the passive engagement of the electronic media.

As poets we are few, and sometimes it feels like a siege. But poetry has existed from the very beginning and has proved itself to be remarkably durable and highly adaptive, even if it hasn't changed much over the course of human history. In the beginning it was intense, compact language, spoken or chanted or sung, then eventually written down, and several thousand years later it's still pretty much the same thing. This anthology, comprising work from the poets of 204 countries, seems to confirm the theory that poetry is a naturally occurring function of all languages, and is alive and well in the world. As if it were an anthropological inevitability, all cultures seem to have developed some form of charged and shaped expression, one which goes beyond the basic giving of information or acts of everyday communication. Other than that, it's impossible to generalise about the style, character and subject-matter of what lies between these covers; please enjoy it for its wild variety, as a global snapshot of poets and poetry in the early days of the 21st century, and as record of a most exceptional happening.

SIMON ARMITAGE

PREFACE

*'It is a happy thing that there is no royal road to poetry. The world should
know by this time that one cannot reach Parnassus except by flying'*

— GERARD MANLEY HOPKINS

On the 31st of May last year, just before 8.30 A.M., Simon Armitage
went on the BBC's *Today* programme and asked for the world's help.
The call was to find poets from all 204 Olympic countries for Poetry
Parnassus. By the time I got into the office that morning, we had
dozens of responses; by the next day it was over a hundred. I trailed
the nominations as the story seemed to inch its way around the globe,
people waking to it on the World Service in New Zealand, people
talking on their lunch breaks in the Philippines. When we closed the
nomination form four months later, the count was over 6,000. Letters,
postcards, emails and online recommendations had come in from almost
every country in the world.

What this became was one of the greatest spreadsheets on earth,
filled with thousands of international poets, rappers, praise singers,
storytellers, griots and spoken word artists writing and performing in
over 100 languages. What this list of names became was hours, days,
weeks of working with the Saison Poetry Library to fill each square
with poems, biographies, articles and links. What this research became
was mornings, afternoons and evenings reading and listening to
Romanian prose poetry; Latin American surrealism; protest poems
from Belize and Papua New Guinea; love poems from Latvia; pastoral
poems from Kyrgyzstan, Estonia and Australia; Islamic Hip hop from
the Tunisian uprising; protest rap from West Africa, children's poetry
from the Pacific Islands and some of the most wonderful titles for
collections such as Saadia Muffareh's *When You're Absent, I Saddle
My Suspicion's Horses*, or Tusiata Avia's *Wild Dogs Under My Skirt*.

It has been a discovery of voices, with many days spent exploring
the contemporary poetry scene in Malta, the Arab Gulf, the Balkans...
Each country and region required a retuning of the ear, a border
crossing, a different root to the rhythms and references. We have
been able to uncover the world through its keenest, most eloquent
observers. The Poetry Parnassus festival itself will be like a spell for
us, where the anthologies, books, magazines and pamphlets all wake
from the shelves and poets step out of them.

I never doubted that we'd find poets from all 204 Olympic countries,
perhaps because I suffer from perennial optimistic delusion. My thinking

was that if it is perfectly normal for hundreds of athletes to flock from every country in the world, then why not poets? – why not one of the richest, most democratic and ancient of art forms?

We found living poets from almost all of the 204 Olympic countries. Of these poets about 160 will be in London at the end of June. All the poets' work will be represented at Southbank Centre during the festival and in *The World Record*.

We have tried to make the selections reflect the wide variety that we had recommended to us. Poets coming to Southbank Centre include world greats as well as poets who aren't as well known to UK audiences, like former court poet to Kim Jong-il, Jang Jin Seong (North Korea), who once received a £7,000 Rolex watch from the leader. After becoming disillusioned with the regime, Jang Jin Seong crossed the Tumen River carrying 70 of his poems, fleeing to China and then South Korea, without being able to say goodbye to his family.

It is the vast generosity of strangers that has made Poetry Parnassus possible. We have a lot to celebrate, especially here in the UK. Without the wealth of translators, publishers, magazines, organisations and festivals, without their unwavering dedication, vim and support, none of this would ever have been possible. What we will have this year, from the 26th June to the 1st of July is recognition of their work and the possibilities to come, in a week that has over 100 free events and about 300 poets, translators, musicians and singers coming together from around the world for a festival that will make history. Poetry Parnassus will be the largest poetry festival ever staged in the UK. For anyone who is unable to make it to the Southbank Centre in London, groups of the poets are also touring the UK from 2nd to 15th July, giving readings in Bristol, Cambridge, Derry, Edinburgh, Hebden Bridge, Ludlow, Manchester, Much Wenlock and at Ledbury Poetry Festival, Liverpool Arabic Arts Festival, Stratford Poetry Festival and Way With Words Festival. Produced with Speaking Volumes, this tour covers a range of venues, from festivals to libraries and detention centres.

We would like to thank the thousands of people around the world who have made this anthology happen by recommending poets online, emailing us and sending postcards. A special thanks goes to all the translators, editors and Parnassus poets, as well as the organisations, publishers, magazines and festivals across the globe who support and promote international poetry, without you Poetry Parnassus and *The World Record* could never have happened.

I would firstly like to thank Neil Astley, co-editor of *The World Record*, whose tireless work, knowledge, generosity and patience has made the impossible possible. Unfortunately we can't thank everyone by name, but would like to thank you all and the following people in particular: Lara Akinnawo, Martin Alexander, Laura Aldis, Arturo Arias, Simon Armitage, Sharmilla Beezmohun, Cristobal Bianchi, Stewart Brown, Benedicte Brusset, Alexandra Büchler, James Byrne, Jane Camens, Julio Carrasco, Janet Charles, Judith Chernaik, Frank Chipasula, Circulo de Poesía, Bea Colley, Martin Colthorpe, David & Helen Constantine, Philip Cowell, Anna Crowe, Nia Davies, Kwame S.N. Dawes, Diana Der-Hovanessian, Gordon Dickinson, Bronwen Douglas, Maggie Eggington, Mia Farlane, Raúl Figueroa Sarti, Steven Fowler, Emma Gallagher, John Gallas, Phindile Gamezde, Chloe Garner, Jacques Gedeon Taritong, Kadija George, Patrice Gerrard, Nathalie Handal, Sarah Hickson, Elizabeth Hodgkinson, Rachel Holmes, Amanda Hopkinson, Sarah Hymas, Naomi Jaffa, Angela Jarman, Vincent M. John, Ilya Kaminsky, Matthew Keeler, John R. Keene, Jude Kelly, John Kinsella, Bas Kwakman, Alexis Levitin, Eleanor Livingstone, Cat Lucas, Sarah Maguire, Vera Maquêa, Lorraine Mariner, Robyn Marsack, Chris McCabe, Stephan McCarty, Michael McKimm, Chris Merrill, Carrie Messenger, Drusilla Modjeska, Yemisi Mokuolu, Jonathan Morley, Jon Morrison, Marc Mottin, Evan. M. Mwangi, Anne Naupa, Margaret Obank, Pascal O'Loughlin, Di Owen, Patty Paine, Palmer Judith, Judith Palmer, Pamela Park, Mark Lindsay Pearson, Craig Perez, Allen Prowle, Faustina Rehuher-Marugg, Fernando Rendón, Samuel Riviere, Peter Rorvik, Joyce Rounds, Jozsef Sakovics, Sarah Sanders, Michael Schmidt, Puneeta Sharma, Samuel Shimon, David Shook, Daniel Simon, Sophie Sladen, Adam J. Sorkin, Anne Stamford, Jana Stefanovska, Sarah Stewart, Marie-Angele Thomas, Miriam Valencia, Sharlene Versfeld, Cristina Viti, Tony Ward, Stephen Watts, Benito Wheatley, Natalie Wisdom, Gina White, Chrissy Williams, Thomas Wohlfahrt, Martin Woodside, Penny Woollard and Afia Yeboah. Please accept our apologies if we have missed anyone from this list.

ANNA SELBY

Recommended by pen

This book has been selected to receive financial assistance from English PEN's Writers in Translation programme supported by Bloomberg. English PEN exists to promote literature and its understanding, uphold writers' freedoms around the world, campaign against the persecution and imprisonment of writers for stating their views, and promote the friendly co-operation of writers and free exchange of ideas.

Each year, a dedicated committee of professionals selects between six to eight books that are translated into English from a wide variety of foreign languages. We award grants to UK publishers to help promote, market and champion these titles. Our aim is to celebrate books of outstanding literary quality, which have a clear link to the PEN charter http://www.englishpen.org/membership/charter/and promote free speech and inter-cultural understanding.

In 2011, Writers in Translation's outstanding work and contribution to diversity in the UK literary scene was recognised by Arts Council England. English PEN was awarded a threefold increase in funding to develop its support for world writing in translation and, as of April 2012, the programme will also fund translation costs directly.

This book is dedicated to all translators

AFGHANISTAN

REZA MOHAMMED

Literal translation from the Dari by Moheb Mudessir
Final translated version by Sarah Maguire

Rain

If it rains
my friends will be stuck at home
wearing the shoes of the dead.
The gates to the city are sealed.
Pillar by pillar
its relics
break in their mouth.

*

We have hidden our dead
in the cellar
until the day of vengeance.
They are buried
under boxes of gunpowder
and ancestral rage.

If it rains
the day of vengeance
will be postponed once again.

Rain is a crime.
Rain ruins dreams.
If it rains
the rain will purge my blood
from the streets.

ALBANIA

LULJETA LLESHANAKU
Translated from the Albanian by Henry Israeli & Alban Kupi

No Time

You asked for death, you were tired.
You asked for it so easily
as if calling for the white horse
with a bag of oats.
You did not know your destiny lay
in a bullet, dripping with blood,
extracted from your body.

It was December 1950.
The murder notice
blackened newspapers like a rotted tooth.
The river froze to a razor's edge
olive trees nearly snapped
beneath the weight of their dark fruit.

Death came silently, without a grave.
We were even afraid of your body.
On my palms were bloody scratches, thorny roses.
I did not know where to hide them.

You died during the revolution.
There was no time to bury you.
You left simply, as quietly as those moments when
wearing a decrepit soldier's coat
we wait on a platform for the next train.

ADEL SOLEÏMAN GUÉMAR

Translated from the French by Tom Cheesman & John Goodby

Eyes closed

1

and so at last I left
wounded from head to foot
dreams all fuddled
– but still intact I tell myself intact –
revived by the brilliantly nubile showers

I took my time in the early morning
to sip my mint tea in a corner café
before catching a flight to the far side of the world
three hours away from the cemetery-republic
where I'd spent my life waiting for a miracle

I cast a last glance back
at the electrically-operated gates
of the new masters' plush residences
thrown up in haste
as if to evade the evil eye
and any possible reawakening of ghosts of justice

2

odours of the *terroir* that keep breaking in
make me recall the vertigo of being dangled
from the topmost floor above a city
travestied but so beautiful still
above the heads that throng its streets
lit by the fires of sham celebrations
above a sea tied up
by small boats all adrift
above the bars packed with hardened informers
and night clubs run by torturer NCOs
above incessant aftershocks from a censored earthquake
hunted into the narrowest crevice

of the tectonic plates of my memory that survive
the time of dry heaves flooded in blood

3

I swigged from dubious bottles
I smoked everything forbidden

it's so quiet I seem to eavesdrop on
the voices of my childhood
singing in chorus

I sat myself down on the ground
I wiped clean the white marble of a spat-upon
tomb and I fell asleep

4

your hand seeks me in the night
timidly it wakes me
and halts at my heart
lingering there
clutch and caress both

your hair it covers my face
I inhale perfume of the ocean
the hennaed Sahara of your passions
the breath of the trees of virgin forests
in spring when they're for being lost in

on your back I trace the flowers
I've yet to give you
and your tender insurrectionary eyes
you've bewitched me with

I broke my watch
vain attempt to bring time to a stop

ANDORRA

ESTER FENOLL GARCÍA

Translated from the Catalan by Anna Crowe

'Between your fingers...'

Between your fingers
what's left of the threads
that used to bind us
weaken
absurdly.

Today I shall leave off hoping
since I alone
want it to happen,
mildly disturbed
I struggle to ressemble
every coherent person
I know,
struggle
to send every sin
back to hell.

ANA PAULA TAVARES
Translated from the Portuguese by Richard Zenith

Bitter as Fruit

> *You tell me things as bitter*
> *as fruit...*
>
>   KWANYAMA

Beloved, why have you returned

with death in your eyes
and without any sandals
as if someone else were dwelling in you
in a time
beyond
all time

Beloved, where did you lose your metal tongue
with its signs and proverb
with my engraved name
        where did you leave your voice
        soft as grass and velvet
        and studded with stars
Beloved, my beloved
what has returned of you
is your shadow
split in half
is a you before you
words as bitter
as fruit

NOTE: It is a tradition, among men of the Kwanyama people, to carry in their mouths a leaf-shaped strip of metal ornately engraved with signs and sayings and used to produce whistling sounds.

LINISA GEORGE

The Brown Girl in the Ring

For most of my childhood,
I wanted to be the brown girl,
The pretty brown girl in the ring.
I knew I could never be the white girl,
So I dreamt and wished to be the brown girl.

Brown girl, with the long straight curl,
Hair I could twirl,
A pretty brown girl.

But I would never look like the brown girl,
A lesson that would take me most of my teenage years to learn.
From pressed hair, to chemically relaxed hair,
Even mismatched brown and purple contacts,
Anything to be the brown girl.

Brown girl, with the long straight curl,
Hair I could twirl,
A pretty brown girl.

But what I was running from,
Ran straight at me.
I didn't realise,
The true me,
I could never flee.
Why couldn't I be a brown girl?
Mom and Dad said I was pretty.
My grandparents said I looked like an empress.
Yet the outside world,
Ordered me to stay inside.
In the magazines I read no one looked like me,
Either they were white girls or brown girls.

Brown girls, with long straight curls,
Hair they could twirl,
Pretty brown girls.

I never went anywhere,
I was too scared to be seen in the public.
If you were darker than a brown girl,
You were practically unnoticeable.
I was Toni Morrison's Sula,
Wishing for the bluest eyes ever, and the chance to be a brown girl.

A brown girl, with the long straight curl,
Hair I could twirl,
Pretty brown girl.

In time I would develop breasts and discover make-up.
Since I wasn't a pretty brown girl,
I decided to transform myself into a sexy black girl.
Tits pushed up high,
Ass stuck straight out,
Short skirts pass the knee,
War-painted coloured face,
Everyone did look at me.
But still I wasn't a brown girl, with the long straight curl,
Hair I could twirl,
Pretty brown girl.
One night Mama Africa visited me in a dream,
With a stern voice she accused me of being utterly disrespectful,
Cursed me for not understanding the definition of beauty, my beauty.
'My child you are a labour of love.
Your skin is woven from soil from the richest land.
Your eyes, ears, nose and lips tell the tales of your royal ancestors,
Queens whose presence diminishes any Cleopatra's.
Kings whose strength and wisdom outweigh that of Samson and Solomon.'

So then who am I?

I am not a brown girl,
With the long straight curl,
Hair that could twirl,
Pretty brown girl.

I am a black girl,
Different from them all,
Rising above with every fall.
I stand 50 feet tall,
With my short kinky curl,
One that I could twirl,
I am an extremely sexy,
Highly educated,
Overbearingly motivated
Soaring high above without wings,
I am the PRETTY BLACK GIRL in the ring.

ARGENTINA

MIRTA ROSENBERG
Translated from the Spanish by Julie Wark

Intimate Bestiary

If someone wanted to be a tortoise
it would be me:
to fashion from a conical section
the prehistoric hub of my election
lodged in the dorsal spine.

Being a tortoise
has something ideal:
it sports wrinkles from its youth
and in a sense literally real
grows bigger with the years
– more years
more bulk.
Post-matrimonial,
without family ties
once its eggs are laid

31

like each and every woman
naturally daughter of the moon,
nevertheless
not a single schism
between her and her hearth gods lies.

With all these lows and highs,
for me
who is in me
– without balm pure pressure to go –
it matters little that her progress
on the surface is slow:
that
would give endurance to me
making me able to enter the sea
– that covers two thirds of the world's ground –
knowing that if I go down
I gain velocity.

ARMENIA

RAZMIK DAVOYAN
Translated from the Armenian by Arminé Tamrazian

Yessenin

There is sound in suffering
And there is light in sound
And there is spirit in light

And within the spirit you stand alone
As the troubadour of some endless army.

With kindness, as a brother, you tell me to live,
May the storms never get you,
May the winds never strike you, may no whip ever hit you,

May no one ever hire you
As a slave.
You tell me to live happily
With no wealth, glory and treasures,
You tell me to live a good and honest life,
You tell me to live
As the sweet smell of wheat bread
And to repeat now and then 'we are brothers'.

It is all right, you tell me, do not suffer,
Mountains never kneel in fear of winds –
And you swing
And you rustle
Like some eternal sorrow
Born in some corner of the wide plateau.

It is all right, you tell me, all right, all right, all right,
Look, there was nothing and there will be nothing,
Keep a drop of humanity in your heart
And your clear eyes shall never dim.

I believe you when I look at your pain
And I believe you when I look at your fear
And I carry your cross faithfully
Not knowing who will carry ours
Among tomorrow's crosses.

It is all right, you tell me, do not suffer,
Mountains never kneel in fear of winds
And you swing
And you rustle
Like some eternal sorrow
Born in some corner of the wide plateau

NOTE: Sergei Yessenin (1895-1925), Russian poet, one of the most lyrical
figures in Russian classical poetry, who committed suicide in a hotel in St
Petersburg (then Leningrad) a few years after the Russian Revolution.

ARUBA

LASANA M. SEKOU

We Continue

It is time to continue
And today I greet you here
As if for the first time

Compañeros/Hermanos/Hombres y Mujeres
  Gentes del Sol
  Del Caribe
  De América Latina
Gentes de sangre Africana
  de sangre Indígena
Living through the blood of a world union

But we have lived in the same house
And danced the same dances,
We have loved each other's songs
Without really knowing each other's names –
Brothers and sisters...
Cousins and comrades...
Sufferers and fighters...

Today we begin
To speak for ourselves/
Unleash our tongues from isolation/
Speak our destiny
As we fight for liberation.
In solidarity
Speak of destiny
Inna one tongue
La lengua de libertad
The language of the brave.

Escucha, pueblo
Dime –

Can the killers of Allende
Speak
With the same sweetness and Truth
As our fathers and mothers?
Name them, here
Alive for the Living Struggle
In the eternal flame of Liberty

Accabre.
José Martí.
Toussaint.
Duarte *y* Duruo

Bottom Belly, Biassou and Bishop
Queen Mary and the son of Mariana Grajales, Maceo.

Ramón Betances *y* Edward Blyden.
Marcus Garvey *y* Don Albizu Campos.
Caamaño, Cudjoe *y* Karpata
Sandino *y* Farabundo.

Walter Rodney and Bob Marley.
Fédon and Fanon.
Tula and José Lake, the patriot

Marryshow, Delgrès, *y* Che
Limpera *y* Guillén.
Henrique Dias *y* Emiliano Zapata.
Names without meaning
If we have no meaning...

And the people –
Yes, always the people
Where lies the only Truth
Where blood and sweat and laughter
Nourishes the Lands
That feeds this Culture
To forge this wreath of freedom song/
To fight down the dictators, *los gorilas*/
To turn back *los imperialistas*

Who else can free us?
Who else can feed us?
Who but ourselves... majestic multitudes...

Greetings *Compañeros*,
We have lived in the same house
And danced the same dances...

We have loved/
Yes,
We have loved
Each other's songs...

AUSTRALIA

JOHN KINSELLA

The Ambassadors

In cold weather we are as large
as our clothes make us, warding
off failure with diplomatic immunity,
exploring limits of the plenipotent.

We describe for our hosts the place
we come from: it's large and many
weathers threaten its coastlines. Inland
is an entirety inside an entirety,

an infinitum. An island, yet it is endless.
Yes, there is a great heat that underlies
all extremes. Yes, we retain red dust
under our fingernails years after

arriving in the Great City. Our
tastes are not lavish – we will acquire
books and tickets to the theatre,
and sack galleries for their spiritual

worth, but keep social standing
out of discussions. We *will* visit Saint Paul's
and wonder over Donne's sermons,
but no hint of Apostolic Nuncios

will haunt our office. We will offer
up raw materials, generations
of the well-fed. We will admire
the Old Country's astrologers

gazing up through smog,
bringing heaven uncomfortably
close to earth. Back home, our
skies are *so* wide and *so* shining...

we remind our hosts at moments
of triumph – 'Water Music'
on the Royal Barge, the Sex Pistols'
performance of 'God Save the Queen' –

our skies are *so* wide and *so* shining.
The embassy ends before it's begun
and yet is never complete – the skull
we bring with us shines through canvas,

our skin, and as we ascend the stairway
to hand in our resignation, the skull
comes into focus – *so* wide, *so* shining,
so willing to trade across harrowed oceans.

EVELYN SCHLAG

Translated from the German by Karen Leeder

Lesson

I wanted to list
What I have learned
How I hold a cool
Name in my hand when
I touch the doorknob how
I turn the road sign around
Kill the fish by striking
Their heads on the stone
I have practised till I have
The knack and how I change
Dresses while the splashes of
Gill-blood are drying
From red to black

The cat which was sitting
On my lap laid his paw
On the back of my hand
And I did not know whether
It was to calm me or because
He so believed in the dead fish

AZERBAIJAN

NIGAR HASAN-ZADEH

Translated from the Russian by Richard McKane

'I knocked at someone's door...'

I knocked at someone's door –
        didn't find...
Whether people, or beasts
        I went up.
Some gave claws, some gave
        looks...
Not the stranger but the friend
        did not forgive.
Along an alley, between heaven
        and earth,
not right, nor left
        but straight.
Open wide the window to hurricanes,
        under the wing
a new wound to add to
        the old wounds.

I knocked at someone's door, my Darling,
to listen, to believe in your voice...

CHRISTIAN CAMPBELL

Vertigo
(for Gwendolyn Brooks and Kiah)

A little girl twirls in the airport,
in the line for New York. She looks
like five and already cocks out her chest.
She is adorned with womanish things,
pink plastic bangles and ruffled socks.
She opens and closes her denim jacket
like wings, as she whirls. She will come
back with more pink things (with which
to twirl). Her lips are pursed big-woman
style (she has the kind of top lip with nerve
enough to curve over the bottom one). She is
the colour of coconut candy. Her face
slopes slightly. Her cheeks are full.
Her eyes wear the seriousness
of sun. She answers to her name
and also to Precious. Her name
might be Precious. She does not fear
her smallness. She likes her Bajan
ways. The spinning is all that counts.
She is already not soft and her forehead
Is broad and African. If twirling and
smiling went together, she would give
one wide with dimples and her tongue
between her teeth. Singing goes with
twirling and this requires fierceness.
She knows how to hold on to the beauty
of a thing. She acts this way. You'd want
to say 'she is a wailing dervish'
or 'she is a rainstorm collecting'.
You'd want to say 'her hair is sectioned
like the parishes' or 'look at Oya's
grandchild'. But she is just twirling,
which her singing tells and tells. It is just that.

Her plaits are countless today, full
of bluebird barrettes. All else are staring,
sensible and still. The girl gives a whirl.

QASSIM HADDAD
Translated from the Arabic by Khaled Mattawa

Poets

Poets draw nature before it prefigures itself
and they invent
and build a hut abandoned by a gang of thugs.

They sing sometimes
and they form a road so water can take the shape of a river.
They instill in mud the memory of the trees.
A bird discovers its colours in the phrases of a poem,
and picks its rare name.

When poets leave sleep behind
the young thugs begin their rampage.
They romp a little
and they throng as if nature is ambushing them.
They storm and they thunder.

And their limbs begin to thin as if the seasons
were all about to start,
as if childhood selected its shapes suddenly,
and eyes
gaze only at the perseverance of nature.

And the young thugs commit their sins
sip by sip
the way poems clash against the triumph of time

Creatures offer gifts
and take their tempting shapes
as if a tongue
         made creation. And people,
still startled by their inception,
face the thin ice adorning their mirrors to see
what the poets have done to our feeble dreams.

Poetry maligns speech
and the young thugs commit forgivable sins
the way an infant scratches a breast then weeps to it
the way a text breaks its intentions.

Then the apple of love descends
enamouring a woman with a lost lover,
the way the wolf divulges the myth of the bloody shirt
and the innocent brothers confess their crime
and nature forgives a careless creator
                then praises him.

BANGLADESH

MIR MAHFUZ ALI

My Salma

Forgive me Badho, my camellia bush,
when you are full of yourself and blooming,

you may ask why, having spent so many years
comfortably in your breasts I still dream of Salma's

just as I did when I was a hungry boy in shorts,
her perfect fullness amongst chestnut leaves.

The long grass broke as I ran, leaving
its pollen on my bare legs.

When the soldiers came, even the wind
at my heels began to worship Salma's beauty.

            *

A solider kicked me in the ribs. I fell
to the ground wailing.

They brought Salma into the yard,
asked me to watch how they would explode

a bullet into her. But I turned my head away
as they ripped her begooni blouse,

exposing her startled flesh. The young solider
held my head, twisting it back towards her,

urging me to spit at a woman
as I might spit a melon seed into the olive dust.

            *

The soldier decorated with two silver bars
and two half-inch stripes was the first to drop his

ironed khaki trousers and dive on top of Salma.
His back arched as she fought for the last leaf

of her dignity. He laughed as he pumped
his rifle-blue buttocks in the Hemonti sun.

Then covered in Bengal's soft soil, he offered
her to the next soldier in line.

They all had their share of her,
dragged her away out of the yard.

I went in search of Salma,
amongst the firewood in the jungle.

            *

Stood in the middle of a boot-bruised field,
working out how the wind might lead me to her.

Then I saw against the deepening sky
a thin mangey bitch, tearing at a body with no head,

breasts cut off in a fine lament,
I knew then who she was, and kicked

the bitch in the ribs, the same way
that I had been booted in the chest.

BARBADOS

ESTHER PHILLIPS

Near-Distance

At last the heart makes its way
past sadness, regret, grows at ease
with shadows that move like
humble servants about the room,
sweeping up words where
they had fallen as dust motes,
unconnected from anything
we meant to say;

brushing the edge off memory,
turning it face downwards,
tending its slow seepage
into the daily habit
of absence under one roof.

VALZHYNA MORT

Translated from the Belarusian by Franz Wright & Elizabeth Oehlkers Wright

Belarusian I

even our mothers have no idea how we were born
how we parted their legs and crawled out into the world
the way you crawl from the ruins after a bombing
we couldn't tell which of us was a girl or a boy
we gorged on dirt thinking it was bread
and our future a gymnast on a thin
thread of the horizon was performing there
at the highest pitch
bitch

we grew up in a country where
first your door is stroked with chalk
then at dark a chariot arrives
and no one sees you anymore
but riding in those cars were neither
armed men nor
a wanderer with a scythe
this is how love loved to visit us
and snatch us veiled

completely free only in public toilets
where for a little change nobody cared what we were doing
we fought the summer heat the winter snow
when we discovered we ourselves were the language
and our tongues were removed we started talking with our eyes
and when our eyes were poked out we talked with our hands
and when our hands were cut off we conversed with our toes
and when we were shot in the legs we nodded our heads for yes
and shook our heads for no and when they ate our heads alive
we crawled back into the bellies of our sleeping mothers
as if into bomb shelters
to be born again

and there on the horizon the gymnast of our future
was leaping through the fiery hoop
of the sun
screwed

BELGIUM

ELS MOORS

Translated from Flemish by Willem Groenewegen & Joshua Clover

'I am the gardener with an alibi...'

I am the gardener with an alibi
and a purple jumpsuit
I maintain the premises
where the golf balls rise and fall
and the body often lies
at the far end of the arc

in a glass booth I sell ice cream
to the visitors
until I am a tree
lightning-struck

I gather a field around me

mornings an orange plastic basket in my hand
I go barefoot into the street
to bring in the milk

I do not walk on thin ice

when I spread my legs
I pretend they are wings

EVAN X HYDE

About Poems

We didn't know
no better
we was small
we was slaves
so they said
we they said
will teach you
about poems
poems is like this
trees by Joyce Kilmer
God can make a tree
poems by a fool like me
poems is like this
they have to rhyme
in every line
and every time
poems must be nice
so we tried to write poems
while we was still small
and was slaves
and we was slaves
and they said good, that's poems
but after we get big
and fight for freedom
and write
the way we feel
hunger in the eyelashes
of our eyes
and hatred give us fever
they said NO
those is not poems
they is hatred
they is violence
they is not nice

neither proper
nor correct
most uncourteous
so we said all right
it's not poems
it's AMANDALA
AMANDALA they said
what's that?
and we said
it's what we call
poems by men like me
God can still make a tree

BENIN

AGNÈS AGBOTON
Translated from Gun into Spanish by Agnès Agboton,
and from the Spanish by Maya García Vinuesa

'They remain lying on the earth...'

They remain lying on the earth
the dark bodies of men
after a useless death
and in the hidden heart of the
others
the flame of hatred is still
burning
ignorantly awake.
Useless hatred.

Inside a calm refuge
of beautiful walls
all has changed;
two important men have smiled
to each other,
they have shaken hands.

Again, all is useless,
the struggle of the living,
the death of the dead.
Again, all is useless,
the hunger...

ANDRA SIMONS

Week of the Dog

I *50,000 Dogs Killed in China*

here in london, during that week
i on the southern end of
the porcelain tub, he on the northern
our blue walls reflecting off the still clear water
we care not for summer shortage
steal we do, guiltless moments
highbury humming around us
the water grows to chill
seven days our bodies lie baptised
silent underneath
he lathers and washes my mess of hair
i shudder under the jug.

II *Forecasters Expect Seven Atlantic Hurricanes*

shrivelled this morning and rinsed out
onto the floor from the bath too deep for one
flows a river dampening and staining my feet
canine red, i howl as i shiver dry.

BHUTAN

SONAM CHHOKI

New Year dusk

two black figures on the bridge
are old wooden posts
what else have I mistaken
in the year just closed

BOLIVIA

MARÍA SOLEDAD QUIROGA
Translated from the Spanish by Ronald Haladyna

The Yellow House

The house
                        yellow
windows everywhere without panes
pure air
not stone nor brick nor wood
                        yellow.
no flowers
no colour on the walls
                everything yellow
scaffolds
of an interwoven presence.

This is the house
yellow
a closed walnut
open to the tides.
Slowly light
constructs it:
solid walls
summer through the windows
and colour that ascends
             serpent of gold
along the naked walls
and encloses it.

BOSNIA AND HERZEGOVINA

ADISA BAŠIĆ

Translated from the Croatian by Ulvija Tanović

People Talking

> *They never said a bad word about the people who did this
> to them. Except for expressing disbelief at what was done to them.*
>
> JEAN-RENÉ RUEZ, Chief Investigator for Srebrenica
> speaking about the survivors

Ignorance

He says: Cross yourself!
And I cross myself.
But I didn't know
so I used my whole hand.
And then he takes
the blunt edge of the axe
to my hand.
But, believe me, girl,
I didn't know

51

Natural disaster

They brought us here
to a complex:
a bunch of houses and
garages.
You go into one, into another,
into a third.
And then you come out dead.

Revenge

I know who killed my wife and
son and
daughter.
I know, one of them came back.
Opened a bakery.
But I make sure
I never buy anything there.

Showering

They sway like algae
as the guards wash them with
fire hoses.
About thirty men I
don't know. All naked.
And Hajra, the bank
teller, among them.
To this day,
as far as I know,
the bodies have not been found.

Occupation

I used to be a lawyer.
Today, I'm a victim.

Birthday

We all gathered
there. In front
of the car battery factory.
And it was hot, July.
Next to me
on the asphalt
at the same time
a child was being born.

Survivors

Twice
quietly
so mother wouldn't hear
and get a fright
I took father
off
the gallows.

(Ključ, Sanski Most, Prijedor, Foča, Sarajevo, Srebrenica)
Noted down by Adisa Bašić, Sarajevo.

BOTSWANA

T.J. DEMA

Neon poem
Thoughts after Amiri Baraka's Black Art

Poems *are* bullshit, unless they teach
Poems serve no purpose unless they reach
The audience they are written for
The ears they are meant for

You could write the perfect love poem
Tell us how you teased her
Till she let you touch her
But if she cannot remember you
Then friend, your poetry didn't do what it was supposed to
For I've heard war poems
That hid behind fancy syllables and metaphors
Quietly comfortable with the thought of coming to blows
Over why they should fight for anything at all
Once I wrote a hope poem, one of those there is a future type poems
But it never spoke till what few wishes we had left, broke
I've even seen live poems
That wait till the audience is gone
Then begin humming softly as a song
Murdering any sense of rhythm they might have had at all
I'm thinking of crafting an it's too late poem
I'll build it up till it sounds like metal bats against tin cans
Loud and outrageous, still might be too little too late
Because this generation
This generation wants fast poems
That can out race us, out face us
Maybe even take us to where we've never been
Quick as sin
A look at me poem
That screams out to the world
You can't even speak your mind
Yet you still believe that you, and you, and you
Are free
From something or someone
Any one give me a neon poem
Black- red-white- yellow- purple- pink even lime poem
That will teach all other wannabe poems
How to grow up and become real type poems
Because poems
Poems are bullshit, unless they teach
They serve absolutely no purpose unless they reach
Some one

BRAZIL

PAULO HENRIQUES BRITTO
Translated from the Portuguese by Idra Novey

Quasi Sonnet

There is nothing that leads to nothing.
Even to sit in a room, quiet and nude
as Blaise Pascal, will have some effect

on Tanzania maybe, or on New Guinea,
just as the beating wings of a lepidopter –
according to the proverb about butterflies in Peru –

could incite a tidal wave in Shanghai,
or knock down an Iraqi helicopter.

And so we become ourselves, *hypocrite lecteur*,
at the very least accomplices, you and I.

BRUNEI DARUSSALAM

ANONYMOUS
Translated from the Malay

'A twist of hair...'

A twist of hair
stitches softly
puffed flour
on a pan.

I lower my
pinced fingers
at it in a thin
flour-cloud.

Carefully. The hair
must not prick
deeper or
slip away.

And the flour
must not hush
off the edge
by breath or dab.

A delicate matter
needs the same
exact line
to put right.

BULGARIA

KAPKA KASSABOVA

How to Build Your Dream Garden
(Mandála, Ecuador)

Year one. At the end of a dusty road, find a malarial swamp.
Drain and fill with earth. Get sick. Curse the day you came.

Year two. Construct a wooden cabin with shells for doorknobs,
        mist for glass.
Lie and listen to the waves. Remember, you were sick *before* you came.

Year three. Plant seeds. The earth muffles the past with leaves
and roots. Now wait for someone to come and understand.

Year four. The coloured birds of paradise arrive, the iguanas balance
on the plants. Lost strangers come and never leave. Smile knowingly.

Year ten. Stop counting, isn't this why you came? Now dream to the beat
of waves the only dream that's left, dream that the garden goes to seed,

the iguanas grow to monsters and gore the strangers in the dust.
The locals talk for generations. And the sea, the sea takes care of
      everything.

BURKINA FASO

MONIQUE ILBOUDO

I suffer

I suffer
From a lack of means
From SAP
That come and go
From the devaluation
That humiliates me
From the IMF
That crushes me
From a value system
That excludes me
From the single-mindedness
That smothers me.

I suffer
From the aid
Generous or disguised
From the pity
Feigned or sincere
From the arrogance
Malicious or mocking

I suffer
From the look
That discriminates against me
From chartered flights
That turn me away

I suffer
From being a dumping ground
From eating leftovers
From dressing in rags
From thinking the thoughts
Of Others

I suffer
And I am not proud
Of my powerlessness.

NOTE: SAP: Structural Adjustment Program. IMF: International Monetary Fund.

BURUNDI

KETTY NIVYABANDI BIKURA
Translated from the French by David Shook

Three tribes

Three tribes,
Three beautiful smiles,
Three young destinies.
Three little girls,
Three bursts of laughter tickle the mango tree...

They play in a circle holding hands,
Their sandals and fears cast to the wind...
Three playful dreams,
Three songs.

One, two, three, they hop,
Their small braids bounce toward the horizon.
One, two, three, they hop,
Six little feet land on the feverish earth;
Freshly raped by her son,
Fecund and bearing infamy in her womb.

One, two, three, and the eroded earth opens.
Roaring and gaping,
Festering with little monsters,
She swallows all three songs.

Three bits of childhood fly apart.
Three shredded dreams, three muted laughs.
Three smothered destinies, three crushed buds.
Three unfinished songs...

One, two, three identical wails rise to the skies of disaster.
Three silhouettes clad in black wraps lengthen, hair shaved, souls scorched.
Three mothers.
Three wounds.
Three hearts split forever.
Hutu. Tutsi. Twa.
Three tribes. Just one pain.
A single river of tears that flows and flows, toward infinity.

And such silence...
Silence burdensome and scarlet with the blood of innocents.

CAMBODIA

KOSAL KHIEV

Why I Write

I write 4 men, women, and children. any 1 who ever felt alone, any1 who
    ever felt disowned, i write for the bones buried in a country i call home,
i write for u the listener so listen up
take a step back and imagine the bigger picture
cuz i write the real so feel me
i write for inner city street kids
struggling to find their place in a world to concern with race
i write for the momz and pops shops
strugglng to stay atop cuz the dopeboyz got the block on lock
cant compete with the drama
so i write soap operas
about single mothers and brothers
about the struggle and hustle
the bustling city where empty bellies rumble
like silent earthquakes we shake
hungry like young lions
we defying the odds
prayin to God Lord give us the strength to carry on
so i write to redefine the stars
naw, none of that hollywood glitz and glamour
or them stones that shimmer and glimmer
but
some of that earthy residue that comes thru when one is being true
so i write to the few
hoping i get trickled down to the masses
i wanna spark the world and get reborn in its ashes
i wanna unfog their glasses and make em see the sons and daughters they
    abandoned to be bastards
know that we grow like molasses
i point to the north like davie jones compass
just follow the sounds of trumphets and listen up
i write for love
for wind chimes when they dangle and jangle
moving passionately like two doing the tango

i write for the sweet taste of mangos
cuz this is that tropical heat
sun blistering
skin glistening
while drinkin coconuts under the cabana
while i listen to the sound of ur sleep
beauty like the everglades
i write to the beat drums of runaway slaves
engrave in the ecthings of oaktrees
so even when time pass we last like classic oldies
weathering the elements
yeah
i write for the essence of soul
for the old
cuz experience is wisdom and wisdom is gold
Behold
i write for the gorillas in the congos
for the nomads in the jungles following the rhythm of the bongos
yeah
i write for the warriors stretched out in the far corners of asia
malaysia, cambodia, afghan, iran, iraq, and deep africa
i write for the souls lost i attica
i write for california
the golden state where we holding weight
struggling to hold on to faith
cuz they steady packing us in prisons till we're old and grey
so i write for those in blue thats doing all day
tehachapi, new folsom, corcoran, pelican bay
all the way to susanville, high desert, and back down this way
calipat, lancaster, soledad, ironwood
and so many more built into cesspools
so i write about wats less cool
less fake
so less take a moment of silence for the fallen and press pause
okay
thats enough
lets get back to the cause
lets get back to these walls
built to separate and generate hate
built to execute and induce waste
so i write from a place of pure bass
all the five elements put together to produce faith

i write for men women and children
anyone whoever felt alone
anyone whoever felt disowned
i write for the bones in a country i call home
i write for u the listener so listen up
take a step back and imagine the bigger picture
i write the real so feel me

CAMEROON

PAUL DAKEYO

Translated from the French by Patrick Williamson

'So we will emerge from exile...'

So we will emerge from exile
A swarm of bees
A tidal wave
That ebbs to the horizon
Flayed by wind
Like so many stars hoisted
To the very centre of the sky
We will emerge from exile
Like a raging volcano

I will take you to walk
On the shore
Along the coast
When the breeze skims
The sea
The never-ending sea

I will offer dawn
The magnitude of love
And your snuggly
Sun-beaten
Body

And so we will go
Across the smooth sand
Of my land
Alone in love
Just as the incoming tide
Lulls the worn reefs

CANADA

KAREN SOLIE

Migration
(for Cathy)

Snow is falling, snagging its points on frayed
surfaces. There's lightning
over Lake Ontario, Erie. In the great central
cities, debt accumulates along baseboards
like hair. Many things were good
while they lasted. Long dance halls
of neighbourhoods under the trees,
the qualified fellow-feeling no less genuine
for it. West are silent frozen fields and wheels
of wind. In the north, frost is measured
in vertical feet, and you sleep sitting because it hurts
less. It's not winter for long. In April
shall the tax collector flower forth, and language
upend its papers looking for an entry adequate
to the sliced smell of budding
poplars. The sausage man will contrive
once more to block the sidewalk with his truck,
and though it's illegal to idle one's engine
for more than three minutes, every one of us will idle
like hell. After all that's happened. We're all
that's left. In fall, the Arctic tern will fly
12,500 miles to Antarctica as it did every year

you were alive. It navigates by the sun and stars.
It tracks the earth's magnetic fields
sensitively as a compass needle and lives
on what it finds. I don't understand it either.

CAPE VERDE

CORSINO FORTES

Emigrant

Translated from the Portuguese by Sean O'Brien & Daniel Hahn

Every evening, sunset crooks
    its thumb across the island
And from the sunset to the thumb
    there grows
    a path of dead stone
And this peninsula
    Still drinks
All the blood of your wandering body
From a tenant farmer's cup

But when your voice
    becomes a chord on the shore's guitar
And the earth of the face and the face of the earth
    Extend the palm of the hand
From the seaward edge of the island
    A palm made of bread
You will merge your final hunger
    with your first

From above there will come
The faces and prows of not-voyage
    So that herbal and mercury
Extract the crosses from your body

The screaming of mothers carries you
                    now
To the seventh corner
      where the island is shipwrecked
      where the island celebrates
Your daughter pain
The pain of a woman in childbirth

So that all parting is power in death
      all return a child's learning to spell

No longer do we wait for the cycle
      Pulp from good fruit, fruit from good pulp
      The earth
            breathes in
                  your green speech

And there before your feet
                    should be
                        a tree on a hill

And your hand
            should sing
                  a new moon in my heart

Go and plant
            in dead Amilcar's mouth
This fistful of watercress
And spread from goal to goal
            a fresh phonetics
And with the commas of the street
      and syllables from door to door
You will sweep away before the night
The roads that go
            as far as the night-schools
For all departure means a growing alphabet
      for all return is a nation's language

They await you
            the dogs and the piglets
            at Chota's house
            grown thin from the warmth of the welcome

They await you
    the cups and semantics of taverns

They await you
    the beasts
    choking on applause and sugarcane

They await you
    faces that explode
    on the blood of ants
    new pastorals to cultivate

But
    when your body
        of blood and lignite, on heat

Raises
    Over the harvest
Your pain
And your orgasm
    Who didn't know
    Who doesn't know
        Emigrant
That all of parting is power in death
And all return is a child learning to spell

NASARIA SUCKOO-CHOLLETTE

Just Long Celia

It was long Celia they called me
Not Ntozake
Or Mamma Zulu
Or even Nanny

Just Long Celia

Just Long Celia longing for freedom
Just Long Celia hoping for home
Just Long Celia free

Unna hear dem drums?

Naseberry sweet dem words was
Just like to bite in
And let dem run sticky down my chin

free   free   free

Unna hear dem drums?

Dis my Sunday offering
Dis my boxin day dinner
Dis my candle wood

It's in the wind that's fiddlin through the wattle where the daub has
    worn away
It's runnin mad like ants across the table where heavy cake has just
    been cut
It's spillin out of hushed lips like drunken men pouring another cup
    of sea grape wine

Start a revolution...
Take a puff and pass it around

67

Unna hear dem drums?

You can't kraal my spirit but for a little time
I feel the light you cannot see
And I will swim back home to lay my clutch
Where I began to be

                    And iron wood don't sink

Unna hear dem drums?

Sarah, you gyapseedin duppy
You a blackgyardin tell-tale dead woman
You lie
And 12 white ghosts are fighting over my pickins in fifty lashes

I a woman
I a free woman
I a naked woman
I a torn an tattered woman

But you still cyan't break open my cockspur thorny shell

                And memba what happen when ya rub a "nicka" wrong.

Wake up it's morning

You still tied to that dock
One knot away from
Walking on water

You still taking lashes from
That raging monster
Whose rib you took

You still fighting the reflection
You see in your basin
That is me

Wake up!

Lick dem drums Julia,
Lick dem drums

GLOSSARY:

Unna: Caymanian words coming from the Gullah Language of the Ibo people wunna meaning 'you people'.

Naseberry: Fruit.

Heavy cake: Pudding like cake made from root starches like cassava.

Kraal: Caymanian term for a pen in the water where turtles were kept, coming from the South African word meaning 'dwelling place'.

Iron wood: Very hard wood Caymanians used to make the frame for their wattle and daub houses.

Gyapseedin': Catching news.

Blackgyardin': Maligning someone's character.

Cockspur: Prickly vine with very thorny brown shells that hold nicker nuts. The vine is often called lion bush in Africa because it's so thorny it keeps lions out of the tribal villages.

Julia: Aunt Julia, Caymanian icon, 103-year-old female drummer with her own unique style of drumming and homemade drum. She wrote many of Cayman's traditional folk songs. Still performing today.

CENTRAL AFRICAN REPUBLIC

ANONYMOUS

Translated from the Sango

2 Termite Skyscrapers

2
termite
skyscrapers

he tries
to separate
his
eyes

the man
who
minds

2
termite
skyscrapers

comes home
with
nothing
and
a
headache.

CHAD

NIMROD
Translated from the French by Patrick Williamson

The cry of the bird
(for Daniel Bourdanné)

I wanted to be overcome with silence
I abandoned the woman I love
I closed myself to the bird of hope
That invited me to climb the branches
Of the tree, my double
I created havoc in the space of my garden
I opened up my lands
I found the air that circulates between the panes
Pleasant. I was happy
To be my life's witch doctor
While the evening rolled out its ghosts
The bird in me awoke again
Its cry spread anguish
In the heart of my kingdom

ALEJANDRA DEL RÍO

Translated from the Spanish by Thomas Charles L. Rothe

In Jan Neruda's Tavern

> *Poor Catullus, stop your nonsense*
> *and accept the loss of what you see is lost*
>
> CATULLUS

A Czech of extraordinary scale sways me in his rhythm of moulded metals
teaching me with a mellow accent to say
red flower in winter

A giant Czech is grateful for the light contact of our fingers

A huge Czech begins to wane as he drinks more

A small Czech could drown in his own tears
maybe confessing domestic problems

A petty Czech sleeps off his drunkenness on my shoulder
while he makes himself invisible he murmurs some words of gratitude

Before disappearing he offers one more glass of Becherovka.

CHINA

YANG LIAN

Translated from the Chinese by Brian Holton & Agnes Hung-Chong Chan

from What Water Confirms

4

in Hackney   the river is a hidden god
only seen when the autumn floods rise   under the streets
glaciers keep grinding in the rebated trench
a woodblock *Waterways Classic Annotated* bows to the meaning of
          wandering
this day uniquely, once only, exists

soaked with light
pierced again and again by the fluttering of a water bird

Georgia   Victoria   Edward   Elizabeth

          what if it was the Kingdom of Wei or the Tang Dynasty?

a brass fireplace where the ashes of the dead drift
a pair of ivory-white eyeballs gaze after his footsteps
a string of small parks' names spread like ripples
          rings of green by the mouth

a chapel   a bell always desperately ringing at the prow
imitating the one on the Whampoa in heavy fog

landforms hold a foundling tight
wrecked cars abandoned at the roadside   distance
is dug away like a motor   what if
one line of Chinese poetry lets the rain empty a room even more

water   dives back to the ancient hearing of the marshes
water   probably weary of flowing too

          missed it   tired too
a red brick wall is like a line running parallel to time

night after night extends   then there's the lonely structure of an
        individual
let him guess that's what he wants   rudder
dries up and cracks in the wind   pearly light thrashes in the
        sleeping oyster
Hackney is like a short Chinese verse   treasuring the moonlight she
        fears
leaves of a calendar turned over   a little plaza with a local accent
holds dirty pigeons to its bosom and breaks into pieces

NOTE: *Waterways Classic Annotated:* A major work of geographical writing by
Li Daoyuan (*d.* 527). Its forty chapters trace the various river courses of
China, providing a wealth of anecdotal and historical material concerning
cities and areas through which the rivers pass.

CHINESE TAIPEI
(TAIWAN)

CHEN LI
Translated from the Chinese by Chang Fen-ling

Nocturnal Fish

In the night I turn into a fish,
an amphibian
suddenly becoming rich and free because of having nothing.

Emptiness? Yes,
as empty as the vast space,
I swim in the night darker than your vagina
like a cosmopolitan.

Yes, the universe is my city.
Seen from any of our city swimming pools above,
Europe is but a piece of dry and shrunken pork,
and Asia a broken tea bowl by the stinking ditch.

73

Go fill in your sweet familial love,
fill in your pure water of ethics and morality,
fill in your bathing water which is replaced every other day.

I am an amphibian
having nothing and having nothing to fear.
I perch in the vast universe;
I perch in your daily and nightly dreams.
A bather bathed by the rain and combed by the wind.

I swim across your sky swaggeringly,
across the death and life that you can never escape.

Do you still boast of your freedom?

Come, and appreciate a fish,
appreciate a space fish that suddenly becomes rich
and free, because of your forsaking.

COLOMBIA

RAÚL HENAO
Translated from the Spanish by the author

Emptiness

One morning I awoke empty

There remained not the slightest trace of
me in the room

My body took indistinctly the form of
whatever object

was in reach

I did not succeed in looking at myself in
the mirror

I could not even locate the bottom of my
pockets

Not one single hair lay on the very white
sheet

Then I opened the room door:

    I had left myself outside.

COMOROS

Salim Hatubou

Translated from the Frenchby by Éva Rogo-Lévénez

And So

So, with naked feet, I took to the path leading to the town. I went
through the villages where I saw all the same poverty. I closed my
eyes and I quickened my steps. I reached the pass. I arrived in town,
out of breath and sweating. I said: I want to leave! The man looked
at me, smiling. He asked me: Have you a strong back and tough arms?
I answered: I'm as solid as the sacred rock of my village, as strong as
the baobab of djinns of my forebears and as loyal as the fisherfolk's
sons. He asked me: Name? I have the name of my father. Date of
birth? I was born in the middle of the year of the great drought. Look
down there, in the harbour, do you see the seagulls? Tomorrow, at
dawn, you will make your way through there and board that ship.

CONGO-BRAZZAVILLE (REPUBLIC OF THE CONGO)

ALAIN MABANCKOU
Translated from the French by Patrick Williamson

'there is nothing worse...'

there is nothing worse
than the grief of black-rhun palms
the sleep of swamps
the silence of passerines

    *

there is nothing worse
than the gossiping
of red ants
the confabs of praying mantis
eyes of agate
in dark lairs
the sky overcast with folded cloth

    *

god turns his back on us

how can one read
the tables of the law
translate the omens
of night
for everything was written

KAMA SYWOR KAMANDA

Translated from the French by Patrick Williamson

The song of resistance

Fanatics advance towards
Life's great fascinations
Under the protective wing of nothingness.
This is also the moment of immense disillusion
When the solitude of being is felt
Like memory voided of its messages
And emptied of images that fuel the fleeting.
Beyond the tumult of war,
A call comes through the flames,
Breaking the bonds that bind men to their manes.
This is the hour in which destinies
Become one with shooting stars
And exhaust all life forces,
Mistaking heroes for martyrs
In the blood and ash.
Bearers of lava and harvests,
We will go forward to the swamps and forests, the seas
And volcanoes, to bring offerings and songs.
We will follow the mutterings of darkness
And the groans of shades
Until the earthly root couples
With heavenly bodies
In the echo of distant mysteries.
We will go forward further than the Gods,
Beyond grotesque visions, to reanimate the spirits
Of all our uprooted dead.
We will go forward, implacable and devoted,
Brandishing lightning like a flare
In the night of our acute suffering
To bring controversy and refutation.
We will go forward, driven by the winds of history,
To free consciences
Subjugated for too long.

The roots of the upside-down tree
Will end up absorbing the rains
At the same time as our hopes
Mingled with the alchemy of our passions.

COOK ISLANDS

AUDREY BROWN

The Trilogy of Two (2) Halves

PART I

like the lady in the photograph (1998)

her came into our life
uninvited

       apparently always there   in another place with another name
                an accident
                 found out on the school yard from others
                 like a web blog on the internet for all to see
her looks like the lady in the photograph
pretty and exotic in that typical
tamure way
            her looks more like him than me
            but fat
            fair with yucky teeth and over
      expressive mouth
            her seems intelligent
            and dictionary nice
        but after something more than her lets on
he says
their friendship
           was conceived from naivety and no idea
           the result
                 a baby older than i
       born to a sky

with no mother or father
a small start elsewhere

with a L O U D arrival of her   here am her
let sing her.

PART II

she the chief executive and her (2003)

she so different
petite   smoker   workaholic
                         with world on she's shoulders
hardly eats   so disciplined   materially focused
          & controllingly beautiful   with synchronised hair
               she born to a body that is a power suit
          everything is perfect
                    except her
                              the pimple
                              on she's upper lip

               her came in the universe before she
               despite all she's prayers
               god never told she about her

               she'll never tell her to her face
               but she's heart says it all

               and she's *d i s t a n c e*
                         her the opposite of she
                         a child of the ocean
                         she of the sun and rising

               her made she's perfect
                         world imperfect
               the
illegitimate

          legitimate
                    press
                                   d e l e t e

PART III

albums of life's time (2007)

mama had a stroke
talofae
                    how does an iron will become melted?
stubborn
mama's mouth places a straight face
as if there is no pain
while eyes juxtapose   as you move mama from the bed to the chair
the fan is working overtime
and the sun is trying to forgive the situation
by keeping as honest as it possibly can
                        while mama is sleeping
                        you open the albums full of pictures
                        and see the life of your family
                        without you
            a lifetime compacted together
            with stories to speak of many times
                        seeing peoples faces in babies
                    and mannerisms of mothers and fathers in
                    children and grandchildren
it's hard to be in two (2) places at once
especially as you were never meant to be here until now
your heart whispers to self
it's not your fault   the albums of life's time
                        pieces the jigsaw *d i s t a n c e* of she
mama is awake now
                it's time for her taele
                you really don't know what you're doing
                but you casually reassure her
                no worries mama
                it's only you
                        her grand daughter
                        her son's eldest daughter
                        older than she
        you can hear the river flowing
        from behind the house
        and feel a certain shelter
        from the trees.

ANA ISTARÚ
Translated from the Spanish by Mark Smith-Soto

Bringing to Light

she came from me
emerged from the deep
the doctor applauded
I came with sea in my belly
like an intense umbrella
globe of the world

I was the sphere rolling in the dawn
my heart beating like a horse
I put it that way

because its mane
perfumed me

my womb moved
in the way herds are moved
I came with my mollusk my poppy
my wild pony
with my round sparrow

I could never not show   I told myself
for our appointment
so here I am
with this festival
jumping at my waist

I danced my rose dance
my wing-beats
mooing like boats do
my womb spinning

she waited for me
hidden in the redness
the doctor was frowning into

I pushed
the world's wind roaring in my forehead
I puffed like a lighthouse
like the sea gods of myth
a royal pomegranate about to blow

I remember how thankfully
César held me by the hair
deeply moved without knowing
whether to crow or envy me
completely turned to my lungs' work
breathing out breathing in breathing out
he watched me from inside his eyes
in a way that will never be repeated
in the whole of his life's life,
watched the landscape of my belly change

and so she
came from me
she came from the deep
blessed us with the slap of her scream
began drinking the sun like a wild beast
made of wool or amaranth

I was in love and laughed
from madness from sparking from my knees
wanting to kiss César's sex, the fleece
of him with tears in his eyes
to pick up my little creature
and run out to lavish her down the streets

what soft rain of milk galloping
the light of the world into my nipple

CÔTE D'IVOIRE

TANELLA BONI
Translated from the French by Patrick Williamson

from Gorée baobab island

here too the sheets where history snoozed
are white and empty

the covers of time alone
                        are green like the last word in the world
when the wind howls
                        day and night at the gates of chaos

then I wrap myself in the words of your look faraway
beyond the sea that separates us infinitely

CROATIA

DAMIR ŠODAN
Translated from the Croatian by Damir Šodan & Stephen M. Dickey

Kamchatka

I dreamed that Kamchatka
had broken off from the mainland
and was floating freely across the sea.

All the media covered the event.
(The Japanese were advised
to remain indoors.)

I ran through the city trying to find you
before the whole world fell apart,
but you were getting ready to go

to the movies with some women
I did not know. One of them stole my
coat. I was so desperate.

I screamed all night long,
but no one could hear me.
As if I'd been long dead.

PEDRO PEREZ SARDUY
Translated from the Spanish by Jean Stubbs

The Poet

The Poet is the type with class
            who is born on some insignificant day
            like October 20 on which Arthur Rimbaud
            was born in 1854

The Poet is the curiously irresponsible type
            practically what has been called
            a serious pathological case
            because he's a city mole and changes
            his skin constantly
            with rare exceptions he always ends up
            being militant for some non-just cause or other
            professing the latest ideas that are *engagées*
            and giving up that self-worship of his
            which is an expression thought up
            by some other poet
            because

The Poet that is he who goes about ordering
          or discovering street poetry is the kind
          who likes to preserve his private life to the full
          and will go to all lengths to defend it
          and always has a pretext
          because

The Poet is the type who doesn't use firearms
          unless they're the harquebuses used
          in the age of enlightenment
          but that's beside the point
          for example if he is born under Libra
          like old Arthur was
          he's unkempt phlegmatic
          neurotic as hell
          hypersensitive
          fit to play golf
          and listen to *Swan Lake*
          but if he's born under Taurus
          he's the kind with violent streak wild
          who never thinks twice
          about joining the guerrilla struggle
          in any part of the world
          – even in the most
          of Babel's hotels in the West –
          and he's a real Don Juan
          even when he's not handsome
          because

The Poet is in love with love
          and knows how to make it only too well
          he practises yoga meditates Zen Buddhism
          and ceremoniously drinks tea
          and ejaculates different coloured stars
          with each orgasm...fabulous...!
          because

The Poet is the COPYRIGHT type who has no faith
          in his glory
          or that of the Nobel Prize
          he knows other languages especially
          Western ones

and buries himself in the country
to study Oriental philosophy
he eats frog's legs and is a connoisseur
of drinks and aromatic herbs
because

The Poet is a paranoid with copious atomic neurones
and makes no literary bones about rejecting
all that is troglodyte and socially calcified
beat par excellence in his latter years
of lyricism he likes to love
as much as he denies all signs of frigidity
in his lover
because

The Poet is a mythological being almost sacred
as he has been ever since prehistoric times
when he rode on his mammoth
with supernatural powers to presage disasters
he never augurs happiness
because he's a doubting dilemma
just like his day and age
although at times he prefers to go off
into the country
to cleanse himself of the refined oil
to the strains of a thin flageolet
and he's so incredulous as to consider
his work superior to that of the singular kind
unmultipliable by two
almost impossible to believe
that he came from a mother's womb
– sorry [Author's note] it's just that

The Poet is the type who is born where
night finds him
what's more

The Poet is the type who always believes in someone
or something and therein lies the contradiction
no ifs and buts
and he's so soft that each day
in his solitude

he goes over all his small failures
so as to build the one-and-only-indivisible-collective
for when it's time for the enchanted dream
because

The Poet is the type to be pitied
but he likes to savour international dishes
and frequently visits
the Volga (Russian food)
the Yang-tse (Chinese food)
the Saint John (American food)
the Fish & Chip Shop (English food)
the Montecatini (Italian food)
the Polynesia (Polynesian food)
the Monseigneur (French food)
the Wakamba (African food)
the Centro Vasco (Spanish food)
La Carreta (Creole food)
because

The Poet is the embittered type who courts trouble
and is always the one to sacrifice himself
to be fucked over and over again
by apocalyptic existence
that is his lot...BAM!
until the moment he acquires
(no, not a Prize...that's not enough)
social standing and holds
his own space
(not in a spaceship either)
he often holds it in diplomacy
(as a diplomat) that is
he becomes according to historical materialism
a being who sells his intellectual power
at a high price and the crises start
in his work of creation
(I don't mean Jesus Christ or Buddha
who saw to it that
the poet is subject to the law of the incessant flow of dharma)
because he wavers in his beliefs and...
well, to continue:
that according to him demand of him

87

certain standards and make him attached to life
(to transform the WORLD to change LIFE)
but there are other who if adapt perfectly
and like their new life as a function-ary
(not from Aryan)
start to travel with importance
or go on their important travels
because

The Poet is the type made for the clouds
                which doesn't mean that
                he's up in the clouds
                but that he needs to fly to travel
                that is to get to know people
                swap emotions and people too
                and he always maintains as he does now that
                there should be an airline
                specially for poets
                something like **POETA DE AVIACIÓN** or
                POETANA AIRLINES CORPORATION
                with Boeings Ilushin and Super DC-10s
                to take them no problem at all
                to any corner of this world
                as the desire or the inspiration moves them
                with no other passport than one of their books
                translated into at least five languages
                [OK...OK, we'll bear you in mind for the next Congress...]
                because

The Poet is the type who needs love affection
                and concern more than any one else in the world
                and he needs to meet lord fog madame notre dame
                mademoiselle le louvre monsieur d'eiffel
                and take a spin on the air metro and sit down
                and enjoy himself in the gardens of Rome
                and drink port and take a minibath in the
                Fontana di Trevi think about Botticelli
                Michelangelo or the genius of Dante
                and throw three coins in so as to sing
                three coins in the fountain
                to visit the ruins of Pompeii
                and those of the old Roman Empire

(seat of incredible battles) to go see
underdevelopment and compare it with his own
his cosa nostra
and that's something else
because

The Poet is the type to detest underdevelopment
    and yet he doesn't help eradicate it
    he thinks that by carrying unforgivably
    silken lectures in his bags
    he's going to de-underdevelop himself
    but it does NOT always happen that way
    it's a joke
    because

The Poet is thoroughly untrusting
    right down to the fallout shelters
    because he knows that when all's said
    and done he'll not be of much use
    when the hour of the comics comes around
    and he's had to emigrate in safari
    most of the time although not to Africa
    but to live in some big old house in
    MONTparnasse-pellier-martre
    well one or other of those mounts or
    along the banks of the Thames
    because

The Poet is the metaphysical type caught up in
        cycle of rebirth and he goes far very far
    to meet with hunger nostalgia and revolution
    but he's a globetrotter
    knows his way around cities like
    Stockholm Geneva Zurich
    Moscow Indianapolis Peking Athens
    Mexico City Brussels New York
    Berlin Havana Barcelona
    because

The Poet is an internationalist
    not of the proletarian but of the poetarian
    he's a being who fights like hell

for the collective freedom
and he likes to be steeped in heartache abroad
but he writes the most although to no avail
to justify his being – the rest is bullshit –
HIS BEING
and it's the worst paid
[this thesis is not universal – Author's note]
but he has more feelings than cats have
because

The Poet is a scaffold across which the sun creeps
barefoot and naked
he returns in one piece
barefoot
dissipating the illusion that comes
out of materialist desires
I am a beggar
an inoffensive kind of being
not needed anywhere
but to quote Walt Whitman…
'Don't cry over me…'

CYPRUS

CHRISTODOULOS MAKRIS

The Impressionists

Round them up, the Impressionists,
even those straddling the margins
of their place and time – idealists
prone to self-harm, hermits opting
to stay unwashed for weeks, students
of the bodies of chocolate pre-pubescent girls –
and lock them in a house loaded
with cameras and microphones. Force them

to speak our language. Offer them a budget
scarcely adequate for food or tools,
and present them with tasks: to construct
a sunrise, say, or to stay under water
for an hour. Insert moles, temptresses, syphilis,
critics; divide them into bedrooms of three;
command the sun to scream overhead daily.
Scrutinise them as they disintegrate
into bedlam or rally round leaders. Then
make them stand up and nominate each other
for execution. (Naturally, the decision
on who survives the vote rests solely
with us.) Repeat the process occasionally
until only one remains – to be declared
The Greatest Impressionist of All Time –
before he, too, is brought before the guillotine.

CZECH REPUBLIC

SYLVA FISCHEROVÁ

Translated from the Czech by Sylva Fischerová & Stuart Friebert

Eggs, Newspaper, and Coffee

Eggs, newspaper, and coffee
are the first lie of the world,
saying that it's
                    in order.

What order, while the whoredoms
of Jezebel, your mother,
and her witchcrafts are many?
said Jehu to King Horam
and shot him
                between the shoulders.

91

What order, when every morning
the ark's built up,
and the animals outrun
      one another,
wheedle money, bribe Noah:
    Brother, let me in!
Noah's taken in,
the ark rocks on pity, on grief,
a swift stream, the Okeanos of weeping,
spits it into the pan of eggs
    in the middle of the morning.
How the animals shout! How fried they are!
    The latest news from the ark! Come and get it!
        they squeak from the pan,
and above them, implacable as Jehu, an angel cries:
What order?
The news of your heart
is black as night,
ugly as a Medusa!

On the waves of a compassionate coffee,
Noah sails the ship on
past shop shutters slowly lifting up,
around rambling flowers
that open and close
their shining petals,
and breathe out pity
which papers
      the world

PIA TAFDRUP
Translated from the Danish by David McDuff

The Whales in Paris

It's probably not Paris that the whales sing about in the great oceans,
but the city is beautiful this morning, where I wake up
after dreaming about ton-heavy, cavorting whales.
On all sides they swam, the gigantic creatures,
my only salvation in the rough sea
was to grab hold of their tails, which were so slippery
that my hands slid the moment the whales altered course
or flapped their tails hard, hurling me far away,
but each time I swam back, grabbed hold again
and in this way managed to survive all night...
On the wall opposite I see now that it's a brilliant morning,
the greetings of the birds suggest the same,
the whales are gone, a woman moves from window to window,
raising the Venetian blinds and opening the windows ajar,
– this I enter in my dream journal.
The sun falls into the woman's kitchen,
where she walks around putting heaps of clothes together.
Each day our lives are invented;
a so far new combination of the known and unknown,
will perhaps arise today —
it depends on what falls into our minds,
falls into us, embraces us with memory-deep gaze,
when we seek an entrance to something
                            that is freedom for the soul —
and will tolerate no limit other than the open sky.

ABDOURAHMAN A. WABERI

Translated from the French by Patrick Williamson

Desire

I am the rustling of the world
the swaying between here and elsewhere
the dumb foliage of the cactus
the coarse wood that covers the gecko
the bed for the world-book
whose pages are as many waves of the quest
endlessly begun again

DANIEL CAUDEIRON

Words for an Expatriate

You say there's a fair bit of sun
in Southend
but you'll never see
it again...
once you see it at Mero –
with a wide, curved mirror
to reflect it, a tall golden lance
that shatters the dwarf coconuts apart,
then goes down revolting
to an inevitable drowning.

It's last bloodshed, as if in defiance
of the remorseless end,
a red soaked banner flung
wide and high
that leaves all wounds,
and momentarily incarnadines the sand;

astounded faces
are shaken
by a wonder, daily, never dull.

DOMINICAN REPUBLIC

CHIQUI VICIOSO

Translated from the Spanish by Judith Kerman

The Fish Swam

> *Everything will have to be reconstructed, intended anew, and the old myths, reappearing, will offer us their spells and their enigmas, with an unknown face.*
>
> JOSÉ LEZAMA LIMA, Myths and Classical Weariness

I

The fish swam
out of the water
and it was common
to encounter birds
in the roots of trees.

II

Free
the sea rose through violet plains
there was no sun

but the light reigned
in that Paradise
under the green absolutism
of an apple tree.

III

Ruah, K'I, divine breath
Kalpa and Purlaya
The nine beginning whispers
Hamsas's rainbow
Sealed alliance between God and his creation
Where Eva originates.

IV

Silicius land
By God's will
Incarnated Golem
One of two faces

Detached from the circular head
Two of four legs
Untied and claiming for a back
Their own essence
For the beginning
Of their crossing.

V

Ouessant/
Surija/
Tula
altars chiselled by the waves
Islands
for the wandering ships of the soul
Finis Terra
in the geography of the unattainable
where I encounter
the foam's in piercing blades.
My sisters of worship the Apsaras.

ECUADOR

SANTIAGO VIZCAÍNO
Translated from the Spanish by Alexis Levitin

from Hands in the Grave

II

Each one of us has learned to live
with the slow cordage of insomnia,
to breathe the final exhalation of the fallen,
to rub against the peeled flesh of the wall.

Each one of us
has the smell of poppies when they open,
the breath of an eye torn from its orbit,
the feeling of hatred and of hunger.

Each one of us
has his laugh like a stem,
and knows of rancid breath and hope.

'Listen to me,' I said,
but their eyes could no longer make out their shadows.

III

An inebriated angel strolls by
shy
as an owl.

The women squeeze their breasts
and a bitter milk comes forth
with which they suckle sombre skeletons, their little ones.

On the other side, spiders,
their feet,
their luxurious palpi.

'Listen to me,' I said,
but it was like a verb from an ancient torrential homeland.

VI

We are deserted,
abandoned to a pusillanimous will.

How have we gotten here,
so surfeited with death?

'To die is an art,' I said,
but that light was not my own.

VII

Don't hold back,
go on with that deceptive stammering.
Forget the pulsing phantom
that dwells on the other side of the wall.
Cling to faith, suborn yourself,
like someone begging alms among famished wolves.

XII

My heart is a bed
where scorpions copulate.
There is no hiding place from this throbbing of the grave.
How long has it been since the ghost
last appeared with its violet light?

We listen to the muteness of the night
and we forget.
Thus is the circle closed.

XVI

Maybe meaning is in gazing till it hurts.
Or in stumbling over the halo of a dream.
Or in letting yourself be carried along
like an abject creature
surrounded by oppression and misery.

But how to know where to crawl
or how to turn to snow,
bloody torridness.

IMAN MERSAL

Translated from the Arabic by Khaled Mattawa

Amina

You order beer by phone
with the confidence of a woman who knows three languages
and who weaves words into unexpected contexts.

How did you find this sense of security
as if you'd never left your father's house?
Why does your presence provoke this destructiveness
that is completely free of intent,
this gravity
that releases my senses from their darkness?
What else should I do
when a shared hotel room offers me
a perfect friend
except to lump my unrefined manners and fling them
at her face as a crudeness I have contrived?

Go ahead, amuse yourself.
I am fair.
I'll let you have more than half the room's oxygen
on the condition that you see me beyond comparisons,
you who are twenty years older than my mother.
You wear bright colours
and will never grow old.

My perfect friend,
why don't you leave now.
Perhaps I'll open the grey wardrobes
and try on your stylish things.

Why don't you go
and leave me all the room's oxygen.
The void of your absence may lead me
to bite my lip in despair
as I look at your toothbrush,
familiar... and wet.

EL SALVADOR

CLARIBEL ALEGRÍA

Translated from the Spanish by Carolyn Forché

Flowers from the Volcano

Fourteen volcanos rise
in my remembered country
in my mythical country.
Fourteen volcanos of foliage and stone
where strange clouds hold back
the screech of a homeless bird.
Who said that my country was green?
It is more red, more grey, more violent:
Izalco roars,
taking more lives.
Eternal Chacmol collects blood,
the grey orphans
the volcano spitting bright lava
and the dead *guerrillero*
and the thousand betrayed faces,
the children who are watching
so they can tell of it.
Not one kingdom was left us.
One by one they fell
through all the Americas.
Steel rang in palaces,
in the streets,
in the forests
and the centaurs sacked the temple.
Gold disappeared and continues
to disappear on *yanqui* ships,
the golden coffee mixed with blood.
The priest flees screaming
in the middle of the night
he calls his followers
and they open the *guerrillero*'s chest
so as to offer the Chac
his smoking heart.

100

No one believes in Izalco
that Tlaloc is dead
despite television,
refrigerators,
Toyotas.
The cycle is closing,
strange the volcano's silence
since it last drew breath.
Central America trembled,
Managua collapsed.
In Guatemala the earth sank
Hurricane Fifi flattened Honduras.
They say the *yanquis* turned it away,
that it was moving towards Florida
and they forced it back.
The golden coffee is unloaded
in New York where
they roast it, grind it
can it and give it a price.
Siete de Junio
noche fatal
bailando el tango
la capital.
From the shadowed terraces
San Salvador's volcano rises.
Two-storey mansions
protected by walls
four metres high
march up its flanks
each with railings and gardens,
roses from England
and dwarf *araucarias*,
Uruguayan pines.
Farther up, in the crater
within the crater's walls
live peasant families
who cultivate flowers
their children can sell.
The cycle is closing,
Cuscatlecan flowers
thrive in volcanic ash,
they grow strong, tall, brilliant

101

The volcano's children
flow down like lava
with their bouquets of flowers,
like roots they meander
like rivers the cycle is closing.
The owners of two-storey houses
protected from thieves by walls
peer from their balconies
and they see the red waves descending
and they drown their fears in whiskey.
They are only children in rags
with flowers from the volcano,
with *Jacintos* and *Pascuas* and *Mulatas*
but the wave is swelling,
today's Chacmol still wants blood,
the cycle is closing,
Tlaloc is not dead.

EQUATORIAL GUINEA

RECAREDO SILEBO BOTURU
Translated from the Spanish by David Shook

Tragedy

> *Africa is one of the continents richest in natural resources but its children
> perish like hens.*

The Okume's leaves
began to fall
little by little
&,
the wind appeared
to take them like ashes
to the cosmos,
on that night.

On that night
the cricket's tender voice
which brightens up the passage
of the lightning bugs in the field
was turned off.

On that night
the water of the Atlantic
dried up
&, the sea's mouth opened
so that Mustafa
would heave his last sigh,
his last breath,
the last beat of his heart
under the brown blankets
of the Red Cross
           with his chimeras.

& in his village
the tigers began to voice
roars that terrified
the children,
perturbed their mothers
&,
the Harmattan arrived
and made teardrops
rain from strong men;
           meanwhile his mother
in her bed
consoled by having him
in the pretty earth,
in the fertile earth,
in the glory.

Northward.

RIBKA SIBHATU
Literal translation from the Italian by Andre Naffis-Sahely
Final translated version by The Poetry Translation Workshop

Mother Africa

Cradle of mankind
baobab of the soul,
in your savannahs
and sacred forests
death dances.

You hear the echo, the scream
of the mother
who delivers diamonds
and receives armoured tanks.

O dying land,
that for decades
has met the elders,
the elders who keep
the ancestral treasures.

When will dawn break
for generous
Mother Africa?

KRISTIINA EHIN

Translated from the Estonian by Ilmar Lehtpere

How to explain my language to you

How to explain my language to you
here and now
by moonlight
beside the spring

I'm sitting with you
handsome Indo-European man
on a big mossy Finno-Ugric stone
the talk half-naked
night-bright between us

I so want to tell you
how pine trees smell in my language
and irises
how water babbles in my language over granite stones
and how crickets get the very last out of their fiddles

Instead we are silent
eyes closed
and we open our mouths just a bit now and then
for some half-naked night-bright words
in a language neither yours nor mine

ETHIOPIA

BEWKETU SEYOUM
Translated from the Amharic by Chris Beckett

Elegy

The fall of every leaf diminishes me,
so when I hear a rustle
I send my eyes out of the window
to look at the trees in the yard.
Alas! where there were woods,
now I see flag-poles standing.
Men have swept nature's nest away
to build their cities.
The melody of the nightingale
has lost its immortality
and I am sitting on a dead land,
writing my elegy in the sand.

FIJI

SUDESH MISHRA

Lorca

When they take him out again in a scene
That echoes the primal scene of his murder,
The dream is the same. A path forks out
Into an orchard. It's a moonless night.
Olives are not screaming for mercy.
Gypsies are not cursing their guitars.

No dog, out of the blue, licks his face as he kneels.
A cicada attempts a note, yes, but insinuates nothing.
If he shivers, it's because of the cold.
His captors have never seen the picture,
But possessing the gift of hindsight
Know exactly what to do. They load their guns.
They take aim. They demand lessons in poetry.

FINLAND

PEKKO KAPPI

Translated from the Finnish by the author

Mariainen

What do I sing, of whom am I singing?
I am singing about the Creator's death
about the death of Mariainen

Deep grave was dug
Deep grave, iron bottom
to the depth of nine laps
to the depth of ten arm lengths

There the Creator was buried
Mariainen put to death
sealed with tin nails
sealed with iron nails

So the Creator is being prayed to
Oh, merciful Creator
Make the sun shine
And God's moon shine

Melt away the Golden nails
Melt away the iron nails
Let the Creator run away
let Mariainen run away too

Mari was running down the road
A hundred saints behind her
A thousand saints behind her

A pile of wood falls across
She bows to the pile of wood
and gives her hand to the pile of wood

The holy crowd is puzzled
What's up with our Mari?

A bridge comes across
She bows to the bridge
and gives her hand to the bridge

The holy crowd is puzzled
What's up with our Mari?

A church comes across
She doesn't bow to the church
and doesn't give her hand to the altar

NOTE: This song is based on a version found in the *Suomen Kansan Vanhat Runot* (the Ancient Poems of the Finnish People anthology). It was sung by a person called 'Tarin akka' (Tari's Hag). You can't find the exact version from there though, because over the years the song has altered in people's mouths. The storyline is the same however. It's a very strange song, because the Creator, God and Mari get mixed up all the time. Oh yes, Mari is Saint Mary. I really like the story: there's an element of 'living death' and this terrible feeling that there's loads of people following right behind you, watching and commenting on what you are doing. But in the end no one has any idea of Mari's mission. Also the aspect of a road and going down the road is always fascinating.

VALÉRIE ROUZEAU
Translated from the French by Susan Wicks

Carpe Diem
(for Susan)

Today two thousand nine in four-line verse
upon the little town wherein I lie
even at pushchair level the sun shines.
Babies like market traders bawl their wares.

I want to catch this Sunday
keep it in the meshes of my net,
a giant silver fish cleaned and ready
this fourth of January, dripping wet.

To gather while I may life's roses
thorns or scales di da di da di dum
to garnish lucky me a bunch of flowers
strolling the stalls and holders strollerless.

Monday can take its time in coming
water running under each bridge away.
For now I pour it bring it to a simmer

GABON

ANONYMOUS
Translated from the Fang

Sun

Dead darkness falls
headlong falling
at your flashlight glare
your beam-eye arrows
shot from your fire-box:
flare-shots
rip her coat
pitch-coat pricked
with star-studs:
your flare-shots
rip her pitch-dark coat.

THE GAMBIA

MARIAMA KHAN

Men and Fame

Some men have conscience
In others, nonsense
Takes over the conscience

Some men are like foul ditches
They swallow even the sand that
Will fill them to extinction

Some men give promises this minute
By the ticking of the next second
It is lost like a post-virginity encounter

Some men desperately sell their souls
To be named for even things ill-fitting for them
The mad desire of the spotlight, is the curse bending them over

They do cut their faces
And by God, if no rescuers are at hand, they will self-drown
In the abyss of a molten bunker.

GEORGIA

MAYA SARISHVILI

Translated from the Georgian by Timothy Kercher & Nene Giorgadze

Let my husband know

Let my husband know

that this, my veil, sprouted from my skull
like milk bursting with fat spurts from a crusty fissure.
The veil, smoke from the flume.
And I, the blackened chimney

or too-hot porch that releases

globules of milk fat   wisps –

floating to high up places from where there's no return.
Let my husband know my mother's soul is a veil –
flown worriedly into my hair to sway me –
but paint

on my flesh still lingers, like a bullet made of diamond.

111

Let my husband know

I'll wear a veil of sweetened pigeon meat on the back of my head,

or instead of a veil, I'll use his letters as covering
as I grow old and transform
like a flower unfolding in boiling water.

GERMANY

JAN WAGNER

Translated from the German by Danielle Janess & Julian Smith-Newman

a horse

> *The well-aimed phrase is a whip*
> *your poem a horse.*
>
> MICHAEL DONAGHY, after Lu Chi

is it a black, a chestnut or a grey,
stallion or mare,
which tramples the garden and makes its way
over the rhubarb and the lavender?

which leaps the triple bar
only to land in the middle
of the battlefield, hitched before
the cart with barrels and the pyramid

golden of hay? the carthorse,
which hauls its kilo-heavy heart
from brabant and the V, light plough
of the wild geese, or the lippizaner, born

as a black, which has the wits to mince
from every field, white and ever whiter,
grows into a triumph, checkmates the whole world,
dazzling as the handkerchief of an emperor?

let it be understood: all two-hundred
and fifty-two bones you can compose
in sleep, know the hoofbeat,
hard knowledge, the precision in the tail,

the grey-brown silhouettes that rub themselves
at night against the pasture fence, haw and gee,
hear the strangled whinny in the graves
of pharaohs and of conquerors.

and yet you are still here, red as a beer-
cabby and cursing, with the sugar stick
brilliance in your pocket and the beast,
which goes neither forward nor back,

reacts neither to your whip
nor to the carrot dangling on a string
before its nostrils like the candle
before an icon. move, you tell it, trembling.

it does not move. it stands there, looks into the land.

GHANA

NII AYIKWEI PARKES

Men Like Me

My mother warned me about laid-back men
like me. Men with lazy leans and sharp eyes,
who love nothing better than an evening
on a street corner tasting the world, slice

by sour slice. Men with rough beards and dreadlocks,
whose hands are comfortable settling into
pockets. Men with a thousand ways to pause
and paint plain days in shades of awe and blue,

who dream in many dialects, smell of spice,
men whose tongues slide easily over lips.
My mother told me to steer clear of wise-
cracking men like me, sun-hardened, with deep

laughs and tattoos, usurping God's calling
as creator, rewriting their own skins.

GREAT BRITAIN

JO SHAPCOTT

Phrase Book

I'm standing here inside my skin,
which will do for a Human Remains Pouch
for the moment. Look down there (up here).
Quickly. Slowly. This is my own front room

where I'm lost in the action, live from a war,
on screen. I am an Englishwoman, I don't understand you.
What's the matter? You are right. You are wrong.
Things are going well (badly). Am I disturbing you?

TV is showing bliss as taught to pilots:
Blend, Low silhouette, Irregular shape, Small,
Secluded. (Please write it down. Please speak slowly.)
Bliss is how it was in this very room

when I raised my body to his mouth,
when he even balanced me in the air,
or at least I thought so and yes the pilots say
yes they have caught it through the Side-Looking

Airborne Radar, and through the J-Stars.
I am expecting a gentleman (a young gentleman,
two gentlemen, some gentlemen). Please send him
(them) up at once. This is really beautiful.

Yes they have seen us, the pilots, in the Kill Box
on their screens, and played the routine for
getting us Stealthed, that is, Cleansed, to you and me,
Taken Out. They know how to move into a single room

like that, to send in with Pinpoint Accuracy, a hundred Harms.
I have two cases and a cardboard box. There is another
bag there. I cannot open my case – look out,
the lock is broken. Have I done enough?

Bliss, the pilots say, is for evasion
and escape. What's love in all this debris?
Just one person pounding another into dust,
into dust. I do not know the word for it yet.

Where is the British Consulate? Please explain.
What does it mean? What must I do? Where
can I find? What have I done? I have done
nothing. Let me pass please. I am an Englishwoman.

KATERINA ILIOPOULOU
Translated from the Greek by John O'Kane

Tainaron

Here the days do not dissolve in the air
They drop into the water
Forming their very own layer
A surface of separation.
A hawk flies above the body of summer
He dives again and again
Feeding and getting drunk on falling.
There is nothing here
Only crazy wind and stones
And sea
A random promise
Sharpens our lust with the blade of the moon.

When I arrived for the first time in this landscape of endings
The wind entered my mouth with such fury
As if I were its sole receptacle
Until all my words disappeared.

Every tree receives the wind differently
Some suffer others resist
(I met a palm tree that gave birth to the wind and distributed it
in every direction)
Others shake all over and change colours.
I of course am not a tree
I sat down and wore the wind as a coat.
I bent my head and looked at the ground.
From its crevices, the roots of thyme
with their hieroglyphics struggled to enter the light.
Then the words came back.

NOTE: Cape Tainaron is the southernmost tip of continental Greece. Ancient
Greeks believed it to be the end of the world.

MAUREEN ROBERTS

A Farewell Song

White clouds, grey streaked
    her early morning hair
        Waiting to be combed by sunrays
           parting locks of clouds.
Her frock swirling coconut branches,
    lifting up high in the early morning breeze
        settling around her knees
           in the glassy translucence
              of aqua seas.

Came to find you
    Speaking soft to me like these island whispers
        and you were gone.
        Rising up with a pre-dawn breeze
           You decided not to wait
              Ten years was too long

Though I might have come sooner
    But couldn't with you gone.

    Came to find you
        baby, child teenager and adult as I am
           but couldn't with you gone.

    Look it rains, sweet smelling, soft and warm
        like your checks on my face
I have grown my hair long for you
    the way you would prefer it.
        I will wear it in plaits
           But who will plait it?

    I have come, as I came before, on other visits.
        I am well, mammy, daddy, all the children
           Everyone is well and send their love.

Came to see you but you had gone away.
Left no address.

Pulling your skirt up
    Placing it between your knees you said,
        'it's time to go. After all I'm weary
I've walked countless steps to Douglastan and back
    I've sifted and sorted enough nutmeg
I've carried enough feed for Nan, the goat, and those damn rabbits
Baked enough bread, bun and coconut tart.
        It's time to rest.'
            Your filmy eyes peering into another sunset
                Across the bay at Gouyave, Benago 1.

The flowers are gone.
    The stubborn rose that climbed over the door
        The pots filled with flowering plants;
            the black sage, the thyme.
The fruit trees, except the tamarind, mango and lime,
    All gone. What without you could survive?
        I came to find you and you were gone.

'Child, life goes on.'

Last time I saw you the sadness in your eyes, as if you knew
    You would not wait for my return
        I can't remember saying goodbye
            I'm searching my memory to find your words,
                to find your smile.

I'm waiting for your visit in a dream
    clearer than cinematic film.
        I know you'll come when time is right
            breathing a soft
                'Bon dieu, eh eh, oui papa.'
                And you'll smile
            Seeing the little girl of four or five

        the child who knew better than to leave you behind
            to go to England.
                The child who wept and screamed

118

'Dada, Dada, come for me Dada, come for me. Don't go.'
'But you going to England, to your mammy.'

And I was gone.

Black child, calypso in my soul,
        red earth dance pounded into the soles of my feet.
            So many partings.

I had a dream one time, that I a skinny black child
        Was walking across dry, sun-cracked savannah
            With my nomad family. Old men with sticks,
                dogs with strange wolf-hound heads,
                    high arching backs and sparse, shaggy coats

Looking for our next home
        Looking for home
            While fierce dogs barked at us.

Who will interpret my dreams?
        Who can know without the gift?
            I only knew I was ancestral dreaming.

And where are you to tell me why and how?
        And what can I, a mere child,
            know of the purpose of adults and this world?
                Who am I and what do I know at the last/
                    Except that this final parting
                        hurts.

CRAIG SANTOS PEREZ

from preterrain

[we] cross with only these possessions
    and look for something familiar yet so much belongs to a separation
unlike definitions i lose what objects mean
    in time i could almost say *we belong to what we lose*
somewhere beginnings persist that were never simply given never simply taken
    maybe this is more than lost cargo maybe this
is only where light comes to breathe from afar no exact location
    disclosed because no breath ends

        return

is it true that you can live with thirst
    and still die from drowning only to have words
become as material as our needs
    I want to ask you is *it still possible to hear our paper skin opening* [we]
carry our stories overseas to the place called 'voice'
    and call

            to know our allowance of water

CARMEN MATUTE

Translated from the Spanish by Pablo Medina

The Fig's Proposal

I propose to you
the sweetness of the fig,
its rosy flesh
folded over a damp self
like a sea creature.

Enjoy the mystery of this fruit,
its mollusc-like feel,
its intimate size.
Smooth and pulpy it
will satisfy your tongue's
desire.

I propose
the fig's delights.
Take a bite of its split,
helpless centre,
taste once again – stubborn –
its flesh containing
honey and deluge.

The delights and sweetness of the fig –
small and overflowing –
is all I propose.
Let your wide mouth linger
in its sweet secret.
Let it ravish, slowly,
the wakened flesh.

Let it bring to your palate
the memory of a primal flavour.

KOUMANTHIO ZEINAB DIALLO
Translated from the French by Helen & David Constantine

Hymn to the brave peasant women of Africa

This evening from my vantage point
At the gates of a savaged age that is answering back
Peasant women of Africa my thoughts are all of you
And for some days now I have been searching
In the belly of the days and in the vomit
Of memories on the slopes of sleep
And in your blue eyes
That water the pale savannah and cause
The fields of maize to sing and our mysterious mountains
To be green again, in your blue eyes
I have been searching for sheaves of words
Among the sheaves of fonio
I see puckers of pain around your eyes
Blood in the pupils between sheaves of flowers
And a rise of fear
Between a sheaf of rice
And a girl who is laughing
In the presence of a patriarch at his prayers
And a virgin crying at the harshnesses
Served to a crucified child

Black devil-women, old as the earth,
Lofty, untameable, your arms have a saving strength
At the gates of a savaged age that is answering back
You are to me great priestesses outfacing the weather
And I match my thoughts to the rhythm of your peasant tread
I salute your courage when your gatherings under the talking tree
Unleash the virtue of the ancestral language
And you demand justice, justice
For the savaged race, you sound out the sky
You dig over the earth for the children of the fugitive rains
I salute you, peasant women of Africa
And I offer you for your bravery
A thousand poems bursting forth like roses in the evening wind

I offer you the laughter of the pastoral flute
Bewitching princess whose voice clothes the mountain tops
And I offer you also the words of the kingly tom-tom
Mad guardian of our vacillating faiths
For this evening from my vantage point
At the gates of a savaged age that is answering back
Too long I've been trying to say
Not knowing enough, but nonetheless trying to say
What all these troubled hearts intend with me
Whose only desire in this world of wrong and harm
Is to say, say again, to myself say it again,
And I laugh that I could say nothing about you
Brave peasant women of Africa

GUINEA-BISSAU

VASCO CABRAL

*Translated from the Portuguese by José Lingna Nafafe,
Ana Raquel Fernandes & Jonathan Morley*

Last Adieus of a Forest-Fighter

That afternoon I left and you remained,
we felt, us two, the *saudade*'s sorrow.
I suffered the bloody truth of your tears.
You're not my only happiness, *amor*,
I left you there for love of Humankind
but, seeing your tears, my heart took upon the pain
you bore, and ached bitterly at your moans,
so yes, it's why I left you and remained.

Believe I never left, that you gave me
the gift of yourself; then this pain and grief
will be no more than nightmares, quickly gone.
Believe I never will forget your love,
and, if I am the one your love burns for,
carry the hope that one day I'll return.

JOHN AGARD

Half-caste

Excuse me
standing on one leg
I'm half-caste

Explain yuself
wha yu mean
when yu say half-caste
yu mean when picasso
mix red an green
is a half-caste canvas/
explain yuself
wha yu mean
when yu say half-caste
yu mean when light an shadow
mix in de sky
is a half-caste weather/
well in dat case
england weather
nearly always half-caste
in fact some o dem cloud
half-caste till dem overcast
so spiteful dem dont want de sun pass
ah rass/
explain yuself
wha yu mean
when yu say half-caste
yu mean when tchaikovsky
sit down at dah piano
an mix a black key
wid a white key
is a half-caste symphony/

Explain yuself
wha yu mean
Ah listening to yu wid de keen

half of mih ear
Ah lookin at yu wid de keen
half of mih eye
an when I'm introduced to you
I'm sure you'll understand
why I offer yu half-a-hand
an when I sleep at night
I close half-a-eye
consequently when I dream
I dream half-a-dream
an when moon begin to glow
I half-caste human being
cast half-a-shadow
but yu must come back tomorrow

wid de whole of yu eye
an de whole of yu ear
an de whole of yu mind

an I will tell yu
de other half
of my story

HAITI

ÉVELYNE TROUILLOT

Translated from the Creole by Lynn Selby

Please

Please
don't ask me to speak of
the earthquake
each single brick
keeps telling me of a misfortune with
no end
I don't recognise the poetry

coming out of my mouth
the words are burdened with the refuse of death
and remnants of grief
they stick to the tips of my fingers
they don't want to leave me
like a band of spirits that has taken over me
they refuse to go
Don't speak to me of January 12th
since that day
I've become a horse that they have
mounted
since that day
I serve them against my will

HONDURAS

MAYRA OYUELA

Translated from the Spanish by Allen Prowle & Caroline Maldonado

Mistress of the house

There are no Cassandras at the bottom of your glass,
there are no Malinches,
nor stealthy Amazons crossing behind you.
It is not Alfonsina who will come
and lead you by the hand
to the suicide sea of lovers.
It is not Lot and his wife who will kiss you
with salty kisses on the back of your neck.
It is not Mary Magdalene awakening in your instincts,
it was not Echo who wept at your window to Narcissus
and the Furies. They never avenge the tears which you spilled for him.
Mistress and sole author of your destiny
you will not dress up as Ophelia,
irremediable,
make-up in place,
putting out the fire from one scene to another,

sole mistress and author of your destiny you
will not light candles to Sor Juan Iñes de la Cruz
praying for him,
for the eternal repose of his embrace,
which you have never asked for,
of his words stifling
the disquiet of your silence.

It will not belong to Queen Maria Isabel that dress you make up out
of remnants,
it's for other Marias:
others, like you, full of grace and disgraces.

HONG KONG

JENNIFER WONG

Glimpse

Brown bread rises
from the toaster.
Time gargles
in a coffee machine.
On the table there's jam,
still sweet, and a soft block of butter.
We stir in milk, then sugar.
This is just one morning.
Outside, a few leaves fall.
There're not many clouds
to be seen, and the day is not that cold,
even a little sunny. Next door
our neighbour unchains his bike,
and you turn to me and say,
'I'll be coming back early.'
We kiss.
This is simple.
And this is one morning.

HUNGARY

ÁGNES LEHÓCZKY

Nárcisz's telephone call in leapmouth

The telephone is the one thing to survive it.
We can speak only briefly.
Yet from the receiver seagulls are pouring out.
Circulating in the narrow tunnels of my ears.
And suddenly I am rolling in the salty air too.
These words are nestlings learning to fly
fluttering – some of them are bound to fall.
So let this be my contour. Washed away.
Your face is a drained watercolour.
Here it rains all the time.
I deserve it. My eyes trickle down the glass of the phone box.
I stuff the gulls, my couriers, into the phone.

Can you hear them?
Short screams. This is the message.
I would rather they shut up – slamming my hand to the receiver.
It occurs to me it is better not to hear them for you.
It is cruel I know.
I haven't got a birthday, do not call.

GERÐUR KRISTNÝ
Translated from the Icelandic by Victoria Cribb

Patriotic Poem

The cold makes me
a lair from fear
places a pillow of
downy drift
under my head
a blanket of snow
to swaddle me in

I'd lay my ear to
the cracking of the ice
in the hope of hearing it
retreat
if I didn't know
I'd be frozen fast

The ice lets no one go

My country
a spread deathbed
my initials stitched
on the icy linen

TISHANI DOSHI

The Adulterous Citizen

*I am an adulterous resident; when I am in one city, I am dreaming
of the other. I am an exile; citizen of the country of longing.*

SUKETU MEHTA, Maximum City

When it comes to it,
there's only the long, paved road
that leads to a house
with a burning light.
A house you can never own,
but allows you
to sleep in its bed
without demanding sex,
eat from its cupboards
without paying,
lie in the granite cool of its tub
without drowning.
And only when the first shards
of day slice through
the blinds
of the basement windows
nudging you
with something of a whisper,
something like, *Maybe it's time to go* –
do you finally drag
your suitcases
up the carpeted stairs,
out the front door,
on to the summer pavements.

It is nothing
like losing a lover,
or leaving behind
the lanes of childhood.
Nothing like scaling

the winged walls of memory
to discover your friends
have packed up their boxes
and vanished.
More like stumbling
into a scene from the future,
where the ghost
of a husband
beckons with pictures
of a family
you no longer recognise,
and other peoples' children
race across the grass,
lulling you into belief
that you can always return like this –
without key in hand,
to lie in the folds of one city,
while listening to the jagged,
carnal breaths of another.

INDONESIA

LAKSMI PAMUNTJAK

A Traveller's Tale

Perhaps every journey begins
by going down the staircase

or trawling through a passage
in your granny's house where

a door might lead to shadows
& ink stains, a fireside of charred

carbon. Folks often mistake
the soul for the spirit, and like the

key that falls to the sand, we
rise to the swarm but forget the

man. Or songs stitched in the sky
long before cities were erected and

signposts staked. The wind may be
unfaithful as light selects its aperture;

we may give praise to the wrong God,
and remember only what illuminates

the field, the glutinous parts of the map.
We scan the spread from the crest of

the earth as though the world were
merely the consequence of some cosmic

spillage, the mountains brittle before the
sun, the sea no more than water leaking

into space. But lately there is no telling
summer from silver, as islands sink and

fish gasp in the black hole of unseasonal
drought. What stories we may find

in our passage through imagining
are buried in dead men's chests or

saved by the moon like the face of
a stray goddess. Such that it comes as a

gentle surprise that the pages that leap
from certain books hint of something closer

to the skin, a mother's fingerprint, or a
bead of sweat that escapes a father's neck,

bent over the very same lines, sending
him places with wide-eyed wings.

IRAN

MIMI KHALVATI

Don't Ask Me, Love, for that First Love
(after Faiz Ahmed Faiz)

Don't think I haven't changed. Who said
absence makes the heart grow fonder?
Though I watch the sunset redden
every day, days don't grow longer.

There are many kinds of silence,
none more radiant than the sun's.
Sun is silent in our presence,
unlike love, silent when it's gone.

I thought that every spring was you,
every blossom, every bud;
that summer had little to do
but follow, singing in my blood.

How wrong I was. What had summer
to do with sorrow in full spate?
Every rosebush, every flower
I passed, stood at a stranger's gate.

Weaving through our towns, centuries
of raw silk, brocade and velvet
have swilled the streets in blood. Bodies,
ripe with sores in lanes and markets,

are paying with their lives. But I
had little time for the world's wars,
love was war enough. In your sky,
your eyes, were all my falling stars.

Don't ask me, though I wish you would
and I know you won't, for more tears.
Why build a dam at Sefid Rud
if not to water land for years?

Though we'll never see the olives,
ricefields, shelter in an alcove
from the sun, in our time, our lives
have more to answer to than love.

SAADI YOUSSEF
Translated from the Arabic by Khaled Mattawa

Occupation 1943

We boys, the neighbourhood's barefoot
We boys, the neighbourhood's naked
We boys of stomachs bloated from eating mud
We boys of teeth porous from eating dates and pumpkin rind

We boys will line up from Hassan al-Basri's mausoleum to the Ashar
      River's source
to meet you in the morning waving green palm fronds

We will cry out: Long Live
We will cry out: Live to Eternity
And we will hear the music of Scottish bagpipes, gladly
Sometimes we will laugh at an Indian soldier's beard
but fear will merge with our laughs, and dispute them

We cry out: Long Live
We cry out: Live to Eternity
and reach our hands toward you: Give us bread
We the hungry, starving since our birth in this village
Give us meat, chewing gum, cans, and fish
Give us, so no mother expels her child
so that we do not eat mud and sleep

We boys, the neighbourhood's barefoot
do not know from where you had come
or why you had come
or why we cry out: Long Live
. . . .

And now we ask: will you stay long?
And will we go on reaching our hands towards you?

IRELAND

SEAMUS HEANEY

The Underground

There we were in the vaulted tunnel running,
You in your going-away coat speeding ahead
And me, me then like a fleet god gaining
Upon you before you turned to a reed

Or some new white flower japped with crimson
As the coat flapped wild and button after button
Sprang off and fell in a trail
Between the Underground and the Albert Hall.

Honeymooning, moonlighting, late for the Proms,
Our echoes die in that corridor and now
I come as Hansel came on the moonlit stones
Retracing the path back, lifting the buttons

To end up in a draughty lamplit station
After the trains have gone, the wet track
Bared and tensed as I am, all attention
For your step following and damned if I look back.

ANAT ZECHARYA

Translated from the Hebrew by Lisa Katz

A Woman of Valour

> *35 soldiers on active duty and several civilian employees at an air base have been conducting sexual relations with a 14-year-old girl over the past year. Many of the suspects claimed during questioning that the girl had told them she was of enlistment age.'*
>
> HANNAN GREENBERG, Ynet News

The first
places your head on his naked lap
and one might think
you weren't being forced but rather
thanked and your head stroked.
The second slides slowly down your back
the feelings are new
and you can still concentrate.
The third inserts three fingers, says
'Don't move.' You don't,
the map of greater Israel
in your eyes.
The fourth moves aside a pile of reports
on air accidents in the south
and takes you from behind.
A great love you think
a great love scorches me
and won't let up.
You raise and lower your arms
your body stretches to the edge of the sky
your hands cupped for the rain.
The unstoppable fifth and sixth
course into you.
The arrogant salt of the earth, avoiding eyes,
those waiting their turn. Soon your body may look beautiful
even to you.

TRANSLATOR'S NOTE: 'A Woman of Valour', *Eshet Hayil* in Hebrew, is a hymn to the woman of the house which is customarily recited on Friday evenings, after returning from synagogue and before sitting down to the Shabbat evening meal. It is a poem twenty-two verses long (Proverbs 31:10-31) and begins: 'A woman of valour who can find? For her price is far above rubies.' (The Jewish Publication Society Bible)

ITALY

ELISA BIAGINI

Translated from the Italian by Diana Thow & Sarah Stickney

from The Guest

I translate your life
through feng shui, recipes,

I glue your vocal cords back together
I tune the voice you had,
the tongue
that was written in your body

that was washed away with bleach, wind, dishwater

I can read it to you   still
in those x-rays that you carry around
as your portfolio to the gallerists,

and in the dust at the bottom of the drawers
and in that one left inside gloves

in all these years of acid rain,
that has cleaned your bones like silverware.

*

Mended nerves
among fog, paperwork, jackets
the interlaced fingers
(veins and arteries crossed)
and after the tension on the phone-line, in the pen:
cakes are active mines at distance,
every noodle a knot, a new debt.

Your world stuck between the lenses,
you, a building
crumbling in an instant.

*

Between us the voice
doesn't travel like
a hairdryer underwater
but it stops like
a switch
turned on or off
at random. We two
are a country
under embargo,
living on parentheses and
silences, on blackouts,
so that when the light
returns, we have already
forgotten what to say each other.

*

You show me your wounds, like a soldier,
your battle
against another you consuming
your eyes, bones
skin
who cut your tendons a while ago,
the cord that holds you,
diver who won't resurface.

*

nkondi

With all that
metal
inside you – world

calamity – you
attract me with fillings,
bracelets.

I slip toward you, with
your marsupial weight
of pills, the

canned wrongs
undergone, to suck on
in winter for memory:

your lips shining with
that axe that exits
your mouth.

*

KEI MILLER

Your dance is like a cure

In this country on a Saturday night
you are usually the best dancer;
it was not so back home.
Here you can dance
dances that have fallen out
of season, like mangoes in February
or guineps at Christmas. It does not matter
in this new country;
they do not know Spanish Town Road,
have never danced into the headlights
of early morning buses... though,
neither have you; you were never skilled
enough back there. You never entered
the middle circle – like a Holy of Holies –
where only good dancers dared venture.
But in this country, you move like fire
amongst the cane, you move like sugar
and like ocean; they say – you are the sharp
swing of a cutlass, they say –
you are like ointment in a deep wound.
They say your dance is like a cure.

RYOKO SEKIGUCHI

Translated from the Japanese by Eric Selland

from Adagio ma non troppo

In front of our screen was the movement of a hand drawing a diagram. As all detours by definition indicate a triangle, a gathering of multiple triangles cannot but be called by the name *stratégie*, the fact itself of the unstable figure superimposed over a map or timetable announces the stories likely to be excluded from the various texts containing the possibility of being written in the future, caught in creases of muslin wedged in between them and trying to turn around, the petite ears taking on a roundness both become clearly visible, and between the biangular earrings swaying immediately below them, now the seventh line heads toward its final destination and, thick and luxuriant, surges dangerously.

> The city has seven hills and observatories, a number of towers and numerous grounds allocated for landscape gardens and botanical gardens, while on the river always float the figures of many ships. The narrow streets form a web like pattern, and it is not unusual for one street to change its name many times over, and there live people also, the many plazas positioned for summer, or simply in order to feel more strongly the external world.

A rendezvous has no other means of communication save by writing or the voice, and much ink has been spent on all the particulars of which one should be aware, the many numbers, names of districts, streets and so on. Whatever the purpose, these things inscribed so essential to meeting, in some cases become an end in themselves, so that a life could be built on dates written toward their form of incompletion, street names read then, without severing the gaze, holding the breath and watching over them, so that we also in reading that life, from time to time come to exist.

On our first meeting, always and only once, the
doors facing the street turn this way, and as if
left open and released, I run across the street.

When afternoon comes to an end in the Estrela Gardens, into the field
of vision from behind, running diagonally up ahead past little children
diving between the knees of an older sibling seated on a bench, and
an elderly couple gazing at a column of ducks at the edge of the pond,
comes the shadow of a young bicycle cutting crossways through the
path, perhaps the usual shortcut on the return home, or so one might
assume as with no trouble at all the figure glides effortlessly by as if
pushed from behind, like the shadow of a bird streaming along without
peddling, the movement of the bicycle's wheels, likely to pass through
Rua dos Poiais de São Bento where that person lives, and their metallic
rotation set in motion one's own axis as well, as if dancing this image
of a revolving encounter wants to fly as far as the corner of Caetano
Palha Street.

At the stand set up below the enormous trees adjacent to the rear
gate of the Jardim Botânico at the hour when the sun hits precisely
from overhead, during that period in my life when I performed the
daily ritual of downing two cups of coffee in rapid succession as soon
as I appeared from the direction of Calçada Patriarcal, I realised that
I had never even once arranged a meeting at this place. This spectacle
which most likely that person has never seen before, this ground on
which those shoes have never tread, though just a small cut-out patch
is already etched in ink along with the black liquid on his body, without
understanding what this means, my heart leans toward the riverbank,
while the line stretching from Rua do Alecrim to Plaça do Principe
Real is pulled swinging through the air as if a long electrical wire or
fishing line had been laid out, and at which I gaze, turning my head
in the shade of the trees.

TRANSLATOR'S NOTE: *Adagio ma non troppo* is the last poem sequence of a book
entitled *Granada Poems*, which Sekiguchi published in 2007. Most of the poems
were written during her summer stays in Granada, and are influenced by the
weather patterns, the history and languages of the region of Andalusia. *Adagio
ma non troppo* was begun in Bordeaux and completed in Granada. The sections
from that poem translated here have as their backdrop the streets and public
gardens of Lisbon.

AMJAD NASSER
Translated from the Arabic by Khaled Mattawa

The Phases of the Moon in London

She and I were talking about the weather, the rusty key that opens conversations here in London. Mrs Morrison, our old neighbour, is the last English woman on our street, where the English have dropped off one by one since the population balance tipped toward the Asian immigrants. She said, 'the London sky was not like this in the past, but must have resembled your sky in India.'

I said, 'I am from Jordan,' but she did not stop at my correction, which she may not have seen as a correction in the first place. In that English manner whose emotional resonances are hard to read, she continued that they too used to see the stars and detect the phases of the moon.

I was not convinced, but I played on in this game of English politeness. I said, 'What caused the stars and moon to disappear and the sky to turn into a blotted sheet even on these nights clear as a rooster's eye?'

'I don't know,' she said. 'Maybe the change in the weather, or our insatiable consumption of electricity, this excessive urbanisation. We light the earth and the sky disappears. You're probably better off in India.'

'In Jordan,' I said.

Again, she did not pause at my correction. She smiled and directed her small shopping trolley toward her house, announcing the end of a conversation that politeness had imposed on two neighbours who otherwise try all they can to avoid each other when they meet at the door.

I wanted to tell her that the skies of eastern cities, bent under military rule and corruption, are also blotted out, and that the stars that freckled our childhood with comets have also disappeared, but I feared to lose the only gift for which she envied me.

AKERKE MUSSABEKOVA

Remember me

Remember me as a passenger on a ship,
I sat with you,
took some pictures,
and slept at time
on your shoulder.
Remember me as the fresh air,
That soothed your heart,
as the drops of rain
that wet your cheeks with gentle tickling,
as the waves of the sea
that raged with strong wind,
as the tulip fields
or as the white snow that dazed you in the sun.
Remember me as a cup of coffee every morning,
And as a handful of candies
That made you happy like a child,
And as a page of a book you keep under your pillow.
Remember me as a melody you catch in every resonance,
as a whisper among a multitude of sounds
and an echo in the silence
which I ask you to listen to.

SHAILJA PATEL

Eater of Death

Inspired by the story of Bibi Sardar, whose husband and seven children were killed at breakfast by US aerial bombardment of Kabul in October 2001. An estimated 20,000 Afghani civilians have been killed by the US in what is now the longest-running war in US history.

One

They came as we ate breakfast, I remember the taste
of black market naan.
Zainab and Shahnaz turned eyes like whirlpools
as I sprinkled them
with precious water.
My children ate slowly
tasting each crumb.
I remember the bitterness
in my throat.

Before we finished
the sky ripped open, vomited
death, everything
fell around us, everything
burned, children screamed, walls shattered,
a voice like a jackal's howled

Kamal Gohar Shahnaz

Sudiyah Zainab Zarafshan

On and on, after all
the other noises
stopped

Kamal Gohar Shahnaz Sadiyah Zainab Zarafshan

145

It split my head, I would have beaten it
into silence.

I raised my hands
to block my ears, my fingers fell
into the well
of a hole in my face,
the howling
came from me.

Two

Three days later,
in the shelter,
thick with the stench
of human waste, of terror,
starvation and nausea
fought like mujaheddin
in my gut.
Aziza, my neighbour,
scraps of rubble
still in her matted hair,
showed me
a package. Yellow
like the bombs. With an
Amrikan flag.
She said:
They say it's food.

Tears gouged tracks
in the dirt on her face,
her mouth twitched, her head jerked
her one remaining hand shook, spittle and words
jumped from her lips:
Food coloured like
the bombs. For the children
still alive
to pick from minefields
with the hands
they still have
left.

And finally
I saw
the savagery
of a people
who would gloat
over those they kill,
who would take the limbs,
eyes, sanity
of their victims
before execution. I cried out
to the shelter roof, dark as a coffin:
Have they no mothers
no children
in Amrika?

Three

On the ninth day,
after Aziza died
still clutching the pack
she refused to open, I
pried it from her lifeless
lacerated fingers, I

ate the food.

The blood and bones and fat
of my children,
in a yellow pack,
with an Amrikan flag.

I ate the names
I'd patted into my belly
as they ripened inside me,
one by one. The names
that angered
their father, who said
in his despair:

What future have they
in this country that's meat
for wolves?

I answered him:

*Each of them
is a miracle of life, I will not
dim their wonder.*

Kamal – perfection, how you bruise
and scrape my abscessed tongue.
Gohar – diamond, precious stone,
now break my loosened teeth.
Shahnaz – princess, red gelatinous heart
of this monstrous American pastry,
I smear you on my mouth.
Sadiyah – blessed one, sink in my stomach,
stone of my womb, I take you back.
Zainab – granddaughter of the Prophet, peace
be unto him, and you, sugar
my saliva, prophesy
what comes to eaters of death.
Zarafshan –
Zar-af-shan, littlest one, I named you
for a mighty river. You taste now
of rancid mud, you taste now
of poisoned fish,
littlest one
you taste
of splintered glass.

Four

Their names will not be remembered,
they are not Amrikan.
Museums will not hold their relics, they are not
Amrikan. No other mother's
children will be slaughtered
in their memory, they are not
Amrikan.

But I?
I have eaten food
from the bowels of hell,

chewed and swallowed
the fragments of my children
and now
I am no longer human.

Now as every nation
seals its borders against us,
now as they gun us down
when we beg for sanctuary,
I will march Amrika
along my tendons, electrify
Amrika through my nerves.
Seal the borders
of my body to pain,
seal my eyes, mouth, belly
to any hunger not
my own.

I rename myself
Amrika. No love
no grief in the world but mine.
And I will keep them safe –
in the cracks of my teeth
in the pit of my pelvis
in the raw raw flesh
beneath my eyelids.

Kamal
Gohar
Shahnaz
Sadiyah
Zainab
Zarafshan

TERESIA TEAIWA

Pacific Tsunami Found Poems

1

The telephone says
The body says
The multinational corporation says

Samoans had taken the sea's friendship for granted
We can't imagine   It's unimaginable
Free phone calls to Samoa   (But only one Samoa)

2

God's minister says
God's children say
God says

The wave was God's way
We can't concentrate on our assignments
I prepared a speech but I will not be reading it

3

Surfer says
Waiter says
Sean says

The sea got sucked down below the reef
What's one metre of water going to do?
Stupid

4

Teddy Bear says
Ute says
Baby says

Hello to the pole

Hello to the tree
Hello to strangers on the beach

5

Solomon says
Viti says
Niue says

Gizo
Floods
Heta

6

New Zealand is scrambling
An Air Force Orion

New Zealand is scrambling
Hercules   staff and supplies

New Zealand is scrambling
Deputy Prime Minister Bill English

New Zealand is scrambling
More Kiwi casualties feared

7

A depression moves
with a weak ridge extending

Then, late in the day,
a cold front sweeps

Strengthening westerly
in the moist westerly

Slow moving over
a cold southwest flow

Cold southerlies spread over
high over, ridge over

Then, late in the day,
a cold front sweeps

JANG JIN SEONG

Translated from the Korean by Sung Young Soon

I Sell My Daughter for 100 Won

Exhausted, in the midst of the market she stood
'For 100 won, my daughter I sell'
Heavy medallion of sorrow
A cardboard around her neck she had hung
Next to her young daughter
Exhausted, in the midst of the market she stood

A deaf-mute the mother
She gazed down at the ground, just ignoring
The curses the people all threw
As they glared
At the mother who sold
Her motherhood, her own flesh and blood

Her tears dried up
Though her daughter, upon learning
Her mother would perish of a deadly disease
Had buried her face in the mother's long skirt
And bellowed, and cried
But the mother stood still
And her lips only quivered

Unable she was to give thanks to the soldier
Who slipped a hundred won into her hand
As he uttered
'It is your motherhood,
And not the daughter I'm buying'
She took the money, and ran

A mother she was,
And the 100 won she had taken

She spent on a loaf of wheat bread
Toward her daughter she ran
As fast as she could
And pressed the bread on the child's lips
'Forgive me, my child'
In the midst of the market she stood
And she wailed.

SOUTH KOREA

KIM HYESOON
Translated from the Korean by Don Mee Choi

Red Scissors Woman

That woman who walks out of the gynaecology clinic
Next to her is an old woman holding a newborn

That woman's legs are like scissors
She walks swiftswift cutting the snow path

But the swollen scissor blades are like fat dark clouds
What did she cut screaming with her raised blades
bloodscented dusk flooding out between her legs

The sky keeps tearing the morning after the snowstorm
A blinding flash of light
follows the waddlewaddling woman
Heaven's lid glimmers and opens then closes

How scared God must have been
when the woman who ate all the fruits of the tree he'd planted
was cutting out each red body from
between her legs

The sky, the wound that opens every morning
when a red head is cut out
between the fat red legs of the cloud

(Does that blood live inside me?)
(Do I live inside that blood?)

That woman who walks ahead
That woman who walks and rips
with her scorching body her cold shadow

Newborn infants swim
inside that woman's mirror inside her as white as a snowhouse
the stickysticky slow breaking waves of blood
like the morning sea filled with fish

KUWAIT

SAADIA MUFARREH
Translated from the Arabic by Nay Hannawi

Distance

Between the room and hall
is a corridor of broken tiles.
So *small*, my mother complains.

Only my aching body knows
how long it really is.

KYRGYZSTAN

ROZA MUKASHEVA
Translated from the Kyrgyz by Hamid Ismailov

Nomad in the sunset

This time he fell in the abyss on his horse, and the Sun fell with him
And his voice never reached us again,
Only a stone inscription remained.
Where was the army headed in a whirlwind,
The raging Saks and Hunnus.

From far ends of Asia they flew over to this end
Horsemen of the boundless Universe.
The whirlpool of stars within their reach,
Offspring of steppe winds and mountain winds.

Life force of flesh sapped by the distance,
Last drop of water stolen by scorching sands.
At times, the tamed eagle would fall in the hands of the enemy
Life passing away in the saddle
Leaving the pensive nomad to grieve, resting sorrowful head on his fingers:
Oh how narrow the paths of this material existence.

I played qomuz, filled with sadness: I had thought I was strong
But the spinning Earth with me on it, turned out to be smaller than the
    eye of a needle.
I heard many tales of death, every battle rushing towards tasting it
The space of the spinning Universe where I dwelt, shrinking to just my
    existence.

Everything in this world is fleeting, all things pass
– the land was divided, the flocks and soul ripped away from me
In the emptiness of the steppe, luring far off fires burned,
As I rode impetuously at lightning speed, the reigns of destiny no longer
    in my hand,
Suddenly not realising: have I been pierced by light or the searing heat
    of the sword?

What far reaches...where would my tribe go now?
Where would it go, where to aim in darkness?
My small clan, that split off from the big tribe
Flung up in a moment like a spark off a horseshoe

The Sun falls into the wound of my heart
Maybe I didn't know that this world's colour is the colour of blood,
like the sunset.
Now I release my soul to be
And my steed, closer than my soul,
I release him too. Be free.

BRYAN THAO WORRA

No Regrets

Maybe one day,
A page will be found,
A song will be heard,
A stroke will be drawn
Filled with explanations.

Maybe one day,
The nuckawi and silapin, beautiful as a field of khao mai
Will be vindicated.

A family will start.

A child will learn the names of a stranger who believed in them
Before they even met.

Maybe one day,
A heart will remember a brother, a sister, a crime, a moment of love,
A chronicle of a city, a haiku from Japan.
A teacher.
A friend on the other side of your eye.

Until then, what is certain?
Night arrives, then day. The moon, the sun, the rain and waves.
A few other things, maybe something someone will write down.
Maybe not.

LATVIA

KĀRLIS VĒRDIŅŠ

Translated from the Latvian by Ieva Lešinska

Come to Me

I was bringing you a little cheese sandwich. It was two in the morning, everybody sleepy, shops closed but in the *I Love You* bar they gave me a little cheese sandwich.

I was in a taxi bringing you a little cheese sandwich 'cause you were lying there sad, perhaps even ill, and there was nothing good to eat in the house. Was real expensive, around one lat, but that's OK.

So I was in the taxi with my little *iluvu*, all squished, practically cold. But for some reason I didn't make it home. Somehow I ended up where all were merry and witty, and starving. So I drank, I sang, but I saved my little sandwich.

Must have been the third day when I could finally treat you to it, you were so angry, you ate the sandwich hardly looking at it. Had I had more courage, I would have said: but you know I love you, you know I admire you. Don't make me say it again.

VÉNUS KHOURY-GATA

Translated from the French by Marilyn Hacker

Widow

The first day after his death
she folded up her mirrors
put a slipcover on the spider web
then tied up the bed which was flapping its wings to take off.

The second day after his death
she filled up her pockets with woodchips
threw salt over the shoulder of her house
and went off with a tree under each arm.

The third day after his death
she swore at the pigeons lined up along her tears
bit into a grape which scattered its down in her throat
then called out till sunset to the man gone barefoot
into the summer pasture in the cloudy mountains.

The fourth day
a herd of buffalo barged into her bedroom
demanding the hunter who spoke their dialect
she shouldered her cry
shot off a round
which pierced the ceiling of her sleep.

The fifth day
footsteps of blood imprinted themselves on her threshold
she followed them to that ditch where everything smells of boned hare.

The sixth day after his death
she painted her face with earth
attacked the peaceful shadows of passers-by
slit the throats of trees
their colourless blood evaporated when it touched her hands.

The seventh day
stringy men sprouted in her garden
she mistook them for poplars
bit the armpits of their branches
and lengthily vomited wood-chips.

The eighth day
the sea whinnied at her door
she washed her belly's embankments
then called down to the river's mouth
where men clashed together like pebbles.

The ninth day
she dried her tears on the roof between the basil and the budding fog
gazed at herself in stones
found cracks in her eyes like those in a church's stained glass.

The tenth day
he surged up out of her palm
sat down on her fingernail
demanded her usual words to drink and the almond odour of her knees.
He swallowed them without pleasure
on his journey he'd lost the taste for tortured water.

LESOTHO

RETHABILE MASILO

The San's Promise

They came from the south
holding the sun in their right hand
like an object of worship,
crossed the Mohokare into the mountains,
leather bags full of ochre
and painting sticks, venom in small phials,
dried meat conserved in leaves. They stayed

159

long enough to paint the fat of the land:
hunt scenes, children hopping in playful circles
round a fire. An ostrich egg and roots
dug up from the desert's giving sand,
hand prints lit like sepals
exploding on grotto walls.

PATRICIA JABBEH WESLEY

The Women in My Family

The women in my family were supposed
to be men. Heavy body men, brawny
arms and legs, thick muscular chests and the heart,
smaller than a speck of dirt.
They come ready with muscled arms and legs,
big feet, big hands, big bones,
a temper that's hot enough to start World War Three.
We pride our scattered strings
of beards under left chins
as if we had anything to do with creating ourselves.
The women outnumber the men
in my father's family, leaving our fathers roaming
wild nights in search of baby-spitting concubines
to save the family name.
It is an abomination when there are no boy children.
At the birth of each one of us girls, a father sat prostrate
in the earth, in sackcloth and ash,
wailing.
It is abomination when there are no men
in the family, when mothers can't bring forth
boy children in my clan.

KHALED MATTAWA

Borrowed Tongue

Maybe I'm a fool
holding two threads,
one black, one white,
waiting for dawn
to tell them apart.
But I'm only practising
my religion which
I neither borrowed
nor stole.
Maybe I'm a fool
thinking of a better answer
than the transplant patient
who said *I'm sorry
someone had to die.*

No, I haven't outgrown
my tongue. It's a coat
your mother gives you,
crimson or cobalt blue,
satin inside, the collar
wide enough to cover
your whole neck.
All winter you wear it
then spring comes
but never goes.
That's Arabic to me.
I wear a white shirt now –
thin grey stripes,
top button gone
and it fits.

LIECHTENSTEIN

ELISABETH KAUFMANN-BÜCHEL
Translated from the German

Free as a Bird

Unattached
With no roots
With no barrier

Free as a bird
I want to be

Despite the fears of freedom
Despite the vulnerability of the unattached
Despite the unfamiliarity of the unknown

Free as a bird
I want to be

Woven into the warmth of the evening wind
Swaying on the willow tree's branches
Carried by the breath of the stars

Free as a bird
I want to be

From here to there
Never missed and never expected
Never recognised and never attached

Free as a bird
I want to be

DONATAS PETROŠIUS

Translated from the Lithuanian by Medeinė Tribinevičius

Ghost Dogs; Way of the Samurai

My first dog was brown and
wild. While I domesticated the
force of gravity, practised
taking my first steps, he would
work himself loose from his chain and run away.
And one time he didn't come back, his name was
Bear.

My second dog was black, which is why
I called him Bear. He was
too weak to escape his chain.
He howled whenever he heard our neighbour play
the concertina. That's why I learned
nothing from that dog. He died near his doghouse
on April twelfth, during Gagarin's
Easter, and one of me grandmothers (who has practically
nothing to do with this discourse)
explained that we were fighting a star war
and if the Americans were to drop a star
on us we would all freeze. I was so naïve, I believed her.

It was impossible not to see that
my third dog would be a legend, which is why
I named him Bear. He had all
the best qualities of a warrior and one
fault – he was too independent:
he would disappear, reappearing only when it got light.
He would often leave me alone,
exposed from behind and only half-able
to fulfil that secret command – to protect myself from the shadows and
the tall-growing plants, wielding a black plastic pipe in lieu of
the sharpest sword.

I asked the I Ching: will I ever be
ordained a warrior? The most positive answer (Nr. 5)
tumbled out, but nothing changed.
And it was only after many years passed that I recognised
from my actions that everything I knew in life I learned
from my dog –
how to escape a collar, how to carry out unimaginable manoeuvres,
how to remain invisible, unintelligible.

LUXEMBOURG

ANISE KOLTZ

Translated from the French by Anne-Marie Glasheen

Prologue

Life is no long quiet river
but a bloodbath

Yet you ask me for
poetry decorated with flowers
with little birds

I'm sorry Ladies and Gentlemen
each of my poems
buries your dead

*

I advance without a net
from one star to another
sliding through black holes
I leap from moons to suns

I rock at the edges
of the earth
already no longer belonging to it

Because this poem is a lie
it has the right to be beautiful

NIKOLA MADZIROV

Translated from the Macedonian by Magdalena Horvat

Shadows Pass Us By

We'll meet one day,
like a paper boat and
a watermelon that's been cooling in the river.
The anxiety of the world will
be with us. Our palms
will eclipse the sun and we'll
approach each other holding lanterns.

One day, the wind won't
change direction.
The birch will send away leaves
into our shoes on the doorstep.
The wolves will come after
our innocence.
The butterflies will leave
their dust on our cheeks

An old woman will tell stories
about us in the waiting room every morning.
Even what I'm saying has
been said already: we're waiting for the wind
like two flags on a border.

One day every shadow
                    will pass us by.

MADAGASCAR

MODESTE HUGUES
Lyrics translated from Malagasy by Dale Hanson with the author

Lavitra (Far away)

I've travelled far to find my dreams
Far away from home to build my life
I've flown the skies and lived my dreams
I've seen mountain tops and valleys wide
Met different people from different places in the world
I'm far from family, friends and home
I'm happy now, but I'll never forget those far away
I think of you all, forever.

MALAWI

JACK MAPANJE

Scrubbing the Furious Walls of Mikuyu

Is this where they dump those rebels,
These haggard cells stinking of bucket
Shit and vomit and the acrid urine of
Yesteryears? Who would have thought I
Would be gazing at these dusty, cobweb
Ceilings of Mikuyu Prison, scrubbing
Briny walls and riddling out impetuous
Scratches of another dung-beetle locked
Up before me here? Violent human palms
Wounded these blood-bloated mosquitoes

And bugs (to survive), leaving these vicious
Red marks. Monstrous flying cockroaches
Crashed here. Up there the cobwebs trapped
Dead bumblebees. Where did black wasps
Get clay to build nests in this corner?

But here, scratches, insolent scratches!
I have marvelled at the rock paintings
Of Mphunzi Hills once but these grooves
And notches on the walls of Mikuyu Prison,
How furious, what barbarous squiggles!
How long did this anger languish without
Charge, without trial, without visit here, and
What justice committed? This is the moment
We dreaded; when we'd all descend into
The pit, alone, without a wife or a child –
Without mother; without paper or pencil
– Without a story (just three Bibles for
Ninety men), without charge without trial;
This is the moment I never needed to see.

Shall I scrub these brave squiggles out
Of human memory then or should I perhaps
Superimpose my own, less caustic; dare I
Overwrite this precious scrawl? Who'd
Have known I'd find another prey without
Charge, without trial (without bitterness)
In these otherwise blank walls of Mikuyu
Prison? No, I will throw my water and mop
Elsewhere. We have liquidated too many
Brave names out of the nation's memory.
I will not rub out another nor inscribe
My own, more ignoble, to consummate this
Moment of truth I have always feared!

MALAYSIA

SHARANYA MANIVANNAN

Dream of Burying My Grandmother Who Has No Grave

We buried her upright, in the stance of warriors.
    My brothers and I driving
out alone to do this, miles and miles
from the memory of warmth, lifting her
   small strong body out of the vehicle
and laying it down
beside the railway track. My gloved hand
brushing frost from her face in the
Siberian winter of a dream in which I
was my mother, and she, mine.

We buried her there without
ritual, lowering her slowly into a furrow,
covering her with fistfuls of ice, hurrying
against the long wail of the approaching train –
the engine of our car left
   running, our shaking hands, a sorrow
     blinding as snow. Near the end,
my brothers stepped away.
I was the last to see that dowager face.
The sting of the ice from her forehead
on my lips all the way back to waking.

Sometimes her love lights my body up
    from the inside out, a love like a good
   vodka. Grandmother whose body rose in
smoke, I carry your sweet burn within me
even into this, the frozen tundra of a life
   with not a stone left standing
     to bear witness.

FARAH DIDI

winds of change

when did all the singing die
and the laughter disappear?
the tide has ebbed;
the land empty
a deathly silence everywhere,

is it the whisper of the wind I hear
in the quiet of the night,
or is it a child cry for its lost father?
her voice just a strain in my ear
now fossilised in time,

the breeze is gone; the sea is still;
the dead calm wrapped like a
cold blanket in the frosty air,
nothing left but echoes
of a prayer,

where is the moon? is there no light
just darkness chills the skies
where are the footsteps
on the sand?
where is the flame
that burnt so bright?
where are the children
of the winds of change
dancing in the night?

yet as sure it shall
the sea will rise,
the laws of nature rules us all;
though for now, the moon may hide,
when cometh the hour,
cometh the tide,
and men must heed its call.

MALI

OXMO PUCCINO
Translated from the French by Helen and David Constantine

'This is a song...' (HIP HOP LYRIC)

This is a song that sups on the tears
Of absence. When the sun appears
Head down I'll stay here till I see
The day's grief coming home to me
Out of a cloud, such a large sorrow
My eyes can't contain it, they overflow.
Dressed in black, these days of grief
They are love's sad afterlife.
All joy is soon put out.
Goodbye, sweet rains. Hello, drought.
Shelter me, sorrow. Grief, be kind
Be the promised comfort, I must find
Strength for the life ahead.

Sadness is a wide slow load. Whatever you try –
Memories, the laughter of children – you can't get by.
As you fell, you clutched at clichés, the old
Past consolations, they gave you no handhold.
In pain in silence you are a closed book
So look for the words, break out and speak
And better divide your trouble and sing
With others than sit in silence alone in pain
Not knowing where you are. Life must
Be lived here on the earth's thin crust
Till the beast who is hungry for us breaks in
We will embrace and live with the living
All the life ahead.

MALTA

IMMANUEL MIFSUD
Translated from the Maltese by Maria Grech Ganado

from A Handful of Leaves from Mallorca

Biel

Standing on the sand, a Catalan poet
opened his arms wide to embrace the sea.
He spoke in waves, and sang in sand.
He meant to say: *this is the Mediterranean,*
from which the mountains that reach the sky
were born. This sea spawns poetry. This
is the sea which scribbles its blue ink
on the rocks in poetry so dark the sea alone
can understand its meaning.

Untitled 1

The sea is a big and virile man
waiting for the first woman to love.
The sea is a beautiful fleshly woman
waiting for the first man so that together
they can change into a poem full of blood
spilling onto the whiteness of a sheet.

Untitled 2

The sea approaches you slowly. Calmly.
with the hushed tones of the sad. With sorrow.
With the slow pace of those who age and wait.
It approaches you to wet you, to love you,
to hold you close, to lull you, to lay you down to sleep.

The sea approaches you slowly. Calmly.

Laia

You play with the water like a little girl;
You roll up your trousers and pull up your hair;
And laugh while you make the pebble skim
over the silent sea of Formentor.

Your eyes are the colour of my overwhelming sorrow
when I consider that this is only yet another trip
like all the other trips which I've collected
and you're another tale without an end.

MARSHALL ISLANDS

KATHY JETNIL-KIJINER

history project

at fifteen I decide
to do my history project on nuclear testing in the Marshall Islands
time to learn my own history, I decide

I weave through book after article after website
all on how the US military once used my island home for nuclear testing
I sift through political jargon
tables of nuclear weapons
with names like Operation Bravo
Crossroads
and Ivy
quotes from generals like
            9,000 people are out there. Who cares?

I'm not mad at all
I already knew all of this

I glance at a photograph
a boy, peeled skin arms legs suspended

a puppet
next to a lab coat
lost in his clipboard

I read first hand accounts of what we call
jelly babies
tiny beings with no bones
skin, red tomatoes
the miscarriages gone unspoken
the broken translations
>   *I never told my husband*
>   *I thought it was my fault*
>   *I thought*
>   *there must be something   wrong*
>   *inside me*

I flip through snapshots of American marines and nurses
branded white with bloated grins
sucking beers and tossing beach balls
along our
shores
and my islander ancestors
crosslegged before a general
listening to his
fairy tale
bout how it's
>   *for the good of mankind*
to hand over our islands
let them blast radioactive energy
into our sleepy coconut trees
our sagging breadfruit trees
our busy fishes that sparkle like new sun
into our coral reefs
brilliant as an aurora borealis woven beneath a glassy sea
>   *God will thank you* they told us
yea
as if god himself ordained
those powdered flakes
to drift onto our skin our hair our eyes
to seep into our bones
we mistook radioactive fallout
for snow

173

God will thank you they told us
like god just been
waiting
for my people
to vomit
      vomit
        vomit
all humanity's sins
onto impeccable white shores
gleaming like the cross
burned into our open scarred palms

at one point in my research I stumble
on a photograph of goats
tied to American ships
bored and munching on tubs of grass
At the bottom a caption read
    Goats and pigs were left on naval ships as test subjects.
    Thousands
    of letters flew in from America
    protesting

    animal abuse.

at 15
I want radioactive energy megatons of tnt a fancy degree
anything and everything I could ever need to send ripples of death
through a people who put goats
before human beings
so their skin can shrivel beneath the glare of hospital room lights
three generations later
as they watch their grandfather their aunty their cousin's life drip
across that same black screen knots of knuckles tied to steel beds
cold and absent of any breath
but I'm only 15

so I finish my project
graph my people's death by cancer and canned food diabetes
on flow charts
in 3D
gluestick my ancestors' voice onto a posterboard I bought from office max
staple tables screaming the millions of dollars stuffed into our mouths
    generation after generation after generation

174

and at the top I spraypainted in bold stencilled yellow
FOR THE GOOD OF MANKIND
and entered it in the school district wide competition called
history day

my parents were quietly proud
and so was my teacher
and when the three balding white judges finally came around to my project
one of them looked at it and said yea
but it wasn't really
for the good of mankind, though
was it?

and I lost.

MAURITANIA

MBARKA MINT AL-BARRA'

Literal translation from the Arabic by Joel Mitchell
Final translated version by The Poetry Translation Workshop

Message from a Martyr

Fire your bullets – our hearts are already ablaze
       In this land, grief wells up from my distress
Fire your bullets – you villain – for I
       Won't play at murder or run away
My blood fertilises and refreshes this land
       And plants a promising generation that is fully conscious
Limbs grow from seeds of shrapnel
       Hands are formed and crowns spring
That bet this land will always be their home –
       In every corner they stand their ground
Wherever I am, this land is my passion
       Nostalgia is fused with this timeless love
I don't care if there are explosions
       I don't mind the annihilating thunder

MAURITIUS

SARADHA SOOBRAYEN

My Conqueror

She circles me with her Portuguese compass
and settles just long enough to quench her thirst.
She discards my Arabian name *Dina Arobi*,
and calls me *Cerné*, from island of the swans.

With the hunger of a thousand Dutch sailors
and a tongue as rough as a sea biscuit she stakes
a longer claim and makes herself comfy,
bringing her own Javanese deer, pigs and chickens.

Defending her lust for breasts and thighs, she blames
the ship's rats for sucking the Dodo from its shell.
Looking past my ebony limbs, she sees carved boxes
and *marron* hands at work stripping my forests.

She renames me in honour of Prince Maurice
of Nassau. A good choice, sure to scare off pirates
keen to catch a bite of river shrimp, flamed in rum.
Disheartened by cyclones and rat bites, she departs.

For eleven years, I belong to no one. I sleep
to the purring of turtledoves. Sheltered by a circle
of coral reef, my oval shape rises
from the coast up to the peaks of mountains.

A westerly wind carries her back. She unbuttons
her blue naval jacket slowly and takes me.
I am her *Île de France*, her *petit pain*.
She brings spaniels. She captures *marrons*

who are pinned down and flogged, each time they run.
She takes her fill in Port Louis, shipping casks
of pure sweetness to the tea-drinking ladies of Europe.
Young Baudelaire jumps ship on his way to India.

176

His stepfather wants to cure him of 'literature'.
Once a poet makes his mark, no tide can wash away
his words: '*Au pays parfumé que le soleil caresse.*'
And what can I say, he was so delicious!

Sadly sweet Baudelaire soon finds himself
in such a profound melancholy,
after seeing a whipping in the main square,
after two weeks, he sails to France, leaving me

a sonnet. With the pride and jealousy of
the British Admiralty she punishes me
with her passion for corsets, sea-blockades
and endless petticoats wide as the Empire.

The oldest profession is alive and thrives
in my harbours; strumpets and exports, cross-
dressing captains and girls in white breeches.
Boys who like boys who like collars and chains.

She brings a pantomime cast of *malabars*
and *lascars* to my shores. Their passage back
to India guaranteed, if only they can read the scripts.
The cane breaks backs. Tamil, Urdu, Hindi, cling

to their skins like beads of sweat. Hundreds of tongues
parched like the mouths of sweet-hearts in an arranged
ceremony. She is kind and ruthless and insists
on the Queen's English. At night Creole verve slips in

and makes mischief. Each time she comes she pretends
it's the first time she has landed here, but she soon
becomes bored. Tired of flogging and kicking
the dogs. She doesn't know which uniform to wear.

'I'm no one and everyone,' she complains.
'And you have no more distinguishing marks
left to conquer, Saloman, Peros Banhos,
Diego Garcia...' She pulls down her Union
Jack, it falls like a sari, around her bare feet.

NOTES:

Marrons: Creole name given to the slaves taken from Madagascar and transported convicts.
Malabars and Lascars: Hindu and Muslim indentured labourers. These names are disparaging terms in Mauritian Creole.

The Saloman Islands, the Peros Banhos Atoll and Diego Garcia were the ancestral homelands for the Chagos Islanders. The UK Government surreptitiously excised the Chagos Archipelago from colonial Mauritius during the negotiations for Mauritian Independence and created the British Indian Ocean Territory (BIOT) forcibly removing the Chagossians between 1965 and 1973. In 1966 the UK Government made Diego Garcia available to the US Government to build a strategic military base, which was named Camp Justice.

MEXICO

ROCÍO CERÓN
Translated from the Spanish by Jen Hofer

from America

Their name was Krusevac, now Cruz. The buildings perspired. It was an island or a mountain littered with shacks. It's a men's affair. The women stored potatoes, constructed the world. An affair of lustreless traces, so it was thought. Sweetly melodious landscapes with accordion in the background. Cleverness. Prow accumulating salt. *Take my arm, sever the ligament: I need to lose my taste for ajvar.* The birds hushed at their step. Oar. In the depths, the fish intuiting. Some graves hold entire families. But these women are safe. All the tongues of Europe disappeared. Earth. Apple candy doesn't smell like cloves. Each letter spells a sojourn. These women are my mothers. From that day forward – America – the skin of my cheeks a prairie.

EMELIHTER KIHLENG

This morning at Joy
(for Sipwoli)

there is an African woman
eating with a white woman friend
an African American man with his
Pohnpeian sister-in-law
a Japanese man
a Filipino with his Mwoakillese wife
a Nahnep U
a candidate for Lt Governor with
his wife and mother
a Pohnpeian businesswoman with her 3 year old son
dipping their fat pankeik into coffee
two white Americans
two ? men
all of us in this little Japanese restaurant
in Ohmine
eating

VASILE GÂRNEŢ
Translation from the Romanian by Adam J. Sorkin and Cristina Cîrstea

Bookmark (1)

toss a golf ball
into the middle of your poetry
for exoticism
and perplex your reader with the news
that today, Shrove Tuesday, you listened
to a profane cantata by Scarlatti
cut short the rebuttal of the bigoted exegete
balanced on stiletto heels to bamboozle God
and tell him you've sprayed the hall of metaphor
(the spray left behind by Cărtărescu
after his perambulations past words in formations)
and above all don't forget to suggest
you've had a humble revelation
the discovery
that you're the only resident in your quarter
to have read Proust

GEORGES FRANZI
Translated from the Monagasque

Many People Say...

Many people say: Once upon a time
As if to mean: these are only stories...
Think what you like, learned progeny,
Our obsession lies in things of the past.

True, all together, we are not large in number
But do you need millions to make a nation?
All you need is strength and devotion
Which we got from our fathers and mothers.

We are from Monaco, everyone must know,
That our heads are as hard as our Rock:
The spirit of the past, even in our time,
We want to keep it; we will not let it go.

In tomorrow's world,
Friends and neighbours, may God make
Our old Romance language
Plough a wider furrow,
And, be it on organ or flute
To sing out joy or sorrow,
Let us dare to conserve the beauty
Of our ever divine mother tongue.

MONGOLIA

HADAA SENDOO
Translated from the Mongolian by the author

It is Not True I Have No Hometown

It is not true I have no hometown
I say so to myself
While I feel sad

It is not true I have no hometown
My hometown is a rising sun
But now it looks like a cool moon
With knitted brows

It is not true I have no hometown
My hometown is stack of hay
Who will turn it over to dry?

MONTENEGRO

ALEKSANDAR BEČANOVIĆ

Translated from the Montenegrin by Tomislav Kuzmanović

Pessoa: On Four Addresses

So, I drew the line. With a sharp stroke.
As always, whiteness waited. I could
feel my legs going relentlessly numb: the night
was making its way through the branches of nearby trees,
bringing frost. I stretch and get up: everything
needs to go quiet, everything needs to become so distant,
for the *persona* to feel relieved. When I abandon
my writing, long-lasting peace enters the room.
Things seem familiar, then.
I'm no longer in the room: my handwriting is
a short line of strokes. The heart's architecture
resembles the architecture of a city: few paths
lead inside, many lead out.
After all, streetlights in Lisbon are cold.
The subject is a puny clerk, a dying instance, a necessity
character: he leaves written marks behind, then.
Then I can even imagine you: somewhere downtown,
near the intersection where the cars are noisier than
usual, with a careful move of your hand you drop a well-
sealed letter into a yellow mailbox.

HASSAN EL OUAZZANI
Translated from the Arabic by Norrdine Zouitni

What If I Unsettled the Homeland?

What if
I unsettled the homeland?
Richter would set its scale
To shake lots of leaves from
The tree of public interest
In which many hide.
The bourgeois and the destitute,
Warlords and frontline troops,
Shepherds and faithful citizens,
Leaders and freedom-fighters.

What if
I unsettled mountains?
Rebels who lost their way
To the battle-front
Would look down from the mountains' heights.

What if
I unsettled death?
Friends whom I had seen off for good
Would return one by one
To sit up all night
Around the table
Of life.

What if
I unsettled truth?
Many lies
Would fall from
Its folds.

What if
I unsettled silence?

A lot of clamour
Would bounce off its guts.

What if
I unsettled the left?
Party militants dreaming
Of the extreme right
Would peep from its sidelines.

What if I unsettled
War?
Many fighters going to death
For the sake of a cause
That concerns
Only their generals
Would fall at the battlefronts.

What if
I unsettled heroism?
Great cowardice
Would emerge at its borders.

What if
I unsettled crime?
It would end up recognising
Its perpetrators.

What if
I unsettled the page?
A lot of war criminals busy
Planting kisses on the foreheads of victims
Would leap from its folds
And open
Other
Darker
Pages.

What if
I unsettled history?
Historians busy
Adjusting its frame
To the size of the state
Would look down from its heights.

What if
I unsettled love?
All the lovers
Who feign further losses
To realise the pain of love,
Would leap from its tales.

What if
I unsettled politics,
Men piling up their countries' losses
To enter the Guinness Book
Through its wide gate,
Would jump off its notebooks.

What if
I unsettled the battlefront?
Generals stirring up more wars
To conclude a truce
Worthy of thousands
Of martyrs
Would emerge from its sidelines.

What if
I unsettled hell?
Angels who had lost their way
To Heaven
Would emerge from its maze.

What if
I unsettled certainty?
A large smile
Would light up the face
Of Uncle Descartes.

What if
I unsettled the wave?
Stories of sailors
Who got lost on the way
To treasures
That existed only in the heads
Of their leaders
Would bounce off its perplexity.

What if
I unsettled friendship?
A lot of enmity
Would fall off its banks.

What if
I unsettled age?
Children messing around with the stars
Would emerge from its wrinkles.

What if
I unsettled the ship?
A lot of opportunists
Seeking escape
And leaving the deluge
Behind,
Alone,
Would jump from its deck.

What if
I unsettled the Forties?
Little Rim
Would peep from the city's outskirts,
While growing
To reach skies I have never touched
And mountains beyond the grasp of
My hands.

TRANSLATOR'S NOTE: Little Rim is the name of the poet's daughter.

MOZAMBIQUE

ANA MAFALDA LEITE

Translated from the Portuguese by Ana Raquel Lourenço

Music Box

I seep into you as a perfume
dressing the skin in odours or the soul in
satin
I want you to enlace me or bind me with many
bows
embrace me with ribbons or transparent threads
bringing you a present brilliant in cellophane
a little girl dressed in fire
enflaming aflame
wants you wrapped up in veils of silk and brocade
enchanted the serpent the flute the magician
man plays
and when he plays me
I open my body
music box
inside
like dancing ballerina

MYANMAR (BURMA)

ZEYAR LYNN
Translated from the Burmese by Ko Ko Thett

Slide Show

Life is back to normal

Next slide

In the West it's a different story

Next slide

Shall we also discuss the issue of the privileged

Next slide

Impossible, I have said it many times

Next slide

Maria Seow, Channel News Asia, Beijing

Next slide

Since I have decided to wear only trousers
Not a single paso has entered my head for ten years
Similarly   a poem or Maung Ba

Next slide

By using traditional technology we continue to
Produce successful shrimp pastes

Next slide

The body parts of the hostages have to be
Matched with their identity cards

Next slide

Shibboleths in lieu of heartbeats
Your call cannot be reached at the moment
What if no one comes when the Great War is staged some day

Next slide

Since thirteen and a half I have made love to ten thousand women
I just wanted to connect with at least one of them

Next slide

Loathing+fear+fear and loathing

Next slide

The laughter I have learned masks those I have suppressed

Next slide

What's life
It's a sexually transmittable disease
Let's share it

Next slide

The lives that have been barely alive and gone

Next slide

Idiocy, air, air, idiocy
No... No...
Life has to be entered from the other door

Next slide

The light that has left saying 'Just a moment.'

Next slide

'We all live in a yellow submarine
Yellow submarine, yellow submarine'

Next slide

To fly through the invisible fence

Next slide

The issue is as simple as that, I reckon. Those who have existed,
spoken and written before me were awe-inspiring and respectable.
They were real scholars and genuinely learned men. I assume that
you gentlemen are listening to me, standing and speaking in front of
you in a similarly courteous way you would to a madman speaking.
Thank you so very much for putting up with, forgiving, watching
and looking at the shadow of a life that has been trying to come to
terms with life in its own way, that has been struggling.

NAMIBIA

MVULA YA NANGOLO

From Exile

From exile when I return
I'm going to beg someone to touch me
Very, very tenderly
And gradually put me at ease
I wish to feel again how life feels

I've not been home for many, many years
For many years I've been out of sight
For many years I've not been touched
And I've learnt to be homesick here in exile
Where life is not so bright

I've not been touched so tenderly
I've been searched by bullets
Going through my camouflage
And leaving my heart so fresh
I wish to feel again how life feels

From exile when I return
I'm going to beg someone
To introduce the newly born babies

190

Help me identify those grown-ups
And lead me to the cemetery
Where friends and playmates have long gone

From exile when I return
I'm going to beg someone
to understand my silence
the letter that didn't arrive
about our clan and tribe
for now I only belong
to my country and nation
still I wish to be touched tenderly
by hand and atmosphere
of people in a peaceful sphere.

NAURU

MAKERITA VA'AI

Rains of Nauru

Rain, symbolic of a loss
of friend or foe
an ally or enemy
a chief or commoner
a native or foreigner
plagued by death
signifies a blessing
willed by the departed
anointing the land
providing water
to aid
abundant growth
showering prosperity
for loved ones
left behind.

YUYUTSU R.D. SHARMA

London Bombings

I didn't desert the Underground
to join the British waterways
or party on the shores of the Northern Sea.

I didn't leave the streets,
Oxford, Piccadilly, Marylebone High Street,
to go into the lonely Room
to read Brontë, Bill or *Da Vinci Code*.

I didn't desert the West End
to go for meadows dotted with sheep.

I moved like William Blake
in the double-decker buses
deciphering terror alphabets
of a script of hidden sleep.

Notting Hill, Tooting, Camden,
Fulham, Wembley, Hammersmith,
I stayed on to join
carnivals of primal ecstasy.

I was there when they brought
their forgotten gods and demons out from their skins.

I fell in love with her
as Elizabeth got drunk and kept swearing,
smearing her purple lipstick
with shaking long fingers all over her mouth

Sitting in her lover's lap,
she kept calling me 'husband'
Husband! Husband!
as her teenage daughter
opposite us lay in waiting.

I was there when they celebrated
the death of Jane's family
and their charade of being
proverbial husband/wife went on
like a morality play
faming the last shame humanity's grandmothers.

It was there that Elizabeth's body
glowed like a hillside hearth in a room where
a statue of the wooden
Krishna broke into a smile.

'Put your Hinduish/Buddhist marks on your forehead
or wear pendants showing your holy gods,
you could be taken as a terrorist and shot five times in the brain...'

But I refused to desert the square
littered with blotches of the dark ink of terror...

I didn't desert the squares of the mighty Pound
to cry secretly in the nearby towns where
under common ground Marx and Freud lay buried....

I moved about fearlessly
under the shadow of Marble Arch
kissed her beneath
the tall column of Trafalgar Square.
and entered immaculate doors
of New Age goddess on the swelling Thames' banks,
daring to risk the Empire's familiar hand,
Prospero's mighty magic wand.

ARJEN DUINKER
Translated from the Dutch by Willem Groenewegen

from The Sublime Song of a Maybe

X

All corners are naked.
All words are naked.
In Córdoba there is a corner where the men piss
When beer has bloated their bellies,
Groaning with relief,
Eyes half open.

There is also a corner like this in Lisbon,
Even the wind that blows in from the Tagus
Cannot clean it out.
I have stood watching,
Surprised at the nakedness of that corner.

From a balcony there was a cry: 'What is it?
Young man, that corner is very special.
Five deaths every year! Take a good look,
And go on home.
Go on home.'
The woman hawked and spat with force.
And I, while I made myself scarce,
Was amazed at the nakedness of that corner.

BILL MANHIRE

Entering America

A line of men, tipped forward, stumbling.
They are taking off their shoes.

This is how you enter America:
under a gun and a stare.

Where a bastard is free to be a big bastard!
You can be sure of a welcome here!

And these men all in line,
coming home in their suits,

with deals in their pockets, with phones-beyond-phones,
whose tired feet have swollen their way
       soared through the heavens –

are made to show the occasional toe,
not to mention their socks,

with those little designs at the ankles,
often, I believe, called 'clocks'.

GIOCONDA BELLI
Translated from the Spanish by Steven F. White

Brief Lessons in Eroticism I

I

To sail the entire length of a body
Is to circle the world
To navigate the rose of the winds without a compass
Islands gulfs peninsulas breakwaters against crashing waves
It's not easy to find such pleasure
Don't think you can get it in one day or night of consoling sheets
There are enough secrets in the pores to fill many moons

II

The body is an astral chart in a coded language
Find a star and perhaps you'll begin
To change course when suddenly a hurricane or piercing scream
Makes you tremble in fear
A crease in the hand you didn't expect

III

Go over the entire length many times
Find the lake with the white water lilies
Caress the lily's centre with your anchor
Plunge deep drown yourself stretch your limbs
Don't deny yourself the smell the salt the sugar
The heavy winds cumulonimbus-lungs
The brain's dense fog
Earthquake of legs
Sleeping tidal waves of kisses

IV

Place yourself in the humus without fear
             of wearing out there's no hurry
Delay reaching the peak
the threshold of paradise
Rock your fallen angel let your usurped sword of fire
lose itself in the thick hair
Bite the apple

196

V

Ocean smell
Pain as well
Exchange glances saliva impregnate yourself
Roll over imprint of sobs skin that slips away
Foot discovery at the end of the leg
Pursue it look for the secret of the passage the heel's shape
Arch of each step bays shaping arched stride
Taste them

VI

Listen to the shell of the ear
How the dampness moans
Earlobe approaching the lip sound of breathing
Pores that rise up to form tiny mountains
Shivery insurrection of skin caressed
Gentle bridge neck go down to the sea breast
The heart's tide whisper to her
Find the grotto of water

VII

Cut through tierra del fuego good hope
Navigate the madness where the seas join
Sail over the algae arm yourself with coral howl moan
Emerge with the olive branch cry undermining
            all hidden tenderness
Let looks of astonishment go naked
Throw down the sextant from the heights of the eyelash
Arch your eyebrows open the nose's windows

VIII

Breathe in breathe out
Die a little
Sweetly slowly die
Come to death against the eye's centre let the pleasure go on
Turn the rudder spread the sails
Sail on turn toward Venus
morning star
– the sea like a vast mercuric crystal –
sleep
you
shipwrecked sailor.

NIGER

ADAMOU IDÉ
Translated from the French

I'm Scared!

I'm scared!
Yes, I do not conceal it from you
I say it: I'm scared!
I'm scared
Of all anthems you sing
Elixirs vomited noisily
Brought forward
I'm scared of your flags
cracking in the wind of your madness
I'm scared!
To you I confess my fear
I'm scared of your erected tents
Sparse in the flowered gardens
I'm scared of your adult games
In the pedestrian corridors
I know that one day
You will shoot me!
I'm scared
Yes, I confess my fear
I'm scared of your gloved hands
Hiding numerous cactus
I'm scared when a child
Claims for life in his cold cradle
I'm scared when he shows ecstasy
I know that one day
You will shoot him!

NIGERIA

WOLE SOYINKA

Her Joy is Wild

Her joy is wild, wild
Wave-breaking she proclaims,
Your strong teeth will weaken
If you nibble the rind.

Her strength is wild, wild
Wild as the love that sings –
This is the last-born; give me
A joyful womb to bind.

The hour is wild, wild
Denies the wispy moments. Yet
When the fist is loosened, when
The knot is cut, you'll find

Skeins of hair. Wild, wild
Her laughter, dreaming that the tribe
Had slain the senile chieftain
That the rite – was kind.

Her words are wild, wild
Shell the future, place the nut
Between my teeth – and I denied her
Nothing, maimed on her vision of the blind.

ENDRE RUSET
Translated from the Norwegian by Sam Riviere

Plum tree

Mine was a mother
of the malevolent variety. I was born
when she planted a tree from a cherry. It died
the day I forced my hand between Constance's thighs.
She gave a small cry and went limp. My tree
was hollow and smelled a bit damp. My mother
was thin enough to climb inside. She stood
in the hollow as I played in the garden. I saw her hand
hanging among the low branches. I felt her eyes
looking from the tangled dead twigs. Wild pigs
chased me all over the garden. I was too
quick and clever for them. I climbed
my mother's tree, the one her father grew
from a fruit stone. The wild pigs
grunted and dug at the roots. My mother
wouldn't come out of the cherry bush. Her hand
went stiff in the rotting foliage. I plucked
obscenely bulging plums from her branches.
Their pink flesh tasted of Constance.
Their clear juice was sour
and stuck to my palms.

OMAN

ZAHIR AL-GHAFRI
Translated from the Arabic by Salih J. Altoma

A Room at the End of the World

In a distant room, at the end of the world
at the end of a stormy night
I remember you now as a phantom
accidentally passing near the fountain of my life
like a feather blown backwards
onto a land I rarely visit

I listen to your absence at the window of truth
The guests are gone
There's no trace of living shadows
nor flowers, either, left on the doorstep

My glance toward you while you are absent
is the repentance of the unfaithful
The sands scatter my dreams on your bed
and remorse perfumes you with the fragrance of water, white like
       the night,

You and I are two banks between which my life
passes as it floats on the glow of eternity
Tonight your fruits are golden
and music starts to play, a soft drizzle
from a distant room at the end of the world

IMTIAZ DHARKER

Honour killing

At last I'm taking off this coat,
    this black coat of a country
    that I swore for years was mine,
    that I wore more out of habit
    than design.
    Born wearing it,
    I believed I had no choice.

I'm taking off this veil,
    this black veil of a faith
    that made me faithless
    to myself,
    that tied my mouth,
    gave my god a devil's face,
    and muffled my own voice.

I'm taking off these silks,
    these lacy things
    that feed dictator dreams,
    the mangalsutra and the rings
    rattling in a tin cup of needs
    that beggared me.

I'm taking off this skin,
    and then the face, the flesh,
    the womb.

Let's see
    what I am in here
    when I squeeze past
    the easy cage of bone.

Let's see
    what I am out here,
    making, crafting,
    plotting
    at my new geography.

PALAU

ANONYMOUS

Translated from the Paluan

The Bungle-man

the bungle-man
thinks
with crewless brains:
like the boat-bob
from Ngerechemai
who tagged
the where-is
of his fishtraps
with a cloud.

RAFEEF ZIADAH

We Teach Life, Sir

Today, my body was a TV'd massacre.
Today, my body was a TV'd massacre that had to fit into sound-bites
 and word limits.
Today, my body was a TV'd massacre that had to fit into sound-bites
 and word limits filled enough with statistics to counter measured
 response.
And I perfected my English and I learned my UN resolutions.
But still, he asked me, Ms Ziadah, don't you think that everything
 would be resolved if you would just stop teaching so much hatred
 to your children?
Pause.
I look inside of me for strength to be patient but patience is not at the
 tip of my tongue as the bombs drop over Gaza.
Patience has just escaped me.
Pause. Smile.
We teach life, sir.
Rafeef, remember to smile.
Pause.
We teach life, sir.
We Palestinians teach life after they have occupied the last sky.
We teach life after they have built their settlements and apartheid walls,
 after the last skies.
We teach life, sir.
But today, my body was a TV'd massacre made to fit into sound-bites
 and word limits.
And just give us a story, a human story.
You see, this is not political.
We just want to tell people about you and your people so give us a
 human story.
Don't mention that word 'apartheid'and 'occupation'.
This is not political.
You have to help me as a journalist to help you tell your story which
 is not a political story.
Today, my body was a TV'd massacre.

How about you give us a story of a woman in Gaza who needs medication?
How about you?
Do you have enough bone-broken limbs to cover the sun?
Hand me over your dead and give me the list of their names in one thousand two hundred word limits.
Today, my body was a TV'd massacre that had to fit into sound-bites and word limits and move those that are desensitised to terrorist blood.
But they felt sorry.
They felt sorry for the cattle over Gaza.
So, I give them UN resolutions and statistics and we condemn and we deplore and we reject.
And these are not two equal sides: occupier and occupied.
And a hundred dead, two hundred dead, and a thousand dead.
And between that, war crime and massacre, I vent out words and smile 'not exotic', 'not terrorist'.
And I recount, I recount a hundred dead, a thousand dead.
Is anyone out there?
Will anyone listen?
I wish I could wail over their bodies.
I wish I could just run barefoot in every refugee camp and hold every child, cover their ears so they wouldn't have to hear the sound of bombing for the rest of their life the way I do.
Today, my body was a TV'd massacre
And let me just tell you, there's nothing your UN resolutions have ever done about this.
And no sound-bite, no sound-bite I come up with, no matter how good my English gets, no sound-bite, no sound-bite, no sound-bite, no sound-bite will bring them back to life.
No sound-bite will fix this.
We teach life, sir.
We teach life, sir.
We Palestinians wake up every morning to teach the rest of the world life, sir.

LUCY CRISTINA CHAU

The Night

Niko, you will never know about the night
until they say Kid Wilson's wrestle will not be broadcasted tonight,
and your father doesn't know what to do with all that frozen beer,
and it is then that everything goes dark;
and it is then when the silence gets inside and right behind you,
it is then when you think of fear
as a strange man who sits down in your bed.

And you, Niko, thinking about this curious sunrise
with the memories of Kid Wilson in his bath robe,
dancing his feet
as his fists cut the air with hard strikes.

You, imagining the celebration of a knock out, Niko
letting yourself be embraced by your father
as a good friend who celebrates another thing,
who celebrates the most beautiful, great and cutest thing;
and at the same time you know you are Kid Wilson,
he is your father at your birth date,
and you cry,
you cry as the day you were born,
because you don't know who Kid Wilson is,
nor his father,
or his mother's mother,
but you hold on, Niko
because it is the only way to avoid
carrying the weight of the night.

PAPUA NEW GUINEA

STEVEN WINDUO

Lomo'ha I am, in Spirits' Voice I Call

Lomo'ha ne walihowi wa
Lomo'ha konglu ye
Nuwo Lomo'ha ne.

I have travelled in those lands
Beyond doors of sacred tombs
Only in the stories of our fore fathers
Did you weep over my dead name when I left
To that unseen *waliwuiya*

Upon my return after years of wandering
Below the horizon of the sea
And between skies of the *waliwuiya*
I see nothing
But myself among the wild trees
In the wilderness of this jungle
I learned about each mark carved on trees
By unknown hands which spoke to me

Lomo'ha! Lomo'ha!
Yenefa waliwuiya
Yenefa waliwuiya
Na whame?

I call: waiting men do you hear me
I am speaking in this strange language
Lomo'ha ne walihowi ne wa
Lomo'ha I am, in spirits' voice I call

I have returned from death
Do you remember me my people
Lomo'ha ne walihowi wa
Hear this living voice cry before I am lost

See these things that I have brought
And do not judge my spirits' voice for my spirit

Lomo'ha ne walihowi wa
Lomo'ha konglu ye
Nuwo Lomo'ha ne

PARAGUAY

LIA COLOMBINO

Translated from the Spanish by Grizzie Logan & Sebastián Peña

from The Side

I burden myself with the windstorm
I adjust the cloud over the cyclops' head
I dream
I break alien words and I populate myself
I touch the fingertips of breath
Yes
Me
that who carries the voice of me
that who inaugurates me and dilapidates me
that precipitates the syllable towards a sea
I dig in the bottom
                my animal

VICTORIA GUERRERO PEIRANO
Translated from the Spanish by Enrique Bernales

The Cyclist
To the dreamers
To the real cyclists

To the one who closes his eyes through the morning

Only a dream   a magnificent light

Has been set up for him   the dreamer   the soul matchmaker

That one that drowns himself in the gratifying madness and raises
        himself
in his beautiful red
bicycle

I am a mediocre biker
I admit it
I am distressed by thinking in the loneliness of the bystanders

In the oblique shining of the morning
And in the thousands of cars that fly over the pavement
Oh! My old red bicycle I bought
a Sunday in the Mauer Park Fair
Fifteen years ago I could have pedalled
Through one or the other side of the wall
And my dream would dream itself distinct

To my Berliner guide I am a constant pain
He goes ahead of me as an indifferent prince
Biking his enormous blue bicycle
– blue as my grandma eyes –
he can't understand my strange dream or my anguish
he has gotten the confidence of an expert biker

Today I ride my bike
And I remember the colour of grandma's eyes
Her beginning in madness   her permanent exile

I close my eyes as I did when I was a little girl
I drop the grip of my bike   I drift it

To fall down is always a possibility to make a fool of yourself or Death

Maybe certain maternal madness
        make me more human along with so many corpses I piled up
        in my adolescence

My core: the little Lu laughs at me
She knows I am afraid
And enjoys and parties when sees the picture
'It is a children's bicycle' – she said

And we smile at each other
And berlín isn't Berlin anymore neither its perfect bikepaths
Nor its hundreds of museums that honour Death
Today is Lima and in Lima people don't bike often
because the bikes are stolen or you are run over by the cars in any
        corner
and there aren't museums to honour the corpses
of my ten, of my fifteen, of my twenty years

I wrote this poem for the one who still dreams
To the one who crossses the borders *happy and undocumented*
To those who revolt against the killers of the world

To the biker that writes a poem everytime he is pedalling

MARJORIE EVASCO

Despedida
(after Ted Berrigan and Federico García Lorca)

> Si muero, dejad el balcón abierto
> FEDERICO GARCÍA LORCA, 'Despedida'

Juan Rulfo is dead. Twenty-one years ago, he moved
With pale thighs to the dream trees of Comala.

Today, he awakens to the light of my room,
Rising to meet my eyes, asking in tender tones:
A donde vas Margarita?

                I want to say to him:
Voy a la casa de Pedro Páramo, in your village
Of the dead who love, lust, kill in passion, or hope
As if the door of life had never slammed shut.

Instead, I tell him of another Margarita, barely 18,
Giving birth to a daughter at high noon, gored
In the belly by the bull's horn, almost bled dry.

Doomed to die at five in the afternoon, her life crossed
The threshold and opened the balcony to the sun.

JACEK DEHNEL
Translated from the Polish by Antonia Lloyd-Jones

The Death of Oscar Wilde

Sometimes he thrust his hand into his mouth to prevent himself from crying aloud with pain, and once he took it out to speak bitterly of the wallpaper, 'It is killing me,' he complained, adding resignedly, as if the worst was over, 'One of us had to go.'

HESKETH PEARSON, The Life of Oscar Wilde

Its pattern wasn't an issue, Oscar, and not only
to the owner and clients, to the priest and Robbie,
but to you too. Forgive it. Because it was not the
motley roses or brownish leaves that you so hated,
but what was there behind them – the wall and the passage,
the courtyard, the sky above you, boulevards and gardens,
the great wallpaper factory, the massed factory workers,
all their wives and their children, their families, their chattels,
distant cities, the ocean, the whole sapphire planet
full of flaws – lands and islands. And back again: rain clouds,
London, Paris, America, silk, satin and velvet,
everything left behind you – and in the next bedroom
two pairs of lovers' legs shaking as tremors ran through them,
like feet over the   of a strange scaffold.

trapdoor

ROSA ALICE BRANCO
Translated from the Portuguese by Alexis Levitin

No Complaint Book

In the beginning was the Word
but now no one answers.
The husband, the lover, the family and friends,
all gather round the grave.
They begin with prayer or a lay equivalent
and quickly pass to supplications and to bribes.
Cemeteries are bureaucratic offices.
That's why there are no answers.
There are nights of little sleep for the wrong reasons.
This night the bed shook three times. Your whispers
in my mouth. Your moist skin. Am I your epitaph?
The family and the others continue to come to the counters
without their paperwork filled out.
The dead no longer belong to answers.
Any adjective decays just like the flowers.
Any sentence breaks apart without a subject.
I am a mere tattoo there on your grave.
In the beginning was the end.

VANESSA DROSS
Translated from the Spanish by Andrew Hurley

The Absent Warrior

What warrior will I turn to
when, grown old,
the cheese no longer issues from my hands,
the goats will not come at my call,
the blood on the temple's linens
no longer reveals to me its secrets,
the automobile leaves me stranded on some avenue?

The complaints against me
will be unbearable,
the mere mention of my age
a disturbance of the time that day.
The circle of the marketplace –
even its smells, its foods –
will turn against me,
and only a handful of the wise women at the glass wall
will want to hear the stories
history has invented for me,
especially in shopping centre and dark trinket evenings.

What good is life on a crutch,
the wood that built it crowned
by the arm's rank fragrance
that belonged, once, to the air?
What good the lacquered wheel on the chair
(its spokes do, really,
resemble a sun – no, two suns)
that rolls on a tightrope through the smoke?
What good are bones melted by fortune,
by salt, by a fire desired but nevermore?

Within the blue amber of that sombre badge
there also lies, weeping,
the warriors' extinction.
Streets, stop-lights,
the sleepwalkers on the sidewalks
and the wheels of the carriage
no longer know the steadfastness of their voices.

And I shall have no one to turn to.

QATAR

SOAD AL KUWARI
Translated from the Arabic by Fatima Mostafawi, with Patty Paine

The Flood

To murder freedom
we don't need generals,
or cannons. We don't need
weapons of mass destruction,
or podiums.

Erect a dictator's statue
in the middle of a crowded square
and watch
the pigeons fall
one by one.
Look how wisdom wears
the hat of obedience.

*

Coffee shops are havens
for intellectuals
and the unemployed escaping
houses haunted by echoes.

Prisons are built
for those who oppose,
for those who step
over the line, or fly
outside the flock.

The city is governed
by tyrants, wars are waged
by devils. The earth, like a grinder,
never stops crushing.

From which alley can we escape?
We are not lab rats
or horses trained for battle.
We are not your last bid
for power.

*

The clouds are aloof
and impede our view.
The cinema closes
our imagination. Quietly,
let's reshape history
along its endless surfaces,
along its endless mountains.

Inscribed on the walls of cafés:
the science of atoms,
acronyms, long arguments
over lexicon, death
of the author and the francophone.
And there, the last word
on reviving democracy
from its deep sleep.

DOINA IOANID

Translated from the Romanian by Florin Bican

The Yellow Dog

Heart in hand I've been walking all over the city, treading the first snow of the year under my feet. And my heart, sprinkled with wine and with vinegar, went on rotting away to the beat of my years – all thirty and seven of them – while the magpies assembled on the drummer-boy's shoulder. Bones alone couldn't save me. Nor could your name, Argentina, you, Land of Promise. Only a big yellow dog took pity on me – humbly walked up to me and ate up my heart, taking his time. Then he left, moving away towards the horizon like an enormous sunflower.

RUSSIAN FEDERATION

ILYA KAMINSKY

Author's Prayer

If I speak for the dead, I must leave
this animal of my body,

I must write the same poem over and over,
for an empty page is the white flag of their surrender.

If I speak for them, I must walk on the edge
of myself, I must live as a blind man

who runs through rooms without
touching the furniture.

Yes, I live. I can cross the streets asking 'What year is it?'
I can dance in my sleep and laugh

in front of the mirror.
Even sleep is a prayer, Lord,

I will praise your madness, and
In a language not mine, speak

of music that wakes us, music
in which we move. For whatever I say

is a kind of petition, and the darkest
days must I praise.

RWANDA

EDOUARD BAMPORIKI
Translated from the Kinyarwanda by Arlette Maregeya & David Shook

from A Cock Crows in Rwanda

Usually, beloved, I crow,
And my name is Rusake the Cock,
The same one most people chow down on,
Especially my delicious neck.
I'm at every wedding,
And on every chief's table,
Everyone likes me.
Let me come crow the story of Rwanda.
I witnessed bad times,
I travelled to many countries,

And in each I asked
Where the tragedy that decimates
The Rwandese came from.
Nations were watching.
Rusake, I'm sorrowful.

Can I ask you for a favour?
Protect me from insatiably hungry people.
I want to crow my troubles, first.
And then those who want to eat me may.
I know that if I leave,
If I leave this place without crowing my troubles,
You won't say anything about it,
You will just enjoy eating Rusake.

Then those that destroy my nation
Will be forgotten in Rwanda
Unless I crow about them,
So that we can remember their mistakes,
So that future generations will not poke me with their fingers.

Let us remember all of us
Our history.
You people, you quarrelled.
Most of you, you fled the country.
Some of you, you stayed in Rwanda,
And you did not like what you found.
I crow to wake you up,
But you stay in your beds,
And I wonder what keeps you from me,
And I feel sorrowful.
Most of you, you are sorrowful,
You remember sad things.
Some of you, you hurry along,
You talk to each other about development,
You go to school together.
Some of you do not know these things.
Even Rusake does not know this –
Which sauce he is prepared in.
Oh, how I dislike the rich!
Those who chose to flee,
Were bullied by the nations,

They couldn't even walk down the street.
You stayed in the bush,
There were no beans to be found,
You had no way to shop,
No way to attend school.
You hair greyed.
Oh! What hunger!
You really witnessed tragedy.

Those of you who stayed in Rwanda,
You have been mastered by hate.
When I crowed that they live together
They turned a deaf ear, refusing to hear.
And I wonder what keeps them from me,
And I feel sorrowful.

Over at your schools
You learned about ethnic groups
Without knowing their origins.
And no one has the time
To criticise that wrong culture.
A nation clothed in forest,
You put yourself together.
You prayed asking God
Why you must stay abroad
Even though you had Rwanda
As your home.

Someone with good dreams
Dreamed you went to fight,
Someone who dreamed while fleeing
Dreamed they saw you all die.

ISHAQ IMRUH BAKARI

Haiti is once again...

History does not
repeat itself   it hangs

Around the neck
like a stone   or a talisman

And now within
the moment that it takes
a guillotine
to settle a score

And now beneath
the rubble of our
window dressing
the cries of orphans choke

Haiti is once again
the hurt   in the soul
the amputation   that never healed
the torch   flame of cane fires
Haiti is once again...

The clocks have stopped
face and arms
lay unidentified
where they stood

The laughter remembered
hangs on a limping
stride amidst the silence
in abundant after-shock

The tears flow
where no water

can be found
it burns in the steam
It stains and seeps
from ragged thoughts
that yearn for maps
to the neighbourhood streets

Haiti is once again...

Somewhere in a museum
it will be recalled

Somewhere the crimes
of Napoleonic brotherhood

Somewhere the compromises
of the new Americas

Somewhere it will
be condemned
to its loneliness
beyond the age of enlightenment

Somewhere the architects
of banana republics

Somewhere the tyrannies
that censure liberty

Haiti is once again...

At the turn of a new century
it is the twelfth of January
and the world is looking
the other way

It is a normal day   with business and its intrigues
                          aid and its debt relief
                          arms dealers and their wars
                          good causes and their epidemics

It was a normal day

in Cité Soleil
and Jacmel
in Port-au-Prince no doubt
at the Citadel

And the world was looking
the other way

until...

the interruption

the disruption

calamity so epic and severe
prophets were born
in deceit and complicity

and as the vibrations
settled into still life
lost words rolled off
the cliffs of corpses

the nameless
spoke their last
in epitaphs sealed in blood
dust and lost possessions

How much less
sure my staggering walk
How much less
certain my world stories

familiar fingerprints
are being left
at the scenes of crime
in the aftermath

Haiti is once again
at the cross-roads

In whose image
the zombification...?

Haiti is once again
at the turn of a new century

In whose image
the deification...?

Haiti is once again
at the threshold
between bondage
and the ease of flight   in search of the ceremonies
                                of our healing...

SAINT LUCIA

DEREK WALCOTT

As John to Patmos

As John to Patmos, among the rocks and the blue, live air, hounded
His heart to peace, as here surrounded
By the strewn-silver on waves, the wood's crude hair, the rounded
Breasts of the milky bays, palms, flocks, the green and dead

Leaves, the sun's brass coin on my cheek, where
Canoes brace the sun's strength, as John, in that bleak air,
So am I welcomed richer by these blue scapes, Greek there,
So I shall voyage no more from home; may I speak here.

This island is heaven – away from the dustblown blood of cities;
See the curve of bay, watch the straggling flower, pretty is
The wing'd sound of trees, the sparse-powdered sky, when lit is
The night. For beauty has surrounded
Its black children, and freed them of homeless ditties.

As John to Patmos, in each love-leaping air,
O slave, soldier, worker under red trees sleeping, hear
What I swear now, as John did:
To praise lovelong, the living and the brown dead.

PHILIP NANTON

Douglas' Dinky Death

An early forbear was probably the bastard
of some Scottish clan. A sheep stealer
sent to cool it in the 'Indies.
In childhood he played at city planner.
The family backyard became
his private metropolis. Comfortable
roads to travel, roads to choose
strung with matchbox houses, petrol stations,
tiny iron cars on rubber wheels.

The last time that we met
he was driving a taxi and selling fish.
With no city to run he was often drunk.
The little cars he so loved
became a beat-up Austin Cambridge
its floor lined with cardboard,
yellowing foam protruding from
a backseat's thick plastic seam.
The smell of dead fish surrounded him.

One early morning outside his mansion
his bent and battered body was hit,
run over by one of those iron cars
on rubber wheels he loved.
He registered a dinky death: small,
insignificant as our reluctant recognition
of some animal's road-wrecked carcass
stiff with *rigor mortis*; a bored glimpse
of fading letters impressed on asphalt
proclaiming political loyalty
or a pot-hole, small enough to drive over.

SAMOA

TUSIATA AVIA

Return to Paradise

My uncle once broke a man's hands
quietly, like you would snap a biscuit
in half

and then another.
No one knows how loud the man screamed
or if he screamed.

My uncle was Gary Cooper's body double
Return to Paradise, 1952.
He'd studied in Fiji and could speak English

but no one needed him to talk
he was afakasi
and white enough to look white.

Cooper didn't come out much in the day
too hot maybe
they shot him mostly at night

so my uncle stood in the sun for the long shots
in those beachcomber shorts and the hat.
What the villagers remember is the church

where Gary Cooper shoots out the stained glass
windows with a gun.
And the machine that pumped water out of the sea

to make it rain.
The boys remember the cigarettes
and the candy that the crew handed out

all through the night so they would stay
and keep them company.
He was Australian, that man

(most of the crew from Queensland).
They must have sent him back there
with his broken hands
and his Lucky Strikes.

AMERICAN SAMOA

SIA FIGIEL

The Daffodils from a Native's Perspective

Apologies Mr Wordsworth,
but I too wandered lonely as a cloud
when I first heard your little poem,
Form 3, Literature class,
that floats on high
o'er vales and hills.
She made us memorise you!
Along with tiger tiger burning bright in the forest
of your other 19th century Romantic friends.

When all at once she'd pull my ear,
each time I started at the alice bush
next to the mango tree outside.
But in the end I became quite the expert
on your golden host of daffodils,
beside the lake,
beneath the trees,
fluttering and dancing
under the piulo tree.

After school
singing, singing
the daffodils,
your precious daffodils,
my precious daffodils;
my only possession at 15,
the one thing I didn't have to share,
not knowing what was *fluttering*
what was *dancing*.
But never mind,
whatever they must have been,
they must have been magical
enchanting even,
because
they too put a smile on my face –
whenever I lie on my mat
oft in pensive mood
trying to find some bliss of solitude
now and then without the
dogs, the roosters, the eyinga,
my eyinga, the village,
my village, the district,
my district, the neighbours,
the neighbours' radio,
their TV,
their big mouth auntie who swears at the kids
because they haven't started suca
and it's already 5 o'clock in the evening.
God I hated that woman!
But smile at her anyway,
the only way for us to watch *Days of Our Lives*.
Do you know what I mean Mr Wordsworth?
Do you know what I mean?

MILENA ERCOLANI
Translated from the Italian by Cristina Viti

A Woman Is a Woman

A woman is a woman...
each time she speaks to you
and says nothing of the ghosts
you would have wanted
to stitch across her lips
and on her shoulders

A woman is a woman...
each time she awakes
and fearlessly enters
the tight circle
that still stamps on her, uses her
and changes her hands and her face

A woman is a woman...
each time she's a mother
with a breast or without,
as painted in a portrait
with colours from the veins,
secretions of sweat and saliva
beating drop by drop
on the beating heart
hurting her
soothing her

A woman is a woman...
when her soul's resin
anoints her giving body,
anoints her caressing fingers,
anoints her deep-dark kisses
and her eyes can look on
unshaded,
her feet walk unfettered by borders...

A woman is a woman
each time she is frightening
in the guise of a hag, no princess,
but a woman's a woman
each time you recognise her as Queen of Flowers,
each time you can see her as only woman,
with no more veils,
no artificial light
no mannered affectation...

Only then,
fertile field,
kneaded soil,
maytime sky,
wellspring song,
she will be *Woman* for you,
when finally you are *Man* once again.

SÃO TOMÉ AND PRÍNCIPE

CONCEIÇÃO LIMA
Literal translation from the Portuguese by Stefan Tobler
Final translated version by The Poetry Translation Workshop

Cataclysm and Songs

Happy what's left of me after I'm gone
If only one of the songs sung
Lives beyond the person singing in me now.
Yet I would not save from the slaughter
A single one of the songs I sang and sing.
Instead from the entrails of oblivion
I would steal the laughter of children
And the age of the proverb.
And so to those who come
I would offer intact the enigma of light

SAUDI ARABIA

ASHJAN AL HENDI
Translated from the Arabic by Ashjan Al Hendi

In Search of the Other

Isabella
She searches for someone else every day;
  and finds me
  And I search for someone else;
    but find her
It is said: that East and West shall never meet
    but Isabella and I
    Meet every day
on our trip in search of others.

NOTE: Isabella is a German girl who was a member of the organising committee in charge of the Arab delegation guests participating in the International Frankfurt Book Fair in 2004.

DIDIER AWADI

Translated from the French

In My Dream

*We know the battle ahead will be long, but always remember that no
matter what obstacles stand in our way, nothing can stand in the way of
power of millions of voices calling for change.*

*I have a dream that one day this nation will rise up
and live out the true meaning of its creed.
We hold these truths to be self-evident that all men are created equal.*

I had a dream that the people will rise
In my dream a girl will rise
In my dream a son will rise
Hand-in-hand the mother rises
In my dream it's black and white
In my dream It's yellow and red
In my dream Everything is full of colour
reds and yellows and blacks and whites
In my dream There's no one who is dominated
In my dream No nations are dominated
nowhere in my dream is there land that's dominated
And the state is the hatred that is dominated
In my dream settlers are removed
In my dream Colonies eliminated

I abolished the colonies of years of earth all colonies
In my dream the racists are eliminated
In my dream Xenophobes are eliminated
In my dream homophobes are eliminated
Anti-Semites and camiste's are eliminated

*I have a dream that one day out in the red hills of Georgia
the sons of former slaves and the sons of former slaveowners
will be able to sit down together at the table of brotherhood.
I have a dream.*

Jo jolimajo
Jolimajo...
Yes we can
I have a dream
Jolimajo...

In my dream I visit Sarafina from Cairo, Cape Mount Sinai
In my dream I leave myself in Dakar, Bamako, Ndjamena, Dar and
     Zanzibar
In my dream visas are all cancelled
All African countries don't have visas
Even Europe eliminates visas
Asia and America abolish visas
In my dream there's no more war for oil
In my dream there's no more war for diamonds
In my dream there's no more war for gold
The civil war is no longer causes so much death
In my dream I am not a dreamer
In my dream I am not a utopian
The dream would be utopia and dreams

I have a dream
Yes we can
Yes we can
I have a dream that one day my four little children will
one day live in a nation where they will not be judged by
the colour of their skin but by their character.
I have a dream today.
Yes we can
Yes we can
I have a dream that one day down in Alabama,
with its vicious racists, with its governor having his lips
dripping with the words of interposition and nullification;
that one day right down in Alabama little black boys
and black girls will be able to join hands with little white boys
and white girls as sisters and brothers.
I have a dream today
Yes we can
Jolimajo...
I have a dream...

ANA RISTOVIĆ
Translated from the Serbian by Steven & Maja Teref

Circling Zero

We are independent women.
We breathe asthmatically
while waiting for new love. We pop pills
of unfulfilled promises. We drown in murky dreams.
Twenty-four hours a day we painfully make love
to a migraine and forgive her
because she is female.

Independent. For our men
we cook dishes taught to us
by their predecessors.
Clitoris-shaped pasta.
Ketchup dripping like menstrual blood
yet promising only the licking of plates.
But still we believe in the arc de triomphe
which rises between the bedsheets
and the kitchen table.

We play them the music
we lost our virginity to.
Pensive among seductive
lingerie, we keep underwear
with the invisible track of old sperm.
We gyrate our hips as if turning a mill:
after a while it drips
only sticky bitterness.

Yet we claim that we no longer believe
in sharing the same breath
between mouths
and more often we're left breathless
yet we claim that we use the centrifuge

of the washing machine
only when sitting on it –
good intercourse may occur.
In the prewash and rinse cycles
instead of clothes we throw in
pieces of our thinned out skin.

Independent women. We censor
our all to soft words.
We support the revision of feelings
and the theory arguing that innocent Eve
was created first, and that Adam
bit into the poisoned apple
because he wished for God to create
two more phalluses from the serpent:
poor thing, he thought one
wouldn't be enough.

Independent, we claim, more than ever.
Yet during lonely nights, in our tight vulva
more and more, we insert a small magical finger,
as if placing a bullet into the chamber
which refuses to fire.
And we smile with sadness in dreamless dreams.
And the safe hand, circling
the soft zero.

SEYCHELLES

ANTOINE ABEL

Your Country

Your country
Is studded with mountains,
Seychelles lad.

With tough granite
With crude gravel
And with coral, your country.

Your country
Wears a belt
Of white beaches loosening in the tides.

SIERRA LEONE

SYL CHENEY-COKER

On the 50th Anniversary of Amnesty International

I had not planned this celebration,
nor stolen from the Greeks the secrets of
weaving laurels, to crown your bold interventions.
After all, you are English, supposedly of mild
temperament; not one to clamour except when
flaring a cricket bat.

But modesty is trite: a lame intolerance
in the vanguard of freedom of speech,
when the voice of a giant has kept humanity's
threatened spirits alive; the poisoned breath checked
in the forests that had encircled them.

Along the Mediterranean, a hock of burning fires rages,
and the cherry gardens – pungent, always a lovers' enclave –
stagger from a battalion of angry words.
Insouciant about brave eloquence, the tabloids are busy
dredging the trenches for the lost handkerchieves of
the young patriots. Tomorrow, they will print for profit the words
the Dead refused to yield to the crouching tanks.

Light has dimmed into insignificance in *The Old Empires*,
but radiant on other spheres. The tired, *Old Order* sneezes,
and men and women in black talk of a new *Spring* as though
it had been orphaned from the streets' fervent voices; as though
it were a chicken killed and dressed for profit on the Stock Market.
But the seasons have not changed: one word ennobles
our dreams, and as earth still marches free and timeless,
you were always there: a wise guardian of the loom,
watching us weave our stubborn words to aid that march.

Drink lustily, then, to your own sagacious age.
Your embouchure speaks for others with candour,
and not in the landscape of *correctness*. In middle age, your
heart still beats with the excitement of a newly married bride;
your suitors were many, but not one for convention,
you married us all – new narratives about life, hope, and courage –
to stun the naked emperors who only drink from their tasteless and
      vainglorious scripts.

237

ALVIN PANG

When the barbarians arrive

lay out the dead, but do not mourn them overmuch.

a mild sentimentality is proper. nostalgia will be expected on demand.

cremate: conserve land, regret no secrets. prepare ashes for those with
cameras.

hide your best furniture. tear down monuments. first to go are statues with
arms outstretched in victory, and then anything with lions.

it is safer to consort with loss, to know the ground yet suggest no mysteries.

purport illiteracy.

have at hand servants good with numbers. err in their favour between schemes.

keep all receipts out of sight. as soon as is proper, embrace their laws and
decline all credit for your own.

confound their historians. give up the wrong recipe for ketupat, for otak.

lay claim to the tongue of roots, the provenance of trees. when the chiku
blooms, tell them it is linden. when linden, tell them it is ginko.

recommend laxatives as love potions. attribute pain to the passage of hard
feelings. there will be a surge

of interest in soothsaying. do not tell them how it will end, or when. progress,
while difficult, is always being made.

on no account acknowledge what your folktales imply.

never deal in the dark unless you can see the whites of their eyes. when
they speak of god

bow your head to veil piety, shame, laughter, or indifference.

dress your children like their long-dead elders. marry your daughters
to them.

soon you will attend the same funerals.

SLOVAKIA

KATARÍNA KUCBELOVÁ
Translated from the Slovak by Clare Pollard

from Little Big City

XXII

my memory can't catch

helpless green shoots
find concrete walls immune
to urban lifeforms

all shades of grey surface
impress from a height
between vertical and horizontal

synapses connect as
shade shifts

my memory can't climb

maybe there is crucial information I've forgotten
that reveals why planes
rearrange

maybe information waits
around the corner

I would find it
if I could

slide across vertical surface

but it isn't sure
it's really there
and how would I climb
down

it's never certain I'm completely

neither inside or

the number of levels beneath me
is not known
I don't remember where I left my car

elevators packed with people
pass

I am surprised at the number of levels
someone steps on my foot

it's never me
who presses the number
maybe that's the failure

I'll hardly come upon the information
this way

even if it's there
they'll step on it

distributors
who choose buy and go
knowing nothing waits

they remember
where they left their car
don't expect anyone

don't listen
to what thunder says
in rainless urban storms

don't distinguish
exterior from interior

don't expect the next day
when they know it comes
and they can choose the right one
for you and your family

choose and buy the right one
next and new
according to needs and desires

they don't have to seek
but avoid
downsize

find
simple shapes and surfaces

vary
grey surfaces

TAJA KRAMBERGER
Translated from the Slovenian by Špela Drnovšek Zorko

Every dead one has a name

Every dead one has a name,
only the names of the living make us falter.
Some names are impossible to utter
without a stammer and a fidget,
some can only be spoken
through allusion,
and some, mostly women's,
are forbidden in these parts.

Every dead one has a name,
engraved in stone,
printed in obituary or directory,
but my name must be undermined,
every few years
soiled and substituted
with another one.

A decade ago
a high-ranking party official warned me:
Stay a poet, as long as there's still time.
Still time?   Time for what?

I have also become a social scientist
and an editor and an organiser
and a translator and an activist
and a university teacher.
Unbearable – all these things –
all trespasses of the old parcel borders
that were drawn by the dirty
fingers of fraternities.

I air all the rooms,
I ignore all the ratings,
I open all the valvelets.

And they have put me out in the cold –
like the dead.
But every dead one has a name.

SOLOMON ISLANDS

JULLY MAKINI

Praying Parents

My parents pray for us
    every night
Long, winding boring prayers
    touring the world over
    blessing our nation and government
Forgiveness for our sins,
Salvation for the lost.

Every night,
Our names are lifted up
    to the Throne of Grace
Each child called by name
Starting with the youngest
    and ending with me.

If prayers could be coloured
    and seen by human eyes
Each night rising like smoke
    from home
    coloured by emotions
Blue smoke for the blue prayers
Grey – when hearts are heavy
White – a praising heart.

Children, with praying parents
    will rebel and do their uttermost
To shake their olos' faith
    when trouble strikes
They are spared, somehow

Children, see the smoking prayers
    wafting upwards, like incense
Learn to do likewise
Pray for your children too.

Tonight, flying above the clouds
Darkness on either side
    infinite depth below
My name mentioned last
    out of the twelve
My heart is comforted
Someone is being asked to
    take care of me.

SOMALIA

ABDULLAHI BOTAN HASSAN
Translated from the Somali by Martin Orwin

Central London

Learning opens closed doors of houses.
As dawn breaks and opportunities
Approach, let me consider central London.

When visiting Leicester Square or Piccadilly
You cannot appreciate it all in days
Or months; you can't get away from the troubled tourists
Carrying cases, deaf to 'Please, let me through'.

You can't get away from the homeless poor on benefits
Who beg every day with 'Please, have you got any change?'
But people don't even throw a few pennies.

The pigeons thrive on good food not grain
As they flock in a flutter you cannot get away.

You can't get away from the rich man looking
For somewhere to park his BMW

Or from the police who stop you and search
Your pockets for fake things or hashish.

You can't get away from the strange bicycles
With a shelter that people climb into and pay for.

In the centre when you stand, cameras all around,
You can't get away from fear and confusion that day.

The bus or train is packed, no place to sit,
You have an appointment, or work: part time or full,
A tight squeeze now, but you must venture on.
Exhausted from it all you want to leave,
The train swings to one side, you're flung together,
You miss the handle, grasp another's thigh,
In broken English 'Please,' you say 'I'm sorry'
But most just don't return the smallest word.

You look at them and everyone is busy
Their heads are buried in the latest paper and books,
Like spies they steal a look at one another,
From under eyelids glances reach across.

Then two of my own enter: all is noise
And talk, you'd think it was a hundred people.
At first I was shy but now I'm more comfortable
As they get louder I say 'Who says that's enough?'
Unintentional, without malice, it's the way they are.
People aren't satisfied by language they don't understand,
Those who know only their only place do not increase in riches.
The key to what you are ignorant of is to learn.

KATHARINE KILALEA

You were a bird

You were a bird before we met. I know that
because over your skew front teeth
your mouth makes a pointy beak.

I saw you first in Dickens' London,
an evening of frosted windows
and how steaming steak.

That night we were drinking,
the chimneys were smoking,
and my lips swelled up

like bread baking in the oven,
I met London in your face,
I smelt wine on your breath

and the shape of your mouth
left me feeling slightly lyrical.
We drank a lot that night

we drank so much
you would have seen it from heaven.
With you there, sitting in my kitchen,

the cooking pots start to sing.
Now the letterbox is a bird
and the telephone is made of birds when it rings.

ELI TOLARETXIPI

Translated from the Spanish by Philip Jenkins

from Still Life with Loops

In the city of D
my friend S
takes me to an art gallery
in which there is a rock
as large as the head of a medium-sized animal
which juts out from the wall,
leaning towards a bowl
from which it could drink
if the head were, for example,
that of a lioness,
who tired of suckling
draws breath and drinks.

None of this would matter
if it were not that my friend S
has brought me to see
some wings that she herself has constructed.
There hangs in the air what looks like
a butterfly
which is suspended from the top of the room
behind the observer.
What is important is that my friend S
has constructed the wings for me,
that I should be the butterfly
that I only have one day left
to tell her otherwise;
that I want
to take the lioness home with me
and fill her bowl with real milk.

SRI LANKA

MINOLI SALGADO

Patriot Games

We have removed the word minorities from our vocabulary
There are only two peoples
The people who love this country
And the small group of people who have no love for the land

We have learned to apply sorrow to trivial events
a lost watch, an unpaid bill, the empty socket of the moon
To say the guns are silent (in the north)
The roads are clear (of squatters and blind bombs)
To observe a silence deep as sil
with our lids coined closed

Fear is a country that makes us foreign to ourselves
a minority vertical and singular as the talipot palm

It takes strength of mind to break the phosphorous siege
into *a humanitarian operation*
Athletic amnesia
to draw the white vans of disappearance
into a mantra of calm
To stay as silent as the silenced press

Fear is the space you live in when there is nowhere else to go
when the alphabet insists
Sri Lanka has now given a beginning
to the ending of terrorism in the world

NOTE: Italicised lines are drawn from the President's parliamentary speech on 19 May 2009, the day after the declaration of the end of civil war.

SUDAN

AL-SADDIQ AL-RADDI
Translated from the Arabic by Sarah Maguire & Atef Alshaer
for The Poetry Translation Centre

Nothing

Before you start reading,
put down your pen:
consider the ink,
how it comprehends bleeding

Learn
from the distant horizon
and from narrowing eyes
the expansiveness of vision
and the treachery of hands

Do not blame me – do not blame anyone –
if you die before you read on
before blood is understood

JIT NARAIN

Translated from the Dutch by Paul Vincent

Working all day, dreaming at night

Working all day, dreaming at night –
Aja's appearance is something like mine.

My ship was not called *Lalla Rookh*
and my country's name became Holland, *meneer.*

I flew KLM, I left Surinam.
When the memory of you arose,
I went in search of history.

The sap of this story is not sacred nectar,
the feeling it gives holds my mind in its grip.

Why he left India, that I can fathom;
that India never left him, is the burden I bear.

MSANDI KABABA

Nayibamba Bophezu Kwemkhono
(Hard Working Women)

Hold on Women of great courage
You have held on so bravely and tirelessly
Hold on Women of great courage, hold on

Women have taken control of their families and their families are
    now living a better life than before.
Women no longer depend on their husbands to pay for their
    children's school fees
They have put poverty to an end
Jealous down, let us give credit where due
Women of this country, you have become bread winners for your
    families
Women of Swaziland, you do not asked for any favours but sought
    for space to nurture, grow and blossom in all areas of life...
A sister, daughter, mother, grandmother, a businesswoman, a teacher,
    a nurse the list is endless.

You have boldly attacked rough situations and you have conquered
You have stood for what you believe in
Your dreams have come true, your wishes have been fulfilled
Hold on Women of great courage, hold on.

Continue women of great courage
Continue holding on and never give up
The family's hope is in you
Hold on women of great courage, hold on

SWEDEN

LAURA WIHLBORG
Translated from the Swedish by the author

Google Search Results

1 Not **a single** day too early.
2 I won't regret it, not for **a single** second.
3 I won't turn around for **one single** time.
4 **One single** fly this morning and I killed it, it's DEAD!!!
5 Love, love for love, love **one single** time.
6 Not **a single** drop of water...
7 Remember that you were born to life to love **one single** time.
8 I haven't received any flowers, not even **a single** little violet.
9 Oh ring-ring, why don't you give me **one single** call!
10 How do you get through the weekend without spending **a single** euro?
11 You've walked this road a thousand times without stumbling over **a single** stone so why would you stumble this time?
12 But – says today's homeopaths – the fact that not **a single** molecule of the curing substance can be found in the medicine doesn't really matter.
13 If you're going to watch **one single** movie this ear – pick *Blood Diamond* with Leo di Caprio.
14 Oh, ring-ring, why don't you give me **a single** call?
15 Then add the fact that most Swedes don't have **a single** crown saved right now...
16. ...because I've never managed to shoot **a single** little moose... But you should now I've tried, every damned weekend.
17 **One single** day.
18 **One single** each year.
19 Not **one single** friend of mine came to visit.
20 One question: has anyone in this forum ever seen **a single** happy insurance adjuster?
21 I don't want you storming in, breaking my boarders without giving me **a single** chance to defend myself.
22 Now spring has come and my eyes are filled with tears but for a whole other reason this time – there is nothing left, not **a single** little spring flower in the flower bed, everything is gone!
23 **One single** second to perceive you.
24 We don't need **a single** wink ot sleep.

25 Only **a single** day left now.
26 An hour or less then the internet shuts down after I've downloaded
one single file with Utorrent, I've got broadband 8mbt and I recently
bought a...
27 We had **one single** night and my heart was burning when he said:
'Well... I'll see you around...'
28 **One single**.

*In order to show you the most relevant results, the poet has omitted some
entries very similar to the 28 already displayed. If you like you can repeat
the search with the omitted results included.*

SWITZERLAND

VALERIA MELCHIORETTO

The Suitcase

My life is divided from kitchen and dining room.
It is a long hallway, walled by peripheral vision:
a living room spacious as a departure lounge.

Here waiting stretches time's muscle
through the weight of shortcomings.
All I carry is a suitcase containing the time of day.

Its lining familiar as my skin, its handle worn,
slightly arched like a collarbone, a potential key
to sagas, the yarn of my emigrating ancestors.

The suitcase is rigid yet made of impressions.
In generations we will have wings, mutate like finches
with beaks as sharp as knives and forks.

    *

I admire the spiders, how homely they are,
never satisfied with a napkin-sized dwelling.
They aim for a tablecloth-sized web,

even though mostly it catches nothing but light,
pure as goodness in the killing of flies.
Only a spider's loom can capture such lumen.

If I could embroider my life with this thread
I would make a needle from one of my unattached ribs
from the twelfth ribcage raw. The needle's eye being vast

and infinitely dilating. I'd thread light through it
as if through the lumen of my arteries,
as if through a gateway to new dimensions.

SYRIA

RASHA OMRAN
Translated from the Arabic by Golan Haji

Ophelia, As I Want To Be

Nobody came to the hall.
The seats have vacated their guests,
The stage is like marble in an old cemetery.
Nothing in the hall but emptiness,
Nothing but faint echoes of the actors' voices
The noisy hands and palms colliding at the finale.

Nobody comes to the hall anymore.
I wipe the stage with what's left of my gown,
As I do every day
Since I came back from my imposed death
To change the role I never wanted.
For hundreds of years I have been wiping the stage,
The seats, the walls and the curtain,
To stand here, proud of my complete nakedness
In my faded stature like one of the brothel women,
With my hair unkempt like a sorceress,
With my eyes painted in the kohl of hatred,

With my heavy grudge like
Time halted in its endlessness,
With my shouting that looks uselessly for listening ears,
With my sharp nails that will scratch your hypocrite sympathy,
With my old dissidence's glass,
My glass that will every day disappoint you
And wound your eyes exactly the way a mirage does.
My indignation will stun you
And panic will strike when you realise
That I am not Ophelia whom you know.
I am neither white nor good,
I am neither the delicate one burdened by sin to commit suicide,
Nor imagination's mirror of your women.
I am Ophelia who loves to be herself.
Shakespeare found me out in an English brothel,
And when he wearied of me
He dressed me in a princess gown
And handed me over to Hamlet.
Whose sins I kept silent about all that time.
For I learnt submission in the brothel.
I knew that he coveted Gertrude,
That he assassinated his uncle to reach the honey that killed his father,
And named me his love,
Inciting jealousy's serpent to eat away his mother's flesh.
But Gertrude's bed was fortified by her passions, so the bed slipped
          away from him.
And when he feigned insanity he drowned me in the river
And forged his mother's death to declare his purification.
But I turn back from my tragic death
To scandalise your vulgar romanticism,
To shake the tedium from the false story.
And here I remain, for hundreds of years,
Preparing the theatre everyday, waiting for your arrival,
Then standing upon the stage in my frank nakedness,
With the truth I have,
With the complete scandal.
While, daily, for hundreds of years,
You have been hiding shame in your pockets
And throwing it away to the first river you see,
Raising the fingers of your purification
When you pass by the theatre
Turning your eyes away from me.

FARZANEH KHOJANDI
Translated from the Tajik by Narguess Farzad & Jo Shapcott

Behind the Mass of Green

When the message came with a smile
that summer was coming,
men, sloshing their way
through puddles of muddy water,
carried on oblivious.
But the roses felt the warm kiss
of summer on their necks.

Chicks roared inside cracking shells,
plums blushed with excitement.
My mother lugged our winter clothes
out of the chest of drawers
and spread them in the sun.
I pulled my heart out of my breast,
and laid it in the sun as well,
my heart, smelling of frost, and musty winter.

Listen, from now on, my heart is married to the sun.
While you draw the curtains over it all,
and fall into mid-morning naps,
I make love with the sun.
I'm certain this love is my virtue but maybe it's the sun's sin –
because someone hurt me, recently,
someone with a ridiculous laugh,
which broke into the quiet night,
got my name so drunk even street girls shouted it.
Look. There is someone behind this mass of green.
Someone whose eyes, right from the beginning of creation
until this moment, saved faith and love.

Someone whose breath is the astonishment of Jesus,
someone whose touch is a loan from Moses,
someone whose voice veils the song of eclipses,
someone who is seated in the palm of knowledge

and in whose hands the half-apple
waits for sweet lips, someone
who has blessed horizons with dust from his feet.
Yes, behind this mass of green there is someone,
and for him I have come back to life.

HAJI GORA HAJI
Translated from the Swahili

Wonders

Wonders occurred
The octopus was trapped in the forest
Which are you explaining to us
Those without wings flew
The wood broke the axe
Whitebait swallowed the cat
I tell you so you know
Should not shock you
Chicks ate the kite
It is a secret inside a secret
The chameleon passed the car
When you consider this
There is another word like this one
Through the eye of a needle
The ant which is tiny
By God's kindness
the monkey was fished at the coast
you our ulemas?
those which fly sat down
what is it if not death?
what is there to say?
many things of today
it is the wonder of the Merciful
it is astonishing if you measure it

It is neither cunning nor judgement
in speed it was behind
in the end you will not finish it
which I also speak
the elephant passed upright
got stuck.

THAILAND

CHIRANAN PITPREECHA

Translated from the Thai by Rachel Harrison

The defiance of a flower

Woman has two hands
To seize tight the essence of life
The twisted sinews are torn by work
Not by preening with glittering silks.

Woman has two feet
To climb toward her dreams,
To stand together, firm
Not to feed from the labour of others.

Woman has eyes
To search for a new life
To look far across the earth
Not to cast amorous glances in flirtation.

Woman has a heart,
A constant flame
Building force, creating a mass,
For she, she is a person.

Woman has a life
To wipe away the traces of wrong with reason
She has value as a free person
Not as a servant of lust.

A flower has sharp thorns
Not bursting into bloom for an admirer
She blossoms to raise
The glory of the earth.

TIMOR-LESTE

XANANA GUSMÃO
Translated from the Portuguese by Kirsty Sword & Ana Luisa Amaral

Grandfather Crocodile
(for Marta B. Neves, Lisbon)

The legend says
and who am I to disbelieve!

The sun perched atop the sea
opened its eyes
and with its rays
indicated a way

From the depths of the ocean
a crocodile in search of a destiny
spied the pool of light, and there he surfaced

Then wearily, he stretched himself out
in time
and his lumpy hide was transformed
into a mountain range
where people were born
and where people died

Grandfather crocodile

– the legend says
and who am I to disbelieve
that he is Timor!

JÉMIMA FIADJOE-PRINCE AGBODJAN

Translated from the French by Janis A. Mayes

Thank You for Being a Woman

Thank you for being a woman
For having been born
To know the pain of childbirth;
For having nursed my mother's breast
To know the joy and happiness of offering my milk;
For having been carried on her back
To learn how to strengthen my back
For having known the tenderness of this maternal heart
To learn how to have a child's heart.

Thank you for being a woman
For being at the school of prudence
Of endurance and of patience
In order to be guardian of the hearth
To insure its protection and fulfilment;
For being a nest of clear and creative thoughts
For being the welcoming earth where grow
          The seeds of the future

Thank you for being a woman
For being beauty and softness
For being light and warmth
For being discretion and lobe
And finally, more than anything,
For being born to give,
To give my Peace for the Peace
OF HUMANITY.

KARLO MILA

Oceania
(for Epeli Hau'ofa)

Some days
I've been
on dry land
for too long

my ache
for ocean
so great
my eyes weep
waves

my mouth
mudflats
popping with
groping breath
of crabs

my throat
an estuary
salt crystallising
on the tip of my tongue

my veins
become
rivers that flow
straight out to sea

I call on the memory of water
and

I
am
star fish
in sea

buoyed by
lung balloons
and floating fat

I know the ocean
she loves me

her continuous blue body
holding even
my weight

flat on my back
I feel her

outstretched palms
legs wide open

a star in worship
a meditation as old as the tide

my arms, anemones
belly and breasts, sea jellies
Achilles fins, I become
free-swimming medusa

my hands touching
her blue curves

fingers tipping
spindrift

a star in worship

a wafer in her mouth

a five-pointed offering

she swirls
counter-clockwise
beneath me, all goddess
all muscle, energy
power, pulse

oh, the simple faith
of the floating

letting go
in order to be held
by the body water of the world

some days
this love
is all I need

TRINIDAD & TOBAGO

ANTHONY JOSEPH

Buddha

my father has four flags planted at the side of his house.
    secret colours.
he would not name them.
he say he been to china, see buddha sit on a throne,
he in a group looking up: at buddha.
he say buddha take a chillum from his waistband, lit it
    and suckt it.
then the pipe pass around everyone in the circle.
    buddha call – 'al – bot!'
an' albert had to pass between guards on both sides had swords
    and kneel down.
an' buddha put a bead necklace round his neck and say,
    'i give you gift, you give no one.'

he say in the spirit world everything have life,
     he say he speaks to trees and animals,
say he seen jumbie with caduceus upon dem head,
say he been to the bottom of the sea/been standing on the guinea coast
and two african man come out of the sea and say,
     'ai you, you eh see you naked?'
and they took him by both hands and into the water
     and washed him.
then give him a gown – half yellow half brown – an' one say
'let this be your shield, this word be your sword'
and with this they transferred secret syllables to his ear.
he say then one take a dagger
     an' chook 'im in he waist/but the blade
would not penetrate the gown. he say,
     'boy sometimes I jus' drink two guinness,
go kick back an' meditate. when I ketch myself i find myself
in ethiopia someway.'
and then he shows me the necklace
     between his shirt.

my father stands, fixes his brim – pours cold coffee dripping in the
     calabash root
and leaves/uphill to bathe
in cold water
but falls asleep face down in his bachelor bed, still in his string vest,
drawers and argyle socks, cradling a bottle of duty free rum

and the sea   blows up
from the horizon

AMINA SAÏD

Translated from the French by Patrick Williamson

'Each day...'

Each day the sun slits its spectre's throat
and rises in a pool of blood

every beginning draws a circle
memory leads to the sea of beginnings
the pier is made of stone the tree of exile
I seek the horizon

on a thread of light
I go towards this place that is you
and what was happens

a star dances on the sky of my forehead
the bird within rises from the banks of the soul
your word is yours mine is my word

you reach the place that I am
and the poem continues to be written

I see your face and the shadow on your face
as with the poem suffering is shared
we commiserate with the tree, with seasons
that are all too brief and with the exile of seasons
with smiles and rifts in the earth
with the misfortune of men and prayers of women

as we would wish the instant takes its dazzled form
time blurs over like a landscape
we live the two halves of our lives
like a journey that will perhaps remember
the names of islands birds ports
of the white wake of boats cities beings
of the cycle of arrivals and departures

TURKEY

RONI MARGULIES
Translated from the Turkish by Saliha Paker & Mel Kenne

The Slipper

One day a few months ago
an old woman appeared
at the entrance of the underground station.
She was begging.

Her clothes were torn but white as white.
She reminded me of my grandmother:
her eyes full of fear,
her last days.

Each time I passed by her
I made a habit of saying 'Good morning,'
and giving her some bread or money.
She never said a word.

The other day I tried to say more,
she looked, but obviously didn't understand.
She took what I gave her,
turned her head the other way.

When I passed by yesterday,
she wasn't at her usual place,
on the ground I saw a single slipper
in faded pink, sequined, on its left side

a blood-red plastic heart.
Tiny and glittering.
As if it would, at any moment
start beating.

TURKMENISTAN

AK WELSAPAR

Translated from the Turkmen by Hamid Ismailov

The Night Dropped the Stars from the Sky

The night dropped the stars from the sky.
Whilst turning into dew, they
permeated the air with mist.
Flickering out their own light,
Hiding the secrets of the metamorphosis
From the eternal stars into water droplets
In the darkness, where the white shadow
Of a horse breathes, with no saddle and no reins.
As if he feels the oncoming
Thunderstorms, being born here,
In a night where I'm present as is the motion of clouds
at my feet. Yes, there is a mystery...
In the silence of the birth of thunder,
It's here – shining as dew; In the grass,
On the leaves – smelling familiar
I hear the thunder, standing barefoot
At my homeland, where I haven't been for a long while
And here I came and suddenly saw
A white horse looking at the sky,
Enlightening the meadow.

SELINA TUSITALA MARSH

Googling Tusitala

brings
hotel kitano tusitala dot com
brings
tusitala bar and grill in edinburgh
brings
tusitala built in 1883 scotland
brings
tusitala publishing house a biography of recent psychodrama books
brings
deviantart tusitala's gallery chicago
brings
tusitala pedigrees for sale – a tibet ansk spaniel, a japanese chin
8 brings
eBay tusitala year book
19 brings
american idle ask your doctor if its right for you
26 brings
morphology of protozoa, approximately 50 slash long in *Holomastigoides*
         tusitala
35 brings
going west festival word of mouth tusitala 11.40–12.00pm
brings
marinez baldo tusitala karonte strumming a spanish guitar
brings
NZ police news a graduating tusitala constable
brings
the man who was thursday by g k chesterton... truth out of a tusitala
         spoke dot dot dot
brings
oxford house calendars with tusitala rosy raymond and storytelling
         slams
52 brings
the sea slug forum reception at tusitala

56 brings
tusitala a sexydirectory
78 brings
afterlife on tusitala ave with gourmet delights and freddie mercury
57,092 brings
the tusitala bookshelf in barcelona@bookcrossing.com – there's no
     wrong way to eat a rhesus

UGANDA

NICK MAKOHA

Who do they say I am?

They say that I am
Three words short of a proverb.
Two beliefs less than a religion.
One god less to believe in.

They say that I am
Three tribes short of a people.
One heart less of a couple
Two breaths closer to death

They say that I am
Three friends short of Judas.
Two betrayals less of Brutus.
One wisdom short of Confucius.

They say that I am
Three sins over temptation.
Two generations behind emancipation.
One prayer beyond frustration.

They say that I am
Three tears short of a river.
Two waters deep of leaders.
One hope less of a believer.

They say that I am
Three chains left of a slave.
Two victories short of the brave.
One coffin right of the grave.

UKRAINE

SERHIY ZHADAN

Translationed from the Ukrainian by Virlana Tkacz & Wanda Phipps

The Sell-out Poets of the 60s

The sell-out poets of the 60s should be happy
that everything turned out as well as it did;
after all, there were many dangerous moments,
but see – they survived, paid their debts,
their battle wounds
only ache during storms,
like monthly cramps.

The sell-out poets of the 60s drag
huge suitcases made of fake yellow leather,
stay in hotels,
hold phone receivers with their shoulders like violins,
and their suitcases are covered with stickers.
The Viet Cong, girl, is our collective unconscious.
You don't really care about me – you'll throw away my crumpled
        phone number.
One more visa in my passport,
one less.

One day stuck in a snowed-in airport
one of them will remember the lectures they gave,
Berlin radio and bridges over the Wisła River.
'Those were good,' he'll think, 'good,
times, not bad – our sell-out 60s,
too bad afterwards there was so much
masturbation and social-democracy on the brain.
Love led us,
love ripped the tonsils from our throats,
like they rip receivers from pay phones.
Poetry is written with the throat
but this throat is constantly hoarse.'

According to all the rules of literature,
according to all the stipulations in the contracts they signed,
they truly fought for freedom,
and freedom, as we know, demands
that we fight for her once in a while –
in trenches, forests
and on the pages of an independent press.

Speaking of poetry,
let us remember all those who remained
on the streets and beaches of the good-old 60s,
all those who did not pass the rehabilitation course
and to this day, clouds hang over them
their structure reminiscent of American free-verse;
let us remember them since what you call time
is a slaughterhouse
where guts are spilled simply because
this is the place to do it;
and only the sell-out poets
survive,
with lungs blown out
by love.

DHABIYA KHAMIS

Translated from the Arabic by Ahir Zaki, with Patty Paine

The History of That Tree

Violence is the guillotine of History
blood is food for Power
skulls are the throne of Time.

Whoever bows in front of someone
facing the wind with a sorrowful expression
leaves blood at the gate of the conqueror.

Give me the freedom to say that
the forest with its Saints is etched on my neck.

No desire to disclose
for the fear of the "other" is my comrade
no lust for militancy
nor need to speak on behalf of "people"
nor to be thrown in the arms of comrades
just to be like them.

Give me a berry's leaf
so that I can cover my eyes and not see the flaws of history.

Give me a morphine injection, or a morsel of
hashish so that I forget all the lessons I've learned.

I take my breath empty handed
and with a broken wing like all Arab citizens.

I expose the day that was yesterday's graveyard
rebelling over its details
sloughing the slogans off my back
that overwhelmed me since my first moment
on this earth.

Nothing can force me to stand by,
and the law, in any case,
is not my law.

I scream in the face of the sun,
on the edge of my path
the mountains have no edges
the valleys are my asylum.
My Arabism is a cloak that can't disguise my loins
who like me are victims
falling like witch's dolls
armed with pins of death and disability.

I will address you in the space of history
why did you deceive me?
I am like a sparrow that goes to its trap
thinking it has wings that flap.

I steal my life from my death
I steal my freedom from my volcanic-tempered executioner.

I am defeated and afraid
like an autumn leaf that fell
followed by the fruitful tree it died upon.

And no one. No one
knows the history of that tree.

MELISA MACHADO
Translated from the Spanish by S.M. Stone

Marjal

'Whoever desires captivity shall have it.'

The tearing bone is not the bone of the abyss.
It is your bone, your blade.
Let us burn, bone dust.
May it be well-loved, cub of the beast we choose.

I. Here, the animal:
loose tongues of the eyes.

The skin, all scales,
all jasmine and fire.

II. The voracious snout drips.

The cutting mandibles
and the silky skin, of back and tail.

'Whoever desires captivity shall have it.'

III. The animal drinking every scale,
every forked tongue.

Blood mended to the claws.

And the cultured tiger,
with ready jaws

IV. The entrail like a brilliant bone.

Faces and turned backs,
the flanks at full speed.

Tense hunger:
swiping.

V. And the deep creatures surrounded them.
'Like winds.'

All the coincident paths.

Hands like sweet-crumbed birds.

VI. The hairy animal left his seed.
Heed how he touched the mouths.

Resplendent organ,
bright gluttony's beast.

He flew toward me and said:
'Your sin shall be clean.'

KAY RYAN

Flamingo Watching

Wherever the flamingo goes,
she brings a city's worth
of furbelows. She seems
unnatural by nature —
too vivid and peculiar
a structure to be pretty,
and flexible to the point
of oddity. Perched on
those legs, anything she does
seems like an act. Descending
on her egg or draping her head
along her back, she's
too exact and sinuous
to convince an audience
she's serious. The natural elect,
they think, would be less pink,
less able to relax their necks,
less flamboyant in general.
They privately expect that it's some
poorly jointed bland grey animal
with mitts for hands
whom God protects.

UZBEKISTAN

HAMID ISMAILOV
Translated from the Uzbek by the author

Garden

I open the door, it turns into a tree,
screeching in the wind,
I shelter from wind and it turns into a tree,
branches crawling as if through a hole,
I plug the hole with palm of my hand, it turns into a tree,
numbing at once
Numbing, I call out to a friend, and my friend turns into a tree,
making noise with his crown,
It seems my soul is tearing apart, it too turns into a tree,
dropping its leaves,
I cry and I breathlessly wait, and my tears turn to a tree,
of fingers grown to the face.
Hardly alive, I turn towards you, and you will too turn into a tree
And through your branches the sunset
Will look not with an eye of a stranger –
As the last in the tribe of trees
At a forlorn and left behind garden.

VANUATU

GRACE MERA MOLISA

Delightful Acquiescence

Everybody loves
a self-effacing
submissive woman

Vanuatu men and women
love self-effacing
acquiescing women.

For better or worse
we force
talented women
into acquiescence.

The power echelons
and hierarchies
thrive
on acquiescent women.

Vanuatu pays homage
to foreign women
womanples ino gat ples.

Vanuatu supports
liberation movements
in other parts of the world.

Half of Vanuatu
is still colonised
by herself.

Any woman
showing promise
is clouted
into acquiescence.
Vanuatu loves
self-effacing, acquiescing
submissive, slavish, women.

BEVERLY PÉREZ REGO

Translated from the Spanish by the author

Escurana

He thinks I am a saint.
He's crazy.
Saints are brown and tiny,
or white as chalk,
and do not scream,
like me under his body.

He thinks I am holy.
I know: he smears me with saliva,
covers me with gauze,
and lights candles.
He says: Make me a miracle.
Then, gathering the twelve members
of his unfaithful body,
I sew, cross stitch,
on the white surface.
It looks like an alphabet, he says,
and the stitches hurt.
The dry thread
prints his flesh.
I'm ready, he announces.
You can read me.
I know what's coming.
I cover my face
as he goes.
Goodbye, *Escurana*.
That is my name
when he walks out my door.

VIETNAM

NGUYEN BAO CHAN

Translated from the Vietnamese by the author

Memory

Memory is playing I-spy
With the things one remembers

It finds a wooden doll
And dreams of the forest

It picks up a shell
And hears the ocean

It sees the early sunlight
And feels warm kisses

It brushes bare skin
And is burned by love's embers

It sips the night dew
And feels an old thirst again

It touches the river
And the ripples run away

It hides itself
And discovers the sky

It turns round
And falls into the abyss...

BRITISH VIRGIN ISLANDS

OREN HODGE

Sharks in Sharp Suits

Sharks in sharp suits sworn to sharp shoot
Anyone who battles against the system
Conniving carnivores carrying contraband like playboys carry condoms
Not knowing neither nor the knowledge necessary to survive in a
        noble world
Sinfully skilful to survive in the septic
It's fearfully futile to refuse it
Judge and jury have already adjudicated their judgment
So everyone involved must now endure it
The rollercoaster ride really seems relentless
But the consistent constant continues to cleverly confuse
As they are the sharks in sharp suits
Sworn to sharp shoot anyone who battles against the system

US VIRGIN ISLANDS

PATRICIA HARKINS-PIERRE

Post Hurricane Open Letter to the Author of 'Easter Wings'

Dear George:
Hurricane winds have passed
leaving me flat
laid low
as the mango tree across my lawn.
I used to dream about wings
but now I don't dream at all.

NABILA AZZUBAIR
Translated from the Arabic by Najwan Darwish

The Closed Game

And now
There are two boxes
we will throw to the sea

My box, the sea entered
Because it was open
Your box, the beach buried
Because you never got out

ZAMBIA

KAYO CHINGONYI

calling a spade a spade

You sly devil. Lounging in a Pinter script
or pitched from a transit van's rolled-down window;
my shadow on this un-lit road, though you've been
smuggled from polite conversation. So when
a friend of a friend has you, poised, on his lips
you are not what he means, no call for balled fist,
since he's only signifyin(g) on the sign;
making wine from the bad blood of history.
Think of how you came into my life that day,
of leaves strewn as I had never seen them strewn,
knocking me about the head with your dark hands.

TOGARA MUZANENHAMO

Smoke

For a brief moment I was lost in a thought
While walking up the flight of stairs to her room –
Her hand leading me up, my eyes catching a flash
Of her bare thighs under a simple yellow skirt –

And I was a boy again, in that small moment,
Holding a present I had longed and wished for –
Bright blue emotions, sparks in mid-ignition
Bursting in my chest – lights never to grow old.

When I think of her leading me upstairs to her bed,
There's always a thought of that one precious Christmas –
The lightweight pig-iron cap-gun, the blind surprise
And spurt of gunpowder-smoke after the big bang.

BIOGRAPHICAL NOTES
& ACKNOWLEDGEMENTS

AFGHANISTAN
REZA MOHAMMADI

Reza Mohammadi is a prize-winning poet from Afghanistan, and is widely regarded as one of the most exciting young poets writing in Persian today. He was born in Kandahar in 1979 and studied both Islamic Law and Philosophy in Iran, before obtaining an MA in Globalisation from London Metropolitan University. His three collections of poetry have gained him many awards, including one from the Afghan Ministry of Culture in 2004 and prizes for being Iran's best young poet in 1996 and 1997. He is also a prolific journalist and cultural commentator. His articles have been published in journals in Afghanistan and Iran, as well as in English by *The Guardian*. ■ 'Rain' from www.poetrytranslation.org, by permission of The Poetry Translation Centre.

ALBANIA
LULJETA LLESHANAKU

Born in Elbasan, Albania in 1968, Luljeta Lleshanaku grew up under house arrest, and was not permitted to attend college or publish her poetry until the weakening and eventual collapse of Albania's Stalinist regime in the early 1990s. She later studied Albanian philology at the University of Tirana, and has worked as a teacher, literary magazine editor and journalist. Winner of the prestigious International Kristal Vilenica Prize (2009), she belongs to the first "post-totalitarian" generation of Albanian poets, but is a 'completely original poet...her poetry has little connection to poetic styles past or present in America, Europe, or the rest of the world... it is not connected to anything in Albanian poetry either' (Peter Constantine). Instead, her poetry responds to the fallout of her country's past and its relation to herself and her family, exploring how these histories intertwine and influence her childhood memories and the retelling of her family's stories. She has published two collections with New Directions in the US, *Fresco* (2002) and *Child of Nature* (2010), both included in *Haywire* (2011) from Bloodaxe in the UK. ■ 'No Time' from *Haywire: New & Selected Poems* (Bloodaxe Books, 2011), by permission of the publisher.

ALGERIA
SOLEÏMAN ADEL GUÉMAR

Soleïman Adel Guémar was born in 1963 and raised in Algiers. He studied electrical engineering at an army-controlled academy, where he endured three months in army prison for 'indiscipline' (wanting to leave). He then spent two years in Paris, working in publishing. He returned to Algeria in 1991 amid signs of democratisation and worked as a journalist for the weekly *L'Evènement* (banned), then as a freelance. Besides reporting on corruption and human rights abuses, he also published numerous stories and won two national poetry prizes. His poems appeared in the Parisian journal *Algérie Littérature/Action* in 2002. By the end of that year he had had to leave Algeria to seek safety for himself and his family in the UK. His collection, *State of Emergency* (Arc Publications, 2007), won a publication award from English PEN. ■ 'Eyes closed' by permission of the author.

ANDORRA
ESTER FENOLL GARCÍA

Born in 1967, Ester Fenoll García is known for her use of different languages in her poetry. She has published two collections, *Esmorzar perfecte* (2006) and *Anticipant Octubre* (2008), and has won several literary awards, including the Premi Grandalla de Poesía in 2005. Teresa Colom, another huge voice in Catalan literature, has praised the freshness of Ester Fenoll's poetry. ■ Anna Crowe's translation of 'Between your fingers' was commissioned by Poetry Parnassus.

ANGOLA
ANA PAULA TAVARES

Ana Paula Ribeiro Tavares is said to be the only contemporary Angolan poet of the post-independence period. One of her country's most important female voices, she writes of Angolan traditions and languages, love and war, sadness and women. Her poetry is influenced by three Angolan poets, Davi Master, Arlindo Barbeitos and Rui Duarte de Carvalho, and the Brazilian poets Bandeira and Drummond. Currently living in Portugal, she is a PhD candidate in literature and teaches at the Catholic University of Lisbon. She has worked in the areas of culture, museums, archaeology and ethnology, cultural patrimony, entertainment and cultural education. ■ 'Bitter as Fruit' from *Ellipsis* (American Portuguese Studies Association), by permission of the author.

ANTIGUA AND BARBUDA
LINISA GEORGE

Guyanan-born Linisa George has lived in Antigua since the age of three, and started writing poetry in secret at the age of six. In her literary and performing arts career, she has been inspired by the example of Maya Angelou. She is a strong advocate of gender justice and is an executive member of Women of Antigua (WOA), responsible for bringing *The Vagina Monologues* to Antigua, and then for producing *When a Woman Moans*, an Antiguan response to Eve Ensler's play. This year she is shooting a documentary film based on her autobiographical poem 'The Brown Girl in the Ring', about a journey to self acceptance. ■ 'The Brown Girl in the Ring' by permission of the author.

ARGENTINA
MIRTA ROSENBERG

Mirta Rosenberg was born in Rosario, Santa Fe, Argentina in 1951. She translates poetry from English and French for a living, and has published translations of writers such as Katherine Mansfield, Derek Walcott, Marianne Moore, Hilda Doolittle, James Laughlin, Seamus Heaney and Louise Glück. She has published several collections of her own poetry: *Pasajes* (1984), *Madam* (1988), *Teoría sentimental* (1994), *El arte de perder* (1998), and her collected poems, *El árbol de palabras* (The tree of words, 2006). In 2003, she was awarded a Guggenheim grant for poetry, and in 2004 she received the Konex Prize for her literary translations. ■ 'Intimate Bestiary' from Poetry International Web © 2008, by permission of the author.

ARMENIA
RAZMIK DAVOYAN

Razmik Davoyan is Armenia's most prominent living writer, with 17 collections of poetry, three children's books, three prose works and a novel published in his own country, and many translations published throughout the world. He published a dozen books in Armenian during the Soviet era, but three significant titles were blocked. His children's poetry book, *Winter Snowflake, Spring Blossom* (1980), published in Russian, sold 450,000 copies in just two weeks throughout the USSR. Born in 1940, he studied philology and history at university, and worked as an editor for a literary magazine before being appointed to a series of government posts, including Advisor to the President of the Republic of Armenia. Razmik Davoyan has received numerous literary awards, including the Order of St Mesrop Mashtots (1997), the President's Prize for Literature (2003), First Degree Medal for Services to the Motherland (2010), and the CIS Interstate Prize for literature (2012). ■ 'Yessenin' from *Whispers and Breath of the Meadows*, tr. Arminé Tamrazian (Arc Publications, 2010), by permission of author and publisher.

ARUBA
LASANA M. SEKOU

Born in 1959, Lasana M. Sekou is a Caribbean poet, short story writer, essayist, journalist and publisher from the island of Saint Martin. One of the most prolific Caribbean poets of his generation, he has published over a dozen books, including *The Salt Reaper*, *Nativity* and *Brotherhood of the Spurs*. He studied mass communication, political science and international relations at Howard University and Stony Brook University in the US. ■ 'We Continue' from *Corazón de pelicano* (Pelican Heart), ed. Emilio Jorge Rodriguez (House of Nehesi Publishers, 2010), by permission of the publisher.

AUSTRALIA
JOHN KINSELLA

John Kinsella is an activist and award-winning poet committed to international poetry. He is a vegan, anarchist, pacifist who believes poetry has an activist role to play. When he was 18 he tried to get a Red Cross passport so as to not have a 'nation', but was refused because he was entitled to an Australian passport and that excluded him. He is anti-nationalist, anti-capitalist, non-competitive and pro-environmental and will be speaking on subjects including eco-poetry and anti-nationalism. He espouses an 'international regionalism' – a respect for regional integrity but with an internationalism informing this. Much of his poetry focuses on 'wheatbelt' Western Australia. John Kinsella has waived all fees and expenses for Poetry Parnassus and is completely independent of any funding sources or sponsorship for this gathering. ■ 'The Ambassadors' from *Armour* (Picador, 2011) by permission of Macmillan Publishers Ltd.

AUSTRIA
EVELYN SCHLAG

Evelyn Schlag was born and raised in Waidhofen an der Ybbs in Lower Austria. She studied German and English literature at the University of Vienna. She divided her time between teaching and writing up to 2002, since when she has been a full-time writer. She has written several novels and volumes of prose fiction, a book of essays, and six poetry collections. Karen Leeder's translation of her *Selected Poems* won the 2005 Schlegel-Tieck Prize for German translation. ■ 'Lesson' from *Selected Poems*, tr. Karen Leeder (Carcanet Press, 2004), by permission of the publisher.

AZERBAIJAN
NIGAR HASAN-ZADEH

Nigar Hasan-Zadeh is an artist and poet from Azerbaijan now living in London. She wrote her first poem at the age of four, and read her poetry in front of large audiences from the age of 15. At 17, she became a student of Azerbaijani M.F. Ahundov University Slavic Department studying Russian Language and Literature. In 2002 she won the Azerbaijan National Academy public prize. Her eastern style of writing has won her the reputation of a poet with a distinctive combination of different traditional writing styles. ■ 'I knocked at someone's door…' by permission of the author.

THE BAHAMAS
CHRISTIAN CAMPBELL

Born in the Bahamas, of Bahamian and Trinidadian heritage, Christian Campbell is a Rhodes Scholar, a Cave Canem Fellow, has held a Lannan Residency Fellowship and is currently a Professor of English at the University of Toronto. His debut *Running the Dusk* (Peepal Tree, 2010) was shortlisted for the Forward Prize for Best First Collection, and won the Aldeburgh First Collection Prize. 'Campbell's imagery slices through fog,' wrote Elizabeth Alexander, 'these poems are nourished by New World etymologies and old-school ways and wisdoms.' ■ 'Vertigo' from *Running the Dusk* (Peepal Tree Press, 2010), by permission of the publisher.

BAHRAIN
QASSIM HADDAD

Born in 1948, Qassim Haddad is a Bahraini poet who is well-known in the Arab world. He published his first collection in 1970 and has since published a further 24 books of poetry and prose. His published work includes a book of poetry and paintings, *Majnun Laila*, and a book of poetry in collaboration with Saudi photographer Saleh al-Azzaz. In 2007, Haddad prompted controversy when he reworked the Arabic classics *Layla* and *Majnun*, with Marcel Khalife. His book was criticised by some as being insulting to Islamic morals. Haddad is the co-founder and chairman of the Bahraini Writers' Union. His website is www.qhaddad.com. ■ 'Poets' from *Gathering the Tide: An Anthology of Contemporary Arabian Gulf Poetry*, ed. Patty Paine, Jeff Lodge & Samia Touati (Ithaca Press, 2011), by permission of the author.

BANGLADESH
MIR MAHFUZ ALI
Mir Mahfuz Ali was born in Dhaka, Bangladesh in 1958. He studied at Essex University, and now lives in London. He dances, acts and has worked as a male model and a tandoori chef. As a performer, he is renowned for his extraordinary voice – a rich, throaty whisper brought about by a Bangladeshi policeman trying to silence the singing of anthems during a public anti-war demonstration. He has given readings and performances at venues including the Royal Opera House, Covent Garden, Bedlam Theatre at the Edinburgh Festival, and the National Theatre of Slovenia (Cankarjev Dom) in Ljubljana. His poetry has appeared in *London Magazine, Poetry London, Ambit* and *Index on Censorship*, and has been published by Exiled Writers Ink! and in the anthology *Ten: new poets* (Bloodaxe Books/Spread the Word, 2010). ■ 'My Salma' by permission of the author.

BARBADOS
ESTHER PHILLIPS
Esther Phillips was born in Barbados where she continues to live and work. She heads the English Department at Barbados Community College. Her books include *When Ground Doves Fly* (Ian Randle Publishers, Kingston, 2003) and *The Stone Gatherer* (Peepal Tree Press, 2008). Her remarkable poem 'Just Riffing' sets the tone for the anthology *Stories from Blue Latitudes: Caribbean Women Writers at Home and Abroad*. Her work has appeared in various publications, including *Caribanthology* and *The Whistling Bird: Women Writers of the Caribbean*. She has won both the Alfred Boas Poetry Prize of the Academy of American Poets and the Frank Collymore Literary Award. ■ 'Near-Distance' by permission of the author.

BELARUS
VALZHYNA MORT
Valzhyna Mort is a prize-winning writer from Minsk, Belarus. Her first book, *I'm as Thin as Your Eyelashes*, was published in Belarus in 2005, including poetry, prose and selected translations from Polish and English. She received the Crystal of Vilenica award in Slovenia in 2005, and the Hubert Burda Poetry Prize for young East European writers in 2008. She moved to the USA in 2005, where she currently teaches at Cornell University. Her second book, *Factory of Tears* (Copper Canyon Press), was the first bilingual Belarusian-English poetry book to be published in the USA, and was later translated and published in

Sweden and Germany. She has also been awarded a Lannan Foundation Literary Fellowship and the Bess Hokin Prize from *Poetry*. Her latest poetry book, *Collected Body*, was published by Copper Canyon Press in 2011. ■ 'Belarusian I' from *Factory of Tears* (Copper Canyon Press, 2008), by permission of the author.

BELGIUM
ELS MOORS

Born in 1976, Els Moors studied languages (English and German) at the University of Ghent and 'Text and Image' at the Gerrit Rietveld Academy in Amsterdam. In 2006 her poetry debut *er hangt een hoge lucht boven ons* (there is a high sky above us) was nominated for the C. Buddingh Prize and received the Herman de Coninck Prize for the best debut. It was followed by her prose debut, *Het verlangen naar een eiland* (The longing for an island, 2008) and a book of short stories, *Vliegtijd* (Flighttime, 2010). She is currently working as a teacher of creative writing in Brussels, is translating poetry, and is an editor for the literary magazine *nY*. ■ 'I am the gardener with an alibi...' by permission of the author.

BELIZE
EVAN X HYDE

Evan X Hyde is a writer and journalist from Belize. In 1966 he moved to the US for two years where he was exposed to the teachings of early Black Power activists such as Stokely Carmichael and Malcolm X. Returning home in 1968 to a country in a state of political turmoil, he formed UBAD (United Black Association for Development), which demanded better conditions for Belize's black people and emphasised unity. Along with journalism, he has published a mixture of fiction and non-fiction books, and his poetry has appeared in the Belizean Writers Series. ■ 'About Poems' by permission of the author.

BENIN
AGNÈS AGBOTON

Agnès Agboton is a philologist and narrator of tales and legends in the African oral tradition. Born in Porto-Novo, Benin, she moved to Barcelona in 1978, and studied Spanish at university. She has published two bilingual Gun/Spanish poetry books in Spain, *Canciones del poblado y el exilio* (2006) and *Voz de las dos orillas* (2009). She has regularly acted as a narrator in schools and libraries since 1990, has adapted and translated legends and traditional stories of her land into Spanish and Catalan, publishing these in three collections. She is also the author of three books on Occidental African food, *La cuina africana* (1989), *Àfrica en los fogones* (2002) and *Las cocinas del mundo* (2002). ■ 'They remain lying on the earth' published in *Wasafiri* 56 (Winter 2008), by permission of the author.

BERMUDA
ANDRA SIMONS

Andra Simons is a poet known in Bermuda as one of the top cutting edge artists. He writes, directs and acts for theatre. Several of his plays have been shortlisted for awards, and his 2004 play *Starsongs* received the Golden Inkwell for best short play in the Annual Fifteen Minute Play Festival held in Bermuda. He moved to the UK in 2004, and has released a book of poems called *The Joshua Tales* with Treehouse Press. He is currently working on a collection, *Two Steps on the Water*, and performing in a funk/poetry/punk project with percussionist Stephane Roul, as part of their music duo Amphibia. ■ 'Week of the Dog', first published in *Corpus*, by permission of the author.

BHUTAN
SONAM CHHOKI

Born and raised in the eastern Himalayan kingdom of Bhutan, Sonam Chhoki has been writing Japanese short forms of haiku, tanka and haibun for the past five years. These forms resonate with her Tibetan Buddhist upbringing and provide the perfect medium for the exploration of her country's rich ritual, social and cultural heritage. She is inspired by her father, Sonam Gyamtsho, the architect of Bhutan's non-monastic modern education. Her poems have been published in poetry journals and anthologies in Australia, Canada, Japan, the UK and US. ■ 'New Year Dusk' by permission of the author

BOLIVIA
MARÍA SOLEDAD QUIROGA

María Soledad Quiroga was born in Santiago de Chile in 1957. She has published five collections of poetry and her work has appeared in various anthologies, including *South American Writers* and *Current Bolivian Poetry*. She has served as Bolivia's Minister of Education and Culture, and has been a columnist for *La Prensa* and *Pulso* in La Paz. She has a degree in Sociology, has studied literature, and has also taught creative writing workshops. ■ 'The Yellow House' from *Casa amarilla* (Plural editores, 1998), by permission of the author.

BOSNIA AND HERZEGOVINA
ADISA BAŠIĆ

Poet and journalist Adisa Bašić was born in 1979 in Sarajevo. She has a degree in comparative literature and librarianship and a master's degree in human rights and democracy. She has published three poetry collections, *Eve's Sentences* (1999), *Trauma Market* (2004) and *A Promo Clip for My Homeland* (2011). She is an Assistant Professor of Poetry and Creative Writing at the Department of Comparative Literature and Library Science, Sarajevo Faculty of Philosophy. For a number of years, she has been contributing to BiH weekly *Slobodna Bosna*, with a regular literary review column. ■ 'People Talking' by permission of the author.

BOTSWANA
TJ DEMA

Born in 1981 in Gaborone, Botswana, TJ Dema is a spoken word poet who runs Sauti Arts and Performance Management and is chair of the Writers Association of Botswana. She took part in the 2005-06 British Council and Lancaster University's Crossing Borders project, which gave her the opportunity to read at various festivals and other literary gatherings, such as the Cambridge Seminar on Contemporary Literature and Johannesburg Arts Alive. She has performed in many countries, including France, Denmark, India, South Africa, Malawi and Zimbabwe. A selection of her poetry has been translated into Chinese. She has recently recorded 12 Botswana poets on a multilingual CD, *Dreaming Is A Gift For Me*. ■ 'Neon poem' by permission of the author.

BRAZIL
PAULO HENRIQUES BRITTO

Paulo Henriques Britto is a poet, educator and translator from Rio de Janeiro. Known as one of Brazil's principal translators of British and American literature, he received the National Library Foundation's prize for his 1995 translation of E.L. Doctorow's *Waterworks*. He has translated around 100 books and has published six books of poetry and one of short stories. He currently teaches translation and creative writing to undergraduates and poetry translation and literature in the graduate school at PUC-Rio. *The Clean Shirt of It*, a collection of Britto's poems, was published in 2007 in the Lannan Translations Series from BOA Editions. ■ 'Quasi Sonnet' from *The Clean Shirt of It*, translation © Idra Novey (BOA Editions, USA, 2007) © 2003 Paulo

Henriques Britto, by permission of the The Permissions Company, Inc., on behalf of BOA Editions Ltd, www.boaeditions.org.

BRUNEI DARUSSALAM
ANONYMOUS

■ 'A twist of hair...' from *The Song Atlas: a book of world poetry*, ed. John Gallas (Carcanet Press, 2002).

BULGARIA
KAPKA KASSABOVA

Kapka Kassabova was born in 1973 and grew up in Bulgaria until she was 16. Her family emigrated first to Britain, then to New Zealand where she lived until 2004. She now lives in Edinburgh as a cultural mongrel working on a simplified version of her East European-Kiwi-Scots accent. She has published two poetry collections with Bloodaxe in the UK, *Someone else's life* (2003), including work from two collections published in New Zealand, and *Geography for the lost* (2007). She has also published three novels, *Reconnaissance* (Penguin NZ, 1999), winner of the 2000 Commonwealth Writer's Prize for Asia-Pacific; *Love in the Land of Midas* (Penguin NZ, 2001) and *Villa Pacifica* (Alma Books, 2010), as well as two memoirs, *Street Without a Name* (Portobello, 2008), a coming of age story at the end of Communism, and *Twelve Minutes of Love: a tango story* (Portobello, 2011). ■ 'How to Build Your Dream Garden' from *Geography for the lost* (Bloodaxe Books, 2007), by permission of the publisher.

BURKINA FASO
MONIQUE ILBOUDO

Born in 1959 in Ouagadougou, Monique Ilboudo studied for a law doctorate and later taught at the University of Ougadougou. Besides her poetry she has written on gender issues, including a study, *Droit de cité: être femme au Burkina Faso* (2006), and published two novels, *Le mal de peau* (1992), winner of the Grand prix imprimerie nationale du meilleur roman, and *Murekatete* (2000), which came out of the Fest'Africa project to memorialise the Rwandan genocide. She has served in various capacities for the government of Burkina Faso, notably as Secretary of State for Human Rights. ■ 'I suffer' from *A Rain of Words: A Bilingual Anthology of Women's Poetry in Francophile Africa*, ed. Irène Assiba d'Almeida (University of Virginia Press, 2009), by permission of the author.

BURUNDI
KETTY NIVYABANDI BIKURA
Born in Belgium in 1978, Ketty Nivyabandi spent most of her child-hood in Burundi, where she started to write very early on. She later studied in a Catholic convent in France and an American university in Kenya, among others. In 2009 she returned to the homeland she had missed intensely during her travels. Often questioning Burundi's condition, her poems have been published several times in her country's media. She is co-founder of *Samandari*, a platform for Burundian writers to share their craft. ■ 'Three tribes' tr. David Shook by permission of the author and translator.

CAMBODIA
KOSAL KHIEV
Poet and tattoo artist Kosal Khiev was born in a Thai refugee camp. In the aftermath of the Khmer Rouge war he fled with his family to the USA. At the age of 16 he was arrested in a gang fight, charged with attempted murder and tried as an adult. While serving 14 years in a state penitentiary he was introduced to spoken word poetry by a Vietnam War veteran. Upon his release in 2011, the US government deported him to Cambodia, a country he had never been to. He hopes that one day the USA will repeal the current deportation law so he can be reunited with his family. Until then, he lives as an exiled American in Phnom Penh. ■ 'Why I Write' by permission of the author.

CAMEROON
PAUL DAKEYO
Paul Dakeyo is the founder of Silex Editions, a publishing house in Paris where he has lived since 1969. He was born in Cameroon in 1948 and belongs to the second generation of Cameroonian writers. His work expresses his horror at bloody régimes which have become a feature of political life in modern Africa. His poetry is described as one of liberation and activism. He has published several volumes of poetry, and has co-edited three anthologies of African poetry, notably *Aube d'un jour nouveau* (1981). ■ 'So we will emerge from exile...' from *Soweto, Suns Shot Down* (1977), by permission of the author.

CANADA
KAREN SOLIE
Karen Solie grew up in rural southwest Saskatchewan. Her first collection of poems, *Short Haul Engine*, won the BC Book Prize for

Poetry and was shortlisted for the Gerald Lampert Award and the Griffin Poetry Prize. Her second, *Modern and Normal*, was shortlisted for the Trillium Poetry Prize. Her latest, *Pigeon*, won the Griffin Prize, the Pat Lowther Award and the Trillium Poetry Prize. She served as International Writer-in-Residence at the University of St Andrews in 2011, and is an Associate Director for the Banff Centre's Writing Studio program in Banff, Alberta. Her poems have been published across Canada, in the US, UK, and Europe, and have been translated into French, German, Korean and Dutch. She currently lives in Toronto. ■ 'Migration' from *Farewell to Dreams* from Pigeon (House of Anansi Press, 2009), © 2009 Karen Solie, by permission of the publisher.

CAPE VERDE
CORSINO FORTES

Born in 1933 in Mindelo, Cape Verde, Corsino Fortes is a major figure in Lusophone modernist poetry. His first book *Pão & Fonema* (1974) coincided with the year when Portugal's dictator, Salazar, was overthrown, leading to the decolonisation of the Cape Verde Islands and Portugal's other various African colonies. He writes about the typical Cape Verdean struggles, such as drought in his first book, and emigration in his second. *Pedras de Sol & Substância*, the third book which completed his trilogy, looks forward to an independent Cape Verde where islanders can settle and build the country. He has worked as a lawyer and teacher, was a judge in Angola, and served as Cape Verde's ambassador to Portugal. ■ 'Emigrant', tr. Sean O'Brien & Daniel Hahn for The Poetry Translation Centre, from *Poems* (The Poetry Translation Centre, 2008).

CAYMAN ISLANDS
NASARIA SUCKOO CHOLLETTE

Nasaria Suckoo Chollette grew up in a household without a television. She became an avid reader and learned to express her feelings through poetry. As a student she was inspired by poets such as Rumi, Hafiz, Neruda and Kahlil Gibran, Louise Bennett and John Agard. She later developed an interest in painting and joined the acclaimed Caymanian Artists Association, Native Sons, showing her work at local and international venues. Her writing has won the Cayman National Cultural Foundation's annual Cayfest Literary Competition for several consecutive years, and she has been invited to perform her pieces at various community events. ■ 'Just Long Celia' by permission of the author.

CENTRAL AFRICAN REPUBLIC
ANONYMOUS
■ '2 termite skyscrapers' from *The Song Atlas: a book of world poetry*, ed. John Gallas (Carcanet Press, 2002).

CHAD
NIMROD
Nimrod Bena Djangrang – known as Nimrod – was born in Koyom, in the south of Chad in 1950. Originally a teacher of French, history, geography and philosophy in Chad and the Ivory Coast, Nimrod has published poems and short stories in various periodicals such as *Cargo*, *Mâche-Laurier* and *Revue Noire*. He received the Prix de la Vocation pour la poésie in 1989 for *Pierre, poussière* and the Louise Labbé award for *Passage à l'infini* in 1999. ■ 'The cry of the bird' from *The Parley Tree*, ed. & tr. Patrick Williamson (Arc Publications, 2012), by permission of the publisher.

CHILE
ALEJANDRA DEL RÍO
Alejandra del Río is recognised as one of Chile's most representative voices in the generation of the 90s. She was born in Santiago, Chile, in 1972 and began writing poetry while studying at the University of Chile, where she joined a group dedicated to using poetry as a form of protest. She won her first prize in the Poetry Contest for Unpublished Works organised by the Technical Department of Research at the University of Chile. She currently has a video series on YouTube of her poetry, which plays with lights, shadow and echoes. ■ 'In Jan Neruda's Tavern' by per-mission of the author and translator.

CHINA
YANG LIAN
Yang Lian was one of the original Misty Poets who reacted against the strictures of the Cultural Revolution. Born in Switzerland in 1955, the son of a diplomat, he grew up in Beijing and began writing when he was sent to the countryside in the 1970s. On his return he joined the influential literary magazine *Jintian* (Today). His work was criticised in China in 1983 and formally banned in 1989 when he organised memorial services for the dead of Tiananmen while in New Zealand. He was a Chinese poet in exile from 1989 to 1995, finally settling in London in 1997. Translations of his poetry include three collections with Bloodaxe, *Where the Sea Stands Still* (1999), *Concentric Circles*

(2005) and *Lee Valley Poems* (2009), as well as his long poem *Yi* (Green Integer, USA, 2002) and *Riding Pisces: Poems from Five Collections* (Shearsman, 2008), a compilation of earlier work. He is co-editor with W.N. Herbert of *Jade Ladder: Contemporary Chinese Poetry* (Bloodaxe Books, 2012), and was awarded the International Nonino Prize in 2012. ■ Extract from 'What Water Confirms', tr. Brian Holton & Agnes Hung-Chong Chan, from *Lee Valley Poems* (Bloodaxe Books, 2009), by permission of the publisher.

CHINESE TAIPEI (TAIWAN)
CHEN LI

Chen Li was born in 1954 in Hualien, Taiwan. Widely regarded as one of the most innovative and exciting poets writing in Chinese today, he is the author of eleven books of poetry and a prolific prose writer and translator. With his wife Chang Fen-ling, he has translated the works of many poets into Chinese, such as Heaney, Hughes, Paz, Neruda and Szymborska, and has published over a dozen volumes of translations. He is the organiser of the annual Pacific Poetry Festival in his hometown. His poems have been translated into several languages in book form, including *Intimate Letters: Selected Poems of Chen Li*, translated into English by Chang Fen-ling. ■ 'Nocturnal Fish' (Bookman Books Co) by permission of the author.

COLOMBIA
RAÚL HENAO

Raúl Henao was born in Cali, Colombia, in 1944. He has published many poetry collections, including *Combate del Carnaval y la Cuaresma* (1973), *La Parte del León* (1978), *El Bebedor Nocturno* (1977), *El Dado Virgen* (1980), *Sol Negro* (1985), *El Partido del Diablo - Poesía y Crítica* (1989), *El Virrey de los Espejos* (1996) and *La Vida a la Carta* (1998). His work is also included in many international anthologies and has been translated into English, French, German, Swedish, Romanian and Breton. He has lived in Venezuela, Mexico and the US ■ 'Emptiness' from *La vida a la Carta*, reprinted by Festival Internacional de Poesía de Medellín, copyright © 1998 by the author.

COMOROS
SALIM HATUBOU

Salim Hatubou was born in 1972 in Hahaya, Great Comoro. When he was 10, he moved to Marseille in France, where nostalgia for his previous life and homeland inspired his future poetry, which centred on identity and memory. As a teenager he wrote short stories and articles which were published in various journals and magazines. His current work deals with both the French and Comorian society, and his poetry is studied by schools in both countries. He works as a writer for several magazines, including *Respect* and *Kashkazi*. He has published 20 books. ■ 'And So' by permission of the author.

CONGO-BRAZZAVILLE (REPUBLIC OF THE CONGO)
ALAIN MABANCKOU

Alain Mabanckou is a novelist, journalist, poet, and academic born in 1966 in the Republic of the Congo. Currently a professor of literature in the US, he is best known for his novels and non-fiction writing depicting the experience of contemporary Africa, and the African diaspora in France. His controversial writings have been criticised by some of his peers in the African and Diaspora literary world. ■ 'there is nothing worse...' from *The Parley Tree*, ed. & tr. Patrick Williamson (Arc Publications 2012), by permission of the publisher.

DEMOCRATIC REPUBLIC OF CONGO
KAMA SYWOR KAMANDA

Kama Sywor Kamanda was born in Luebo, Democratic Republic of Congo (then the Belgian Congo) in 1952. His poetry has been translated into many languages, including English, Japanese, Italian, and Greek. He has received several major prizes and distinctions, including the Paul Verlaine Prize from the Académie française (1987), the Louise Labbé Prize (1990), the Black Africa Grand Prize for Literature (1991), and the Théophile Gautier prize (1993) from the Académie française. In 2005, the International Council for Francophone Studies (Conseil international d'études francophones) conferred the prestigious Maurice-Cagnon Certificate of Honour upon him for his unique contribution to world francophone literature. ■ 'The song of resistance' from *The Parley Tree*, ed. & tr. Patrick Williamson (Arc Publications 2012), by permission of the publisher.

COOK ISLANDS
AUDREY BROWN-PEREIRA

Audrey Brown-Pereira was born in 1975 in Rarotonga and is of Cook Islands Maori and Samoan descent. Her poetry appears in *Mauri Ola* (2011), *Trout* (2006), *Whetu Moana* (2003) and *Mana* (2000). Her work draws on visual and aural elements, as can be seen in her collection with new media artist Veronica Vaevae, *Threads of Tivaevae: Kaleido-*

skope of Kolours (2002), her New Zealand Fringe Festival performance piece *Teuki: Past with the Present* (2002), art catalogues *Akara ki Mua* (2001) and *Inei Konei* (1998), and the experimental film *The Rainbow* (1998). An Auckland University graduate, she lives in Samoa with her young family and has just completed a new collection, *Passages*. ■ 'The Trilogy of Two (2) Halves' by permission of the author.

COSTA RICA
ANA ISTARÚ

Ana Isarú is a poet, actress and dramatist who has published six poetry books. *La estación de fiebre*, her collection of highly erotic poetry, has been published in Madrid (Colección Visor), and in Paris (Editions de la différence) in a bilingual version. In the USA, Unicorn Press has also published *Fever Season*, a selection of her poems. Some of her work has been translated into German, Italian, Dutch and Swedish. Her plays have been performed in 17 countries in Latin America, the US, Canada, Portugal and Spain. In 1990 she won a John Simon Guggenheim Memorial Foundation grant. ■ 'Bringing to Light' from *Fever Season and Other Poems*, tr. Mark Smith-Soto (Unicorn Press, Greensboro, NC, 2010).

CÔTE D'IVOIRE
TANELLA BONI

Born in Abidjan, Tanella Boni studied in Toulouse and at the University of Paris. She became a professor of philosophy at the University of Abidjan, and also writes poems, novels, short stories, criticism and children's literature. She served as President of the Writers' Association of Côte d'Ivoire from 1991 to 1997 and organised Abidjan's International Poetry Festival. In 2005, she received the Ahmadou Kourouma Prize for her novel *Matins de couvre-feu* (2005) about her compatriots' inability to come to terms with the demons of intolerance, discrimination and prejudice. ■ Extract from 'Gorée baobab island' from *Gorée île baobab, Le Bruit des autres* (Ecrits des Forges, 2004).

CROATIA
DAMIR ŠODAN

Born in 1964, Damir Šodan is a poet, playwright, editor and translator who has worked as a translator for the UN for over 15 years in The Hague, where he still lives. His books include three poetry collections, *Glasovne promjene* (Sound Changes, 1996), *Srednji svijet* (The Middle World, 2001) and *Pisma divljem Skitu* (Letters to a Wild Scythian, 2009), and *Drugom stranom* (Different Drum, 2010), a much discussed and acclaimed anthology of contemporary Croatian neorealist poetry. He has translated many American poets and prose writers into Croatian, including Richard Brautigan, Raymond Carver, Leonard Cohen, Allen Ginsberg and Charles Simic, and compiled and translated an anthology of New York poets under the title *Broad-way* for the Zagreb-based *Quorum* magazine (1999). ■ 'Kamchatka' from *Srednji Svijet* (The Middle World), tr. Stephen M. Dickey (Naklada MD, Zagreb, 2001).

CUBA
PEDRO PÉREZ SARDUY

Pedro Pérez Sarduy is an Afro-Cuban poet, writer, journalist and broad-caster, now based in London, who worked for the BBC World Service (1981-94). His novel, *Las criadas de la Habana* (The Maids of Havana), was published in 2002, and in English translation in 2010. Together with Jean Stubbs, he edited *Afro-Cuba: An Anthology of Cuban Writing on Race, Politics and Culture* (1993), and wrote *Afro-Cuban Voices on Race and Identity in Contemporary Cuba* (2000). His latest book of poetry, *Malecón Sigloveinte*, was published in Cuba in 2005. ■ 'The Poet' by permission of the author.

CYPRUS
CHRISTODOULOS MAKRIS

Christodoulos Makris was born in Nicosia, Cyprus, in 1971. He studied in Manchester and has lived in Lancashire, London and Dublin. He is now based in north county Dublin where he works for the public library service, and blogs at http://yesbutisitpoetry.blogspot.com. His poetry collections are *Spitting Out the Mother Tongue* (Wurm Press, 2011), *Round the Clock* (Wurm Press, 2009) and *Muses Walk* (yes but is it poetry, 2012). ■ 'The Impressionists' from *Round the Clock* (Wurm Press, 2009), by permission of the author.

CZECH REPUBLIC
SYLVA FISCHEROVÁ

Sylva Fischerová is one of the most formidable Czech poets of her generation. A distinguished classicist who teaches at Charles University in Prague, she writes poetry with a vivid imagination as well as hist-orical reach, and was first published in English as a young poet by Bloodaxe in 1990. Born in 1963 in Prague, she grew up in the Moravian town of Olomouc, the daughter of a non-Marxist philosopher whose works were banished under communist rule. She has published six volumes of poems in Czech, and her poetry has been translated and published in numerous languages, most recently by Bloodaxe in *The Swing in the Middle of Chaos*, co-translated by her with Stuart Friebert. ■ 'Eggs, Newpaper, and Coffee' from *The Swing in the Middle of Chaos: Selected Poems*, tr. Stuart Friebert and Sylva Fischerová (Bloodaxe Books, 2010).

DENMARK
PIA TAFDRUP

Pia Tafdrup was born in 1952 in Copenhagen. She has published over 20 books in Danish since 1981, and her work has been translated into many languages. In 1991 she published a celebrated statement of her poetics, *Walking Over Water*. She received the 1999 Nordic Council Literature Prize – Scandinavia's most prestigious literary award – for *Queen's Gate*, published in David McDuff's English translation by Bloodaxe Books in 2001. Also in 2001, she was appointed a Knight of the Order of Dannebrog, and in 2006 she received the Nordic Prize from the Swedish Academy. In 2009 she won the international Jan Smrek Prize (awarded to non-Slovak, foreign poets) for her poetry. Her latest work translated into English is *Tarkovsky's Horses and other poems* (Bloodaxe Books, 2010), combining *The Whales in Paris* (2002) and *Tarkovsky's Horses* (2006). ■ 'The Whales in Paris' from *Tarkovsky's Horses and other poems*, tr David McDuff (Bloodaxe Books, 2010).

DJIBOUTI
ABDOURAHMAN WABERI

Abdourahman A. Waberi, born in Djibouti City in 1965, is a poet, novelist, essayist, academic and short story writer whose work has been translated into more than ten languages. He has received several honours including the Stefan-Georg-Preis 2006, Heinrich-Heine-Universität, the Grand prix littéraire d'Afrique noire in 1996 and the Mandat pour la Liberté prize from PEN France in 1998. In 2005, he was included in the '50 Writers of Future' selected by French literary magazine *Lire*. ■ 'Desire' from *The Parley Tree*, ed. & tr. Patrick Williamson (Arc Publications 2012), by permission of the publisher.

DOMINICA
DANIEL CAUDEIRON

Daniel Caudeiron a poet and playwright from Dominica known for writing one of PAT's (People's Action Theatre) first local plays, *Speak Brother Speak*. He published a book of poems in Dominica in 1973 and helped to produce the literary pamphlets *Free Your Mind* and *Washeen*, amongst others. Unable to contend with the tight confines of Dominican politics and attitudes, he moved in 1975 to Canada, where is an active writer, music promoter, and radio and television personality in Toronto. His play *More About Me* was staged by Black Theatre Canada in 1979. ■ 'Words for an Expatriate' by permission of the author.

DOMINICAN REPUBLIC
CHIQUI VICIOSO

Sherezada 'Chiqui' Vicioso was born in Santo Domingo in 1948. She is a poet, playwright and essayist, and has also been a columnist. She has a BA in Sociology and History of Latin America from The City University of New York (Brooklyn College), took an MA in Design Education Programs at Columbia University and studied in Cultural Project Management Getulio Vargas Foundation in Rio de Janeiro, Brazil. She was Director of Education Pro Familia (1981-85), Consultant to the UN Programme for Development of Women (1986-87) and National Programme Officer with UNICEF Women. She has been a columnist for the newspaper *Listin Diario*, a contributor to *The News* and directed the literary page *Number bewitched, El Nuevo Diario*. At the beginning of the 80s she founded the Circle of Women Poets. In 1988 the Dominican Society of Writers awarded her the prestigious Golden Caonabo and later, in 1992, the Department for the Advancement of Women gave her the Gold Medal of Merit for Outstanding Women of the Year. She was the first Dominican woman to win the National Theatre Prize of the Dominican Republic, with her play *Wishky Sur*. ■ 'The Fish Swam' by permission of the author.

ECUADOR
SANTIAGO VIZCAÍNO

Santiago Vizcaíno's first book of poetry, *Destruction in the Afternoon* (2008), won the Premio Proyectos Literarios Nacionales award from the Ecuadorian Ministry of Culture. He only began sending out his work a year ago, but already over 20 of his poems have taken by *Bitter Oleander, Connotation Press, Dirty Goat, Lake Effect, Per Contra, Saranac Review*, and *Words Without Borders*. He studied Communication and Literature at the Catholic University of Ecuador, and has an MA in Cultural Studies and Literary Heritage Management. ■ Extract from 'Hands in the Grave' from *Destruction in the Afternoon* (Ministerio de Cultura del Ecuador, 2008), by permission of the author.

EGYPT
IMAN MERSAL

Iman Mersal is the author of four volumes of poems in Arabic. She was an editor for the cultural and literary reviews *Bint al-Ard* and *Adab wa Naqd* in Egypt for several years before leaving for North America. She relocated to Boston, Massachusetts, in 1998, and from there to Edmonton, Alberta, Canada, where she works as assistant professor of Arabic literature at the University of Alberta. Translations of her poems appeared in *Paris Review*, *American Poetry Review*, *The Kenyon Review* and *Michigan Quarterly Review*. Her poems have been translated into numerous languages, including English, French, German, Spanish, Dutch and Italian. *These Are Not Oranges, My Love*, a selection of Mersal's work translated into English by Khaled Mattawa, was published by Sheep Meadow Press in 2008. ■ 'Amina' from *These Are Not Oranges, My Love* (Sheep Meadow Press, NY, 2008).

EL SALVADOR
CLARIBEL ALEGRÍA

Claribel Alegría was born in Nicaragua in 1924 to Salvadoran parents, and forced into exile during her infancy because of their human rights work. She herself was exiled from El Salvador for her powerful poetic dissent. She has published over 40 books of poetry, fiction and non-fiction, and her work has been translated into many languages, most notably in English in *Luisa in Realityland* (1987), translated by her late husband, US-born Darwin Flakoll, and *Sorrow*, an exquisite record of her grief after her husband's death, translated by Carolyn Forché (1999). She received the Casa de las Américas prize for *Sobrevivo* (I Survive) in 1978, and the Neustadt International Prize for Literature in 2006 ■ 'Flowers from the Volcano' from *Flowers from the Volcano*, tr. Carolyn Forché (University of Pittsburgh Press, 1982), by permission of the publisher.

EQUATORIAL GUINEA
RECAREDO SILEBO BOTURU

Recaredo Silebo Boturu is a poet, playwright, actor, and theatre director from Equatorial Guinea whose work touches on different themes within the context of his nation's folk and oral traditions. As co-founder and director of the theatre company, Bocamandja, he has shared his work with audiences in Equatorial Guinea, Europe, and Latin America. His award-winning writing and cultural articles have been published in the *Afro-Hispanic Review* and in both Equatoguinean and Spanish publications. His collection of poetry and plays, *Luz en la Noche* (Light in the Night), was published in 2010. ■ 'Tragedy' from *Luz en la noche* (Verbum Biblioteca Hispanoafricana, 2010), by permission of the author.

ERITREA
RIBKA SIBHATU

Ribka Sibhatu was born in Asmara, Eritrea, in 1962. She left because of the oppressive dictatorship, and has since lived in Ethiopia, France, and now Rome. She is an expert on immigration politics as well as the Eritrean folk tradition. In 1993 she published a bilingual book of poems and stories based on her life experience, *Aulò: Songs and Poems from Eritrea* (Sinnos). In 2004, Sibhatu published *The Missing Citizen* (EDUP), a critical work analysing the Italian media's representations of immigrants. Her collection of Eritrean folk stories and fables, *The Exact Number of Stars*, was published by Sinnos in 2012. ■ 'Mother Africa' (uncollected poem) by permission of the author.

ESTONIA
KRISTIINA EHIN

Kristiina Ehin was born in Rapla, Estonia in 1977. She has published six volumes of poetry in her native Estonia and has won a number of prizes there, including Estonia's most prestigious poetry prize. She has also published three books of short stories and has written two plays. Five books of her poetry and three of prose have appeared in Ilmar Lehtpere's English translations, including *The Drums of Silence* (Oleander Press, 2007), a collection of selected poems in English translation, which was awarded the Poetry Society Corneliu M. Popescu Prize for European Poetry in Translation in 2007, and *The Scent of Your Shadow* (Arc, 2010), a Poetry Book Society Recommended Translation. She has taken part in many international festivals and her work appears regularly in English translation in leading Irish and British literary journals, and has been translated into 20 languages. ■ 'How to explain my language to you' from *The Final Going of Snow* (Modern Poetry in Translation, 2011).

ETHIOPIA
BEWKETU SEYOUM

Bewketu Seyoum is a young Ethiopian writer from Gojjam, southwest of Addis Ababa. He studied psychology at Addis Ababa University and published his first collection of poems, *Nwari Alba Gojowoch*

(Unmanned Houses) in 2000, a year after graduating. Since then, he has published two further poetry collections and two novels, and has narrated short stories on CD. In 2008 he received the best young writer award of Ethiopia from the President. Some of his poetry has appeared in *Modern Poetry in Translation* (The Big Green Issue, 2008) and *Callaloo* (2011). ■ 'Elegy' from *Modern Poetry in Translation* by permission of the author.

FIJI
SUDESH MISHRA

Sudesh Mishra is a descendant of a community of Indians shipped to Fiji between 1879 and 1916 to work in plantations during British colonial rule. His award-winning poetry often centres on the theme of migration, with an undercurrent of irony, rage and sadness. *Rahu*, his first published book of poetry, received the Harri Jones Memorial Prize for Poetry. He completed his English Literature PhD at Flinders University in Australia. He has published several collections of his poems and is currently Associate Professor in Literature, Languages and Linguistics at the University of the South Pacific. ■ 'Lorca' by permission of the author.

FINLAND
PEKKO KAPPI

Pekko Kappi plays the *jouhikko*, the ancient Finnish-Karelian bowed lyre. His music has been described as 'swaying between the foul and lovely — dirty and pure... The old songs of unwritten tradition, timeless and dark stories mediate in his mouth.' He started playing the *jouhikko* in 1997 in the Ala-Könni-institute of Kaustinen, and has been studying the tradition ever since with the master players of Finland, Estonia and Sweden. Kappi has performed with different *jouhikkos* in diverse ensembles and theatre productions. His debut recording, *Kalastaja ja kaivostyöläisia*, was released in 2001. He also co-produced the album *Hiien Hivuksista: Jouhikko Music from Finland* (2003). His first full-length album *Jos ken pahoin uneksii* was released in 2007, and followed by *Vuonna '86* in 2010. ■ 'Mariainen' by permission of the author.

FRANCE
VALÉRIE ROUZEAU

Valérie Rouzeau was born in 1967 in Burgundy. She has published a dozen collections of poems, including *Pas Revoir*, which was translated by poet Susan Wicks and published by Arc under the title *Cold Spring in Winter*; it was shortlisted for the 2010 Griffin Poetry Prize, and won the Scott-Moncrieff prize for translation. She has translated works by Sylvia Plath, Ted Hughes and William Carlos Williams and the photographer Duane Michals. She lives mainly by her pen through public readings, poetry workshops in schools and radio broadcasts, and now lives in a small town near Paris, Saint-Ouen, well-known for its flea-market. ■ 'Carpe Diem' from *Quand je me deux* (Éditions Le Temps qu'il fait, 2009), by permission of the author and translator.

GABON
ANONYMOUS
■ 'Sun' from *The Song Atlas: a book of world poetry*, ed. John Gallas (Carcanet Press, 2002).

THE GAMBIA
MARIAMA KHAN
Mariama Khan was born in Gambia. Her first collection of poems, *Futa Toro*, was published in 2003. In 2004, she co-published another volume, *Juffureh: kissing you with hurting lips*, with Bamba Khan, her brother. They also co-authored *Proverbs of the Senegambia*. She also works as an African film producer and director. She set up a non-profit organisation, Documentary Film Initiative (DFI), which produces socially engaged media. Her documentary films have been screened in a number of countries around the world. One of her films, *Sutura*, won a prize in the 2008 United Nations Population Fund Agency's (UNFPA) Pan-African Film Festival. ■ 'Men and Fame' from *Lyrics of the Ghetto*, by permission of the author.

GEORGIA
MAYA SARISHVILI
Maya Sarishvili was born in Tbilisi in 1968, and is one of the most prominent women writers in Georgia today. She won Georgia's most prestigious literary award, the SABA Prize for Poetry, in 2008, for her collection *Microscope*. She is also the author of *Covering Reality* (2001), another poetry collection, as well as three radio plays. Her work has appeared in *Crazyhorse, Versal, Quiddity, Nashville Review, Asheville Review, Plume, Guernica* and other publications. Her poems have been translated into many languages and she has taken part in numerous international festivals, including Poetry International in Rotterdam (2007) and SOTZIA in Tallinn, Estonia (2008). ■ 'Let my husband know' by permission of the author and translators.

GERMANY
JAN WAGNER

Jan Wagner was born in 1971 in Hamburg. He is a poet, translator and literary critic. He has published four published poetry collections, including *Achtzehn Pasteten* (Eighteen Pies, 2007) and *Australien* (2010), both from Berlin Verlag, and co-edited the comprehensive anthology of young German language poetry, *Lyrik von Jetzt* (Poetry of Now, 2003). He has also published a selection of essays, *Die Sandale des Propheten* (The Prophet's Sandal, 2011). His poetry has been translated into 30 languages and he has received many scholarships, most recently at the German Academy in Rome. His awards include the Anna-Seghers-Award (2004), the Ernst-Meister-Award (2005), the Wilhelm-Lehmann-Award (2009), Tübingen's Friedrich-Hölderlin-Award (2011) and the Kranichstein Award (2011). He lives in Berlin. ■ 'a horse' by permission of the author and translators.

GHANA
NII AYIKWEI PARKES

Nii Ayikwei Parkes was born in the UK in 1974 and raised in Ghana. He is a performance poet, writer and socio-cultural commentator who has performed his poetry in the UK, Libya, Mozambique, the Philippines, Rwanda, Ghana, the US and across Europe, and was an Associate Artist-in-Residence with BBC Radio 3 in 2005. In 2007 he was British Council writer-in-residence at California State University, Los Angeles; was awarded Ghana's ACRAG award for poetry; and became one of the youngest living writers to be featured in London's Poems on the Underground programme with his poem 'Tin Roof'. His publications include a poetry collection, *The Makings of You* (Peepal Tree, 2010) and a novel, *Tail of the Blue Bird* (Cape, 2009). ■ 'Men Like Me' from *The Makings of You* (Peepal Tree, 2010), by permission of the author.

GREAT BRITAIN
JO SHAPCOTT

Born in 1953 in London, Jo Shapcott is a poet, editor and lecturer who has won the UK's National Poetry Competition twice, as well as several major literary awards: the Commonwealth Writers' Prize for Best First Collection, the Costa Book Award, the Forward Poetry Prize for Best Collection, and a Cholmondeley Award. In 2011 she was awarded the Queen's Gold Medal for Poetry. She teaches on the MA in Creative Writing at Royal Holloway, University of London. Poems from her three award-winning collections, *Electroplating the*

Baby (1988), *Phrase Book* (1992) and *My Life Asleep* (1998) were brought together in *Her Book* (2000), which was followed by *Tender Taxes* (2001), including her versions of Rilke's French poems, and *Of Mutability* (2010). ■ 'Phrase Book' from *Her Book: Poems 1988-98* (Faber & Faber, 2000), by permission of the publisher.

GREECE
KATERINA ILIOPOULOU

Katerina Iliopoulou is a poet, artist and translator. Her poetry has been translated into many languages and featured in literary reviews and anthologies in Greece and abroad, and she has taken part in a number of international writing and translation programmes and festivals. She has published three books of poetry, including *Mister T.*, winner of the Diavazo award for best debut collection, and has translated the work of Mina Loy, Robert Hass, Ted Hughes and Sylvia Plath (*Ariel*, due to be published) into Greek. As a member of the arts collective *intothepill* she has co-organised projects that bring together poetry and visual arts, and is co-editor of greekpoetrynow.com. ■ 'Tainaron' from *The Book of Soil* (Melani Editions, Athens, 2011).

GRENADA
MAUREEN ROBERTS

Maureen Roberts is a poet and lecturer in Creative Writing. Her first poetry collection, *My Grandmother Sings to Me*, was published by Bogle-L'Ouverture in 2003. She has edited several anthologies, including *Voices in a New Dawn* (2004), a collection of poems, short stories and essays by Grenadian writers (edited with Jean Buffong and Tony La Mothe), and *Writ in Water: a Keats House anthology* (2011), and her own poems have appeared in many anthologies, including *IC3: The Penguin Book of New Black Writing in Britain* (2000). A senior interpretation officer at London Metropolitan Archives, she organises the annual Huntley Conference and curates the Keats Festival at Keats House in London. She is a trustee of Black Cultural Archives and a member of the African Caribbean Women Writers and Scholars. ■ 'A Farewell Song' from *My Grandmother Sings to Me* (Bogle-L'Ouverture Press, 2003), by permission of the author.

GUAM
CRAIG SANTOS PEREZ

Craig Santos Perez is a native Chamoru from the Pacific Island of Guåhan/Guam. He is the co-founder of Ala Press, co-star of the poetry album *Undercurrent* (Hawai'i Dub Machine, 2011), and author of two collections of poetry: *from 'unincorporated territory' [hacha]* (Tinfish Press, 2008), and *from 'unincorporated territory' [saina]* (Omnidawn Publishing, 2010), a finalist for the 2010 *Los Angeles Times* Book Prize for Poetry and the winner of the 2011 PEN Center USA Literary Award for Poetry. Perez received his MFA from the University of San Francisco. He is an Assistant Professor in the English Department at the University of Hawai'i, Manoa, where he teaches Pacific Literature and Creative Writing. ■ Extract from 'preterrain' from *from 'unincorporated territory' [saina]* (Omnidawn Publishing, 2010), by permission of the publisher.

GUATEMALA
CARMEN MATUTE

Carmen Matute was born in Guatemala City. She is a member of the Guatemalan Academy of Language, correspondent of the Spanish Royal Academy (*Academia Guatemalteca de la Lengua correspondiente de la Real Academia Española*). Her books include eight poetry collections as well as *Muñeca Mala* (short stories) and *El Cristo del Secuestro* (novel based on the actual kidnapping of a daughter during the 1980s repression, with co-author Elizabeth Andrade). Her poetry has been translated into English, French, Italian and Swedish, and her literary work has been published in anthologies in the US, UK, Italy, Colombia, Spain, Costa Rica, Sweden, Argentina, Venezuela and Guatemala. She was a visiting writer at Yaddo, Saratoga Springs, NY, in 1998. ■ 'The Fig's Proposal' by permission of the author.

GUINEA
KOUMANTHIO ZEINAB DIALLO

Koumanthio Zeinab Diallo was born in 1956 in Labé, Guinea. Her poetry collections include *Comme les Pétales du Crépuscule* (Like Petals at Dawn, Editions La Semeuse-Togo). She is a founding member of the Guinean branch of the PEN Club International, and a member of the International Committee of Women Writers and of several other literary associations. She won the first prize for poetry written in the Pular language in 1990. An agricultural engineer by profession, she has been a development consultant for UNDP (United Nations Development Programme). ■ The translation of 'Hymn to brave peasant woman of Africa' by David and Helen Constantine was commissioned by Poetry Parnassus.

GUINEA-BISSAU
VASCO CABRAL

Born in Farim (then in Portuguese Guinea), Vasco Cabral (1926-2005) was a leading Guinea-Bissauan writer and politician who became minister of economy and finance, minister of justice, and vice-president of Guinea-Bissau, after independence. He studied at the Technical University of Lisbon and was imprisoned in 1953 for his opposition to Salazar's regime. One of the founders of PAIGC (African Party for the Independence of Guinea and Cape Verde), he has been called the first Guinean intellectual.

GUYANA
JOHN AGARD

John Agard is a poet, performer, anthologist and children's writer. Born in Guyana, he came to Britain in 1977. He won the Casa de las Américas Prize in 1982, and a Paul Hamlyn Award in 1997. He was writer-in-residence with the BBC in 1998, working with the Windrush Project, and writer-in-residence at the National Maritime Museum in Greenwich in 2007. His books include five collections from Bloodaxe, *From the Devil's Pulpit* (1997), *Weblines* (2000), and *We Brits* (2006), which was shortlisted for the 2007 Decibel Writer of the Year Award, and *Alternative Anthem: Selected Poems* and *Clever Backbone*, both published in 2009. His anthology *Hello New* (2000), published by Orchard Books, was chosen by the Poetry Society as its Children's Poetry Bookshelf Best Anthology. He lives in Lewes, East Sussex. ■ 'Half-caste' from *Alternative Anthem: Selected Poems* (Bloodaxe Books, 2009), by permission of the publisher.

HAITI
ÉVELYNE TROUILLOT

Évelyne Trouillot lives in Port-au-Prince, Haiti, and teaches in the French department at the State University. She published her first book of short stories in 1996. In 2004 she received the Prix de la romancière francophone du Club Soroptimist de Grenoble for her first novel *Rosalie l'infâme*. In 2005 her first theatre work, *Le bleu de l'île*, received the Beaumarchais award from ETC Caraïbe. Trouillot has also published poetry in French and in Creole. Her latest novel, *La mémoire aux abois*, published in France by Éditions Hoëbeke in 2010, presents a compelling view of the dictatorship in Haiti and received the prestigious award Le prix Carbet de la Caraïbe et du Tout-Monde that year. ■ 'Please' by permission of the author.

HONDURAS
MAYRA OYUELA

Born in 1982, Mayra Oyuela is a poet and cultural manager from Honduras. She has published two books of poetry, *Escribiéndole una casa al barco* (2006) and *Puertos de arribo* (2009), and her work has been featured in several anthologies from North and Latin America and translated into Italian and Catalan. She has taken part in several major American and international festivals. ■ The translation of 'Mistress of the house' by Allen Prowle and Caroline Maldonado was commissioned by Poetry Parnassus.

HONG KONG
JENNIFER WONG

Jennifer Wong's Oxford education in English Literature inspired her debut book, a collection of poems straddling Hong Kong and Oxford as a poetic journey of homelands, cultural upbringing and personal identity. Her poems have been used in creative learning projects, including poetry commissions by the British Council HK, along with learning plans and workshops bringing English poetry into Hong Kong high schools. She has taught poetry at the Chinese University of Hong Kong and served as writer-in-residence at Lingnan University of Hong Kong. Her poems have also been included in anthologies such as *Lung Jazz* (Cinnamon Press) and *Asian Poetry in English* (Math Paper Press). Her second poetry collection is forthcoming from Salmon Poetry. ■ 'Glimpse' from *Lung Jazz: Young British Poets for Oxfam*, ed. Todd Swift & Kim Lockwood (Cinnamon Press, 2012), by permission of the author and publisher.

HUNGARY
ÁGNES LEHÓCZKY

Ágnes Lehóczky is an Hungarian-born poet and translator. She completed her Masters in English and Hungarian Literature at Pázmány Péter University of Hungary in 2001 and an MA with distinction in Creative Writing at the University of East Anglia in 2006. She holds a PhD in Critical and Creative Writing, also from UEA. She has two short poetry collections in Hungarian, *Station X* (2000) and *Medallion* (2002), published by Universitas, Hungary. Her first full collection, *Budapest to Babel*, was published by Egg Box in 2008. Her collection of essays on the poetry of Ágnes Nemes Nagy, *Poetry, the Geometry of Living Substance*, was published in 2011 by Cambridge Scholars and a libretto of hers was commissioned by Writers' Centre Norwich for The Voice Project at Norwich Cathedral as part of the Norfolk and Norwich Festival 2011. She currently teaches creative writing at the University of Sheffield. Her latest collection of poems, *Rememberer*, was published by Egg Box in 2011. ■ 'Narcisz's telephone call in leapmouth' from *Budapest to Babel* (Egg Box Publishing, 2008), by permission of the author.

ICELAND
GERÐUR KRISTNÝ

Gerður Kristný is an internationally published and translated writer of poetry, short stories, novels, and books for children. She won the Icelandic Journalism Award in 2005 for a biography, and then the Icelandic Literature Award in 2010 for her book of poetry *Bloodhoof*, based on an ancient Nordic myth, published in English by Arc in 2012. Her other awards include the Icelandic Children's Choice Awards (2003), Halldor Laxness Literary Award (2004), and the West-Nordic Children's Literature Award (2010). Her play, *The Dancing at Bessastadir*, based on two of her children's books, premièred in the Icelandic National Theatre in Reykjavik in 2011. ■ 'Patriotic Poem' by permission of the author.

INDIA
TISHANI DOSHI

Born in 1975 in Madras, Tishani Doshi is an award-winning poet and dancer of Welsh-Gujarati descent. She worked with the choreographer Chandralekha, with whom she performed on many international stages. She won an Eric Gregory Award for her poetry in 2001. In 2006, she won the All-India Poetry Competition, and her debut collection, *Countries of the Body* (Aark Arts), won the Forward Prize for Best First Collection. Her first novel, *The Pleasure Seekers* (Bloomsbury, 2010), was longlisted for the Orange Prize and shortlisted for the Hindu Fiction Award, and has been translated into several languages. Her second poetry collection, *Everything Begins Elsewhere*, was published by Bloodaxe in 2012. ■ 'The Adulterous Citizen' from *Everything Begins Elsewhere* (Bloodaxe Books, 2012), by permission of publisher and author.

INDONESIA
LAKSMI PAMUNTJAK

Born in Jakarta in 1971, Laksmi Pamuntjak is the author of two books of poetry, *Ellipsis* (2005) and *The Anagram* (2007), as well as a collection of short stories, *The Diary of R.S.: Musings on Art* (2006) and the award-winning *Jakarta Good Food Guide*. She is also the co-founder of Aksara Bookstore in Jakarta. She has taken part in many international literary events and festivals including the National Poetry Festival in Australia, and her poems and short stories have been published in numerous international journals. She was an international jury member of the Prince Claus Awards based in Amsterdam from 2009 to 2012. She lives in Jakarta and just completed her first novel. ■ 'A Traveller's Tale' from *Not a Muse: The inner lives of women, a world poetry anthology*, ed. Kate Rogers & Viki Holmes (Haven Books, Hong Kong, 2009), by permission of the author.

IRAN
MIMI KHALVATI

Mimi Khalvati was born in Tehran, Iran. She grew up on the Isle of Wight, where she attended boarding school from the age of six, and has lived most of her life in England. She trained at Drama Centre London and has worked as an actor and director in the UK and Iran. She has published seven collections with Carcanet Press, including *The Meanest Flower*, shortlisted for the T.S. Eliot Prize, and *Child: New and Selected Poems 1991-2011*, a Poetry Book Society Special Commendation. She was poet in residence at the Royal Mail and has held fellowships with the Royal Literary Fund at City University and at the International Writing Program in Iowa. She is the founder of The Poetry School, where she teaches. ■ 'Don't Ask Me, Love, for that First Love' from *Child: New and Selected Poems 1991-2011* (Carcanet Press, 2011), by permission of the publisher.

IRAQ
SAADI YOUSSEF

Born in 1934 in Abu al-Khasib, a town south of Basra city, Saadi Youssef is one of the most influential poets in the Arab world. He studied Arabic literature in Baghdad and was influenced by the free verse of Badr Shakir al-Sayyab, Shathel Taqa and Abd al-Wahhab Al-Bayyati. He was involved in politics from a young age and left the country permanently in 1979, after Saddam Hussein's rise to power. At the time his work was heavily influenced by his socialist and anti-imperialist sympathies but has since also taken a more introspective, lyrical turn. He has spent most of his life in exile, working as a journalist throughout North Africa and the Middle East, and now lives in London. He has also translated many well-known writers into Arabic, and took part in the PEN World Voices festival in 2007.

Translations of his work include *Without an Alphabet, Without a Face: Selected Poems* (2003) and *Nostalgia, My Enemy* (2012), both from Graywolf Press. ■ 'Occupation 1943', first published in *Poetry* (April 2006), by permission of the author and translator.

IRELAND
SEAMUS HEANEY

Seamus Heaney a world-renowned Irish poet and critic, the winner of the Nobel Prize in Literature in 1995. Born into a farming family in Co. Derry in 1939, he left Northern Ireland in 1972 and has since lived in America, Wicklow and Dublin. He was Boylston Professor of Rhetoric and Oratory at Harvard University from 1985 to 1997, and Oxford Professor of Poetry from 1989 to 1994. His earlier work is collected in *Open Ground: Poems 1966-1996* (1998), and he has since published three further collections, *Electric Light* (2001), *District and Circle* (2006) and *Human Chain* (2010). Much of his prose is collected in *Finders Keepers: Selected Prose 1971-2001* (2002), all these books published by Faber. ■ 'The Underground' from *Open Ground: Poems 1966-1996* (Faber & Faber, 1998).

ISRAEL
ANAT ZECHARYA

Anat Zecharya was born in Tel Aviv. She is a graduate of the photography department of the WIZO Neri Bloomfield Academy of Design in Haifa and the Alma College of Hebrew Culture in Tel Aviv, and is a dance critic for *Yediot Haronot*. She has twice been awarded the Poetry in the Streets Prize from the city of Tel Aviv, and the Sha'ar Poetry Festival Young Poet's Prize. She has published two collections of poetry, *Yafa Ahat Kodem* (As Soon as Beautiful), from Helicon (2008), and *Due to Human Error* from the Bialik Institute (2012). 'Anat Zecharya is an outspoken young poet who writes forthrightly about women's desires. She does not ignore the times when being on either side of the power equation is part of erotic experience, and she casts her light on the way Israeli politics influences Israeli sex lives.' (*Poetry International*). ■ 'A Woman of Valour' from *Yafa Ahat Kodem* (Helicon, 2008) by permission of the author.

ITALY
ELISA BIAGINI

Elisa Biagini lives in Florence, Italy, after having taught and studied in the US for several years. She has published six poetry collections, most recently *Nel Bosco* (2007). Her poems have been translated into many languages, and she has published editions of her poetry in the US and Spain. A translator from English (of Alicia Ostriker, Sharon Olds, Lucile Clifton amongst others), she has published an anthology of contemporary American poetry, *Nuovi Poeti Americani* (Einaudi, 2006). Roberto Baronti Marchiò has described her poetry as depicting 'a domestic, almost everyday world which is also powerfully metaphorical and contained within the limits of a house or a room. In this narrow world, existence becomes contracted and distorted until it is reduced to fragments of the body, revealing gestures, daily objects, and private obsessions, all of which reveal our crude perception of the disaster of human relationships, or the malaise of daily life.' ■ Extract from 'The Guest' copyright © 2004 Giulio Einaudi editore s.p.a., Torino.

JAMAICA
KEI MILLER
Kei Miller was born in Jamaica in 1978. He read English at the University of the West Indies and completed an MA in Creative Writing at Manchester Metropolitan University. His work has appeared in *The Caribbean Writer, Snow Monkey, Caribbean Beat* and *Obsydian III*. His first collection of short fiction, *The Fear of Stones*, was shortlisted in 2007 for the Commonwealth Writers First Book Prize. His debut *Kingdom of Empty Bellies* (Heaventree Press, 2006) was followed by two collections from Carcanet, *There Is an Anger that Moves* (2007) and *A Light Song of Light* (2010). He is also the editor of Carcanet's *New Caribbean Poetry: An Anthology* (2007). He has been a visiting writer at York University in Canada, the Department of Library Services in the British Virgin Islands and a Vera Ruben Fellow at Yaddo, and currently teaches Creative Writing at the University of Glasgow. ■ 'Your dance is like a cure' from *There Is an Anger that Moves* (Carcanet Press, 2007)

JAPAN
RYOKO SEKIGUCHI
Ryoko Sekiguchi is a Japanese and French writer who now lives in Paris. She has translated Pierre Alferi, Atiq Rahimi, Gôzô Yoshimasu, Yoko Tawada, and Jean Echenoz, among others. Her publications in French include *Calque, Deux marchés, de nouveau, Héliotropes* (all published by POL), *Adagio ma non troppo*, and *Série Grenade* (both Bleu du ciel). Three of her books have been translated into English,

including *Héliotropes* (tr. Sarah O'Brien, published by La Presse), *Two markets, again* (tr. Sarah Riggs, Post-Apollo Press), and *Tracing* (tr. Stacy Doris, Duration Press). ■ Poem from *Adagio ma non troppo*, tr. Eric Selland (Bleu du ciel), by permission of the author.

JORDAN
AMJAD NASSER

Amjad Nasser is a poet at the forefront of the Arab poetry scene. Born in Jordan in 1955, he lives in London, where he works as managing editor and cultural editor of *Al-Quds Al-Arabi* daily newspaper. He has published nine volumes of poetry, four travel memoirs and a novel. His work has been translated into French, Italian and Spanish. *Shepherd of Solitude: Selected Poems*, his first English translated work, was published by Banipal Books in 2009. He has taken part in many international festivals, including London's Poetry International. ■ 'The Phases of the Moon in London' from *Shepherd of Solitude: Selected Poems* (Banipal Books, 2009) © Amjad Nasser.

KAZAKHSTAN
AKERKE MUSSABEKOVA

Akerke Mussabekova was born in 1987 in Kyzylorda, a small city of on the banks of Syrdariya River. Her father was a doctor and her mother a teacher. She studied Kazakh National University where she specialised in Translation/English Interpretations. After studying English for 17 years, she visited Canada as part of the Poet in the City project exchange. She currently works as a technical translator at the International Road Project Western Europe-Western China. She is now concentrating on writing her poetry in English. ■ 'Remember me' (English original translated afterwards into Kazakh) by permission of the author.

KENYA
SHAILJA PATEL

Shailja Patel was trained as a political economist, accountant and yoga teacher. Her publishing debut, *Migritude*, based on her acclaimed one-woman theatre show, was an Amazon poetry bestseller and *Seattle Times* bestseller. She has been African Guest Writer at Sweden's Nordic Africa Institute and poet-in-residence at the Tallberg Forum, Sweden's alternative to Davos. She has appeared on the BBC World Service, NPR and Al-Jazeera, and her work has been translated into 16 languages. She has won numerous awards, and is a founding member of Kenyans for Peace, Truth and Justice, a civil society coalition which works for an equitable democracy in Kenya. In 2011, the African Women's Development Fund named her one of Fifty Inspirational African Feminists for the 100th anniversary of International Women's Day. ■ 'Eater of Death' from *Migritude* (Kaya Press, NY, 2010).

KIRIBATI
TERESIA TEAIWA

Teresia Teaiwa is a poet and academic of Kiribati and African American heritage. She was born in Honolulu, raised in Fiji, and obtained her degrees at universities in the USA. She is currently living in New Zealand, and working as a Senior Lecturer in Pacific Studies at Victoria University of Wellington. Her solo CD *I can see Fiji: Poetry and Sounds* (2008) has been described by literary scholar Ku'ualoha Ho'omanawanui as pushing 'far past any preconceived boundaries of what constitutes Pacific literature', 'expansively universal and intimately personal, embodying a new kind of blossoming of two very traditional genres of Pacific artistic expression'. ■ 'Pacific Tsunami Found Poems' from *Going Down Swinging*, 30 (2010), 33-34, by permission of the author.

NORTH KOREA
(DEMOCRATIC REPUBLIC OF KOREA)
JANG JIN SEONG

Jang Jin Seong was a former court poet for North Korean leader Kim Jong-il. After fleeing to South Korea he became a best-selling author and media sensation. A graduate of Kim Il-sung University, he became a favourite of the Pyongyang government and was twice invited to meet leader Kim Jong-il. After realising that he could no longer live under Jong-il's regime, he fled that life and all its relative comforts to cross the Tumen River into China, eventually settling in South Korea. There he has just published a volume of poetry, *For 100 Won, My Daughter I Sell*. Jang Jin-sung uses a pseudonym to avoid endangering relatives left behind in isolated and bankrupt North Korea. ■ 'I Sell My Daughter for 100 Won' by permission of the author.

SOUTH KOREA
KIM HYESOON

Kim Hyesoon was one of the first women in South Korea to be published in a literary journal when her work appeared in *Munhak kwa jisong* (Literature and Intellect) in 1979. She is one of the most important contemporary poets of South Korea. In her experimental work she explores women's multiple and simultaneous existence as grandmothers, mothers, and daughters in the context of Korea's highly patriarchal society. She has won numerous literary prizes and was the first woman to receive the coveted Midang (2006) and Kim Su-yong (1998) awards named after two major contemporary poets. She lives in Seoul and teaches creative writing at the Seoul Institute of the Arts. ■ 'Red Scissors Woman' from *Your First* (Moonhak kwa Jisung-sa, Seoul, 2008), copyright © 2008 Kim Hyesoon, reprinted by Poetry International Web, 2010, by permission of the author.

KUWAIT
SAADIA MUFARREH

Saadia Mufarreh is a poet, critic, and writer who lives in Kuwait. A 1987 graduate of Kuwait University with a degree in Arabic language and education, she has published four collections of poetry, including *He Was the Last of the Dreamers* (1990), *When You're Absent, I Saddle My Suspicion's Horses* (1994), *Book of Sins* (1997) and *Mere: A Mirror Lying Back* (1999). She is a regular contributor to several Arabic newspapers and magazines and serves as art editor of the newspaper *Al-Qabas* in Kuwait. ■ 'Distance' from *Gathering the Tide: An Anthology of Contemporary Arabian Gulf Poetry*, ed. Patty Paine, Jeff Lodge & Samia Touati (Ithaca Press, 2011), by permission of the author.

KYRGYZSTAN
ROZA MUKASHEVA

Roza Mukasheva was born in 1949 in the village of Bokonbaev in the Ysyk Kul region of Kyrgyzstan. After completing secondary school she entered the Institute of Polytechnics and graduated in 1971. For two years she worked at a factory but soon joined a radio company as a journalist. She also worked at a newspaper for children, and later in social work. Since 2003 she was PR manager in the Central Asian Academy of Arts. She currently works as a translator for the magazine *Armeiskii pedsovet*. She is the author of six poetry collections in the Kyrgyz language. In 1978, she received an award from *Soviet Woman* magazine in the best poetry category. ■ Hamid Ismailov's translation of 'Nomad in the Sunset' was commissioned by Poetry Parnassus.

LAOS
BRYAN THAO WORRA

Bryan Thao Worra is a Laotian American writer. His books include *On the Other Side of the Eye, Touching Detonations, Winter Ink, Barrow*

320

and *The Tuk Tuk Diaries: My Dinner With Cluster Bombs*. He is the first Laotian American to receive a Fellowship in Literature from the US government's National Endowment for the Arts. Bryan Thao Worra was born Thao Somnouk Silosoth in Vientiane, Laos in 1973 during the Laotian Secret War (1954-75), and was adopted when he was three days old by an American pilot, John Worra, who flew for Royal Air Lao, a civilian airline company. He was brought to the US in 1973, and reunited with his biological family after nearly 30 years during a visit to Laos in 2003. You can visit him online at thaoworra. blogspot.com ■ 'No Regrets' from *Tanon Sai Jai* (Silosoth Publishing, 2009), by permission of the author.

LATVIA
KĀRLIS VĒRDIŅŠ

Kārlis Vērdiņš was born in 1979 in Riga. He has published four books of poetry: *Ledlauži* (Icebreakers, 2001), *Biezpiens ar krejumu* (Cottage Cheese with Sour Cream, 2004), *Burtinu zupa* (Alphabet Soup, for children, 2007) and *Es* (I, 2008). He is a renowned critic, with an MA in Cultural Theory and a PhD in Philology, and has published many essays on literature as well as translations of European and American poets (including T.S. Eliot, Konstantin Biebl, Georg Trakl, Joseph Brodsky, Walt Whitman), and has also written libretti and song lyrics. His own poetry has been translated in many languages, including collections in Russian and Polish, and appears in the Arc anthologies *A Fine Line* (2004) and *Six Latvian Poets* (2011) ■ 'Come to Me' from *Six Latvian Poets*, ed. Ieva Lesinska (Arc Publications, 2011), by permission of the author and publisher.

LEBANON
VÉNUS KHOURY-GHATA

Lebanese poet and novelist Vénus Khoury-Ghata was born in the northern village of B'sharre, raised in Beirut, and now lives in France. She is the author of 17 novels, including *Une Maison aux bord des larmes*, *La Maestra*, and *La fille qui marchait dans le désert*, and 16 collections of poems, most recently *Où vont les arbres* (Mercure de France, 2011) Four collections of her poems and one novel are available in English in Marilyn Hacker's translation, including *Alphabets of Sand* (Carcanet Press, 2009). Recipient of the Académie Française prize in poetry in 2009, she was named an Officer of the Légion d'honneur the following year, and received the Prix Goncourt de poésie in 2011. ■ 'Widow' from *Alphabets of Sand* (Carcanet Press, 2009).

LESOTHO
RETHABILE MASILO

Born in 1961, Rethabile Masilo is a Mosotho poet who now lives in Paris, where he is a language teacher. His family fled from Lesotho in 1980 to South Africa, where he experienced the harsh realities of the apartheid first hand, before moving to Nairobi, settling in Kenya until the Prime Minister of Lesotho who had threatened their lives was overthrown, and later died. Rethabile and his sister stayed in America to complete their studies, while the rest of his family returned home. He blogs at *Poéfrika* and co-edits the literary magazine *Canopic Jar*. His first collection, *Things That Are Silent*, was published in 2012 by Pindrop Press. ■ 'The San's Promise' by permission of the author.

LIBERIA
PATRICIA JABBEH WESLEY

Patricia Jabbeh Wesley was born in Monrovia, Liberia, and raised there and in her father's home village of Tugbakeh, where she learned to speak Grebo in addition to English. In 1991, she emigrated with her family to the US to escape the Liberian civil war, whose violence and devastation she witnessed first-hand. Vulnerable in their combination of grief and levity, her poems deal with family, community, and war. She has published four books of poetry: *Where the Road Turns* (2010), *The River is Rising* (2007), *Becoming Ebony* (2003) and *Before the Palm Could Bloom: Poems of Africa* (1998). Her many awards include the Crab Orchard Award for *Becoming Ebony* and the Liberian Award 2010 for her poetry. She is Assistant Professor of English at Pennsylvania State University. ■ 'The Women in My Family' from *The River Is Rising* (Autumn House Press, 2007), by permission of the author.

LIBYA
KHALED MATTAWA

Born in Benghazi in 1964, Khaled Mattawa is a Libyan poet renowned for his poetry and literary translation work. In 1979 his family emigrated to the US, where he attended high school in Louisiana, and later studied political science and economics at at the University of Tennessee. He has published four books of his own poetry, *Ismailia Eclipse* (1995), *Zodiac of Echoes* (2003), *Amorisco* (2008) and *Tocqueville* (2010), as well as many distinguished poetry translations including editions of Hatif Janabi, Fadhil Al Azzawi, Saadi Youssef, Maram al-Massri, Iman Mirsal, Journana Haddad, Amjad Nasser and Adonis. He has received many awards of his work, including an Academy of American Poets award, and the PEN award for literary translation and a Guggenheim Fellowship, and his translation of Adonis's *Selected Poems* (Yale University Press, 2010) was shortlisted for the 2011 Griffin Poetry Prize. He is an Assistant professor of creative writing at the University of Michigan, a contributing editor for *Banipal* magazine, and president of RAWI (Radius of Arab American Writers). ■ 'Borrowed Tongue' by permission of the author.

LIECHTENSTEIN
ELISABETH KAUFMANN-BÜCHEL
Elisabeth Büchel (1954-2005) was both a poet and one of Liechtenstein's foremost artists, notable for a style of work which drew on both American expressionism and European contemporary art. She studied art history in the US at Bridgeport University in Connecticut and the University of Tulsa in Oklahoma. ■ 'Free as a Bird' from *Mille Fleurs*.

LITHUANIA
DONATAS PETROŠIUS
Donatas Petrošius was born in 1978 in Bijotai (western Lithuania), and now lives in Vilnius. He has worked in the editorial sections of various national newspapers, and has been a freelance writer since 2008. His poetry collections include *Iš tvermės D* (The D of Doggedness, 2004) and *Aoristas* (Aorist, 2009), winner of the Lithuanian Writers' Union prize for book of the year. His poems have been translated into 20 languages, and he has taken part in many international projects, the latest being *Letters for Miłosz*. ■ 'Ghost Dogs; Way of the Samurai', translation copyright © *Vilnius Review*.

LUXEMBOURG
ANISE KOLTZ
Born in Luxembourg in 1928, Anise Koltz first wrote in German, but found she could no longer do so after the death of her husband, a late victim of the Nazi occupation. After a long silence, she began to write again, but almost exclusively in French. She has also written children's books in Luxembourgish. In 1963 she founded the *Journées littéraires de Mondorf*, to bring together writers from around the world, to develop links between Luxembourg and the international literary scene. A founding member of the European Academy of Poetry, she is also a member of L'Académie Mallarmé (Paris), Pen-Club Belgium

and L'Institut Grand-Ducal des Arts et des Lettres (Luxembourg). In the UK, *At the Edge of Night*, drawing on four of her books, was published by Arc in 2009. ■ 'Prologue' from *At the Edge of the Night* (Arc Publications, 2009), by permission of the publisher.

MACEDONIA
NIKOLA MADZIROV

Nikola Madzirov is a Macedonian poet, essayist, translator and editor. He was born in a family of Balkan Wars refugees in Strumica in 1973. His poetry has been translated into over 30 languages. He won the European Hubert Burda Prize for young East European poets for his collection *Relocated Stone* (2007), has taken part in many literature festivals, and has received several international awards and fellowships, including the International Writing Program (IWP) at the University of Iowa (2008) and Literarisches Tandem in Berlin (2009). A selection of his poetry, *Remnants of Another Age*, was published by BOA Editions in the US in 2011 with a foreword by Carolyn Forché. He is one of the coordinators of the world poetry network Lyrikline. ■ 'Shadows Pass Us By' from *Remnants of Another Age*, tr. Peggy and Graham W. Reid, Magdalena Horvat, and Adam Reed, © 2011 Nikola Madzirov, by permission of The Permissions Company, Inc. on behalf of BOA Editions Ltd, www.boaeditions.org

MADAGASCAR
MODESTE HUGUES

Modeste is a Malagasy singer-songwriter and guitarist whose music is rooted in his hometown of Betroka in the Central Southern region of Madagascar. His music is a distinctive blend of traditional Malagasy sounds influenced by softer South African dance rhythms, with guitar playing and vocals. He has released two albums, *Modeste* and *Fomba / Living our Destiny*, with a third, *Handeha Hody / Going Home*, due out in 2012. He has been featured and played live on numerous BBC radio programmes and has performed at many venues and festivals across the UK and abroad. ■ 'Lavitra (Far Away)' by permission of the author.

MALAWI
JACK MAPANJE

Jack Mapanje was head of the Department of English at the University of Malawi when the Malawi authorities arrested him in 1987 after his first book of poems had been banned, and he was released in 1991 after spending three years, seven months and sixteen days in prison, following an international outcry against his incarceration. He has since published three poetry titles with Bloodaxe, including *The Last of the Sweet Bananas* (2004), and most recently, *Beasts of Nalunga* (2007), which was shortlisted for the Forward Prize for Best Collection. His latest book is his prison memoir *And Crocodiles Are Hungry at Night* (Ayebia Clarke Publishing, 2011). He lives in exile in York with his family, and is currently a visiting professor in the faculty of art at York St John University. ■ 'Scrubbing the Furious Walls of Mikuyu' from *The Last of the Sweet Bananas: New & Selected Poems* (Bloodaxe Books, 2004), by permission of the publisher.

MALAYSIA
SHARANYA MANIVANNAN

Sharanya Manivannan was born in Madras, India in 1985, and grew up in Sri Lanka and Malaysia. Her first book of poems, *Witchcraft* (Bullfighter Books, 2008), was praised in *The Straits Times* as being 'sensuous and spiritual, delicate and dangerous and as full as the moon reflected in a knife'. She is currently working on a book of stories (*The High Priestess Never Marries*), a novel (*Constellation of Scars*), as well as two manuscripts of new poems (*Bulletproof Offering* and *Cadaver Exquisito*). She received the Lavanya Sankaran Fellowship for 2008-09 and was nominated for a 2012 Pushcart Prize. A journalist and columnist, she wrote a personal column, 'The Venus Flytrap', for *The New Indian Express* from 2008 to 2011. She lives in India and can be found online at www.sharanyamanivannan.com ■ 'Dream of Burying My Grandmother Who Has No Grave' from *Pyrta*, Monsoon Issue #1 (July 2010), by permission of the author.

MALDIVES
FARAH DIDI

Farah Didi, a poet from the Maldives, has been writing since she was a child, influenced by her grandmother, an accomplished poet. She left the Maldives to study and live in Britain. She has said that moving to Europe exposed her 'to the harsh realities of race relations, economic competitiveness, power politics', and opened her eyes to the world. Her poetry is now focused on the continuing struggle to establish democracy in her native Maldives, and her poem 'Winds of Change' relates to the crackdown on pro-democracy activists in the Maldives. She lives in Bedfordshire. ■ 'winds of change' by permission of the author.

MALI
OXMO PUCCINO

Born in 1974 in Mali and raised in Paris, Oxmo Puccino is a French hip hop musician, known for his mastery of handling language and concepts in his songs. He began his collaboration with the fledgling rap collective Time Bomb, honing his craft alongside future superstars like Booba and Diam's, and quickly developed into a lyricist with a metaphorical ingenuity far more advanced than his contemporaries, crafting violent yet strangely poetic portraits of urban Paris life and drawing on the street-smart American hip hop of the Notorious B.I.G. and other icons to document life in Paris's 19th arrondissement. He has released five albums since his 1998 debut, *Opéra Puccino*, most recently *L'Arme de Paix* (2009), and is currently working on a sixth, *Roi sans Carrosse*, directed by Vincent Segal (Ballaké Sissoko, Sting...), Renaud Letang (Feist, Manu Chao...) and Vincent Taeger (Pony Hoax), due out in 2012. ■ 'This is a song' by permission of the author.

MALTA
IMMANUEL MIFSUD

Born in Malta in 1967, the youngest in a working-class family of eight children, Immanuel Mifsud started writing poetry at the age of 16, when he co-founded the literary group *Versarti* and began to work in experimental theatre groups. He has published poetry, prose and three children's books. His writing career has oscillated between fame and notoriety, with one of his short story collections banned in 2005 because of the explicitness of his writing, while in 2011 he won the European Union Prize for Literature. In 2005 Maurice Riordan translated his collection *Confidential Reports* (Southword Editions, Cork), and in 2011 Edizzjonijiet Emmadelezio published *Bateau Noir*, a bilingual edition with translations from Maltese into French by Nadia Mifsud and Catherine Camilleri. ■ Extract from 'A Handful of Leaves from Mallorca' by permission of the author and translator.

MARSHALL ISLANDS
KATHY JETNIL-KIJINER

Kathy Jetnil-Kijiner is a poet, writer, and journalist. Born in the Marshall Islands and raised in Hawai'i, she has worked with Youthspeaks Hawai'i, UC Berkeley's Poetry for the People programme, Voices of Our Nations Arts Foundation, and the Pacific Islander collective One Love Oceania. She has reported for the *Marshall Islands Journal*, the Campanil, and the Secretariat of the Pacific Community. Her solo performance piece *Iep Jeltok* has been featured at various solo theatre venues. She now lives in the Marshall Islands and works at the College of the Marshall Islands. ■ 'history project' by permission of the author.

MAURITANIA
MBARKA MINT AL-BARRA'

Mbarka Mint al-Barra' is a Mauritanian poet and teacher who writes mainly in Arabic and who is active in the cultural and literary life of her country, and elsewhere in the Arab world. Like many poets of her generation, she uses dialogue in her poems, and a narrative style to address the realities of Mauritanian society. She also uses free verse in some poems, borrowing images from religious texts, ancient Arab history and classical Arabic texts to portray conditions in her country. The symbolism of the religious stories is particularly effective in a country deeply rooted in Arab-Islamic traditions. ■ 'Message from a Martyr' by permission of The Poetry Translation Centre.

MAURITIUS
SARADHA SOOBRAYEN

Saradha Soobrayen is the reviews editor for *Modern Poetry in Translation*. She was born in London where she works as a poetry editor, mentor and coach, providing professional development for emerging and established writers and artists. She is widely published in anthologies and journals, including *Out of Bounds* (2012), *Red* (2009), *The Forward Book of Poetry 2008*, *Oxford Poets 2007: An Anthology*, *I Am Twenty People!* (2008), *New Poetries IV* (2007) and *This Little Stretch of Life* (2006). She received an Eric Gregory Award in 2004. *The Guardian* named her as one of the 'Twelve to Watch', up and coming new generation of poets. ■ 'My Conqueror' from *Oxford Poets 2007: An Anthology* (Carcanet Press, 2007), by permission of the author.

MEXICO
ROCÍO CERÓN

Rocío Cerón was born in Mexico City in 1972. Her work is experimental, combining poetry with music, performance and video. Her books of poetry include *Basalto* (2002), *Imperio/Empire* (2009, interdisciplinary-bilingual edition) and *Tiento* (Germany, 2011). Her poems have been translated into English, Finnish, French, Swedish and German, and she has performed her work at venues in France, Germany, Sweden and Denmark. ■ Extract from 'America' by permission of Universidad Autónoma de Nuevo León and the author.

MICRONESIA
EMELIHTER KIHLENG

Emelihter Kihleng lives in Wellington, New Zealand where she is working towards a PhD in Pacific Studies at Victoria University. She was born on Guam and raised in Pohnpei Island, Federated States of Micronesia, Guam and in Honolulu, Hawai'i. Her first collection of poetry, *My Urohs*, was published in 2008 by Kahuaomanoa Press. Her poetry can be found in various literary journals throughout the Pacific and US. ■ 'This morning at Joy' from *My Urohs* (Kahuaomanoa Press, Hawai'i, 2008).

MOLDOVA
VASILE GÂRNEŢ

Born in 1958, Vasile Gârnet has published four books of poetry and one novel. His collections include *A Character in the Forgotten Garden* and *Borges Field*. He is the editor of *Contrafort*, Moldova's leading cultural magazine and has served as Moldova's representative to PEN. His poetry has been translated from Romanian into 14 languages, including French, German and Italian. He lives in Chisinau. ■ 'Bookmark (I)' from *Singular Destinies: contemporary poets of Bessarabiam*, ed. Adam J. Sorkin, Cristina Cirstea & Sean Cotter (Editura Cartier, 2003).

MONACO
GEORGES FRANZI

Georges Franzi (1914-97) found his calling early in life and was ordained as a priest in 1940. Recognising the importance of a country's native language in defining its people's identity, he championed the preservation of his ancestral language, Monegasque. In 1976, Canon Franzi was put in charge of a programme that saw Monegasque taught as a compulsory subject in all of the Principality's elementary schools. Monegasque was later included in the baccalaureate exam.

MONGOLIA
HADAA SENDOO

Born in 1961 in Inner Mongolia, Hadaa Sendoo has lived and worked in Ulaanbaatar since 1991. He writes in Mongolian, Chinese and English. His poems have been translated into more than 30 languages, and selected for *The Best Mongolian Poetry*. His many awards include the Mongolian Writers' Union prize. In 2006, he established the *World Poetry Almanac*. His most recent publication in Mongolian is *The Road Is Not Completed* (2011). He has worked as professor of literature at the National University of Mongolia, and is currently the consulting editor of the *International Literary Quarterly*. ■ 'It Is Not True I Have No Hometown' by permission of the author.

MONTENEGRO
ALEKSANDAR BEČANOVIĆ

Aleksandar Bečanović was born in Podgorica, Montenegro, in 1971. He is a writer and film critic, and has published five poetry collections, two books of short fiction and one book of film criticism, and contributed to the film books *501 Movie Directors, 501 Movie Stars, 101 Horror Movies You Must See Before You Die* and *101 Sci-Fi Movies You Must See Before You Die*. ■ 'Pessoa: On Four Addresses' from *New European Poets*, ed. Wayne Miller & Kevin Prufer (Graywolf Press, USA, 2008), by permission of the author.

MOROCCO
HASSAN EL OUAZZANI

Born in 1970, Hassan El Ouazzani is one of Morocco's most significant younger poets. His poems draw largely on mythology, but with a post-modern twist and an emphasis on blending mythical allusions with everyday experience. He belongs to the generation of 1990s poets who made the prose-poem leap into prominence in Moroccan poetry. He has served as secretary-general of the Moroccan House of Poetry, and now works for the Ministry of Culture. He has taken part in many international festivals of poetry, including those in Medellín (Colombia), Trois-Rivières (Canada), Mallorca, Istanbul, Malta and London. ■ 'What If I Unsettled the Homeland' from Poetry International Web, 2010, by permission of the author.

MOZAMBIQUE
ANA MAFALDA LEITE

Ana Mafalda Leite is has been described as a poet whom critics find easier to ignore than to categorise. Her work draws on Portuguese and Mozambican poetic traditions, enriching both with her highly original perspective. Her work attests also to a self-reflexive poetic reworking of the two traditions. She was educated in Lourenço Marques (now Maputo) and later went to university in Lisbon. She is now a professor of Lusophone African Literature at the University of Lisbon. ■ 'Music Box' from *Charrua and Beyond: Poems from Mozambique* (Heaventree Press, 2007), by permission of the author.

MYANMAR (BURMA)
ZEYAR LYNN

Born in 1958, Zeyar Lynn is a prominent contemporary Myanmar poet, translator and writer. He has published five books of poetry and seven Myanmar translations of internationally acclaimed poets including Ashbery, Bernstein, Tranströmer, and a variety of Chinese, Japanese, Australian, East European and Russian poets. He is known for having introduced L=A=N=G=U=A=G=E Poetry/Writing to Myanmar poetry. He has also organised and hosted the annual UNESCO World Poetry Day event in Yangon since 2005. He is a member of World Poetry Movement (Colombia) and currently lives and works as a teacher of English in a private language school. ■ 'Slide Show' from *Bones Will Crow: An Anthology of Burmese Poetry*, ed. James Byrne & Ko Ko Thett (Arc Publications, 2012), by permission of the publisher.

NAMIBIA
MVULA YA NANGOLO

Born in Oniimwandi in 1943, Mvula ya Nangolo was one of Namibia's first black journalists and published poets. After working for most of his life as a journalist – in Europe, Tanzania, Zambia and Namibia – he became National Poet of Namibia and also Special Advisor to the Minister of Information and Communication Technology. In 1995 he published *Kassinga: A Story Untold* (with Tor Sellström), an account of the 1978 massacre of hundreds of Namibians in a refugee camp in Angola by the South African military. His poetry publications include *From Exile* (1976), *Thoughts from Exile* (1991) and *Watering the Beloved Desert* (2008). His work also features in the anthology *When My Brothers Come Home* (1985). ■ 'From Exile' from *Watering the Beloved Desert* (Brown Turtle Press, 2008), by permission of the author.

NAURU
MAKERITA VA'AI

Makerita Va'ai grew up in Samoa and New Zealand, where she attended high school and taught for a year before returning to Western Samoa. She is a graduate of the University of the South Pacific, and was a founding staff member of the Western Samoa Secondary Teachers' College. She served as Director of the University of the South Pacific Centre in Western Samoa and in Nauru, and she helped set up the Nauru Writers' Association. *Pinnacles*, a collection of her poetry, was published in 1993. ■ 'Rains of Nauru' from *Pinnacles* (Mana Publications, 1993), by permission of the author.

NEPAL
YUYUTSU R.D. SHARMA

Yuyutsu R.D. (Ram Dass) Sharma was born in Punjab and moved to Nepal at an early age. He grew up in very religious surroundings and became a shaman at the age of nine, as he was believed to be possessed by a spirit. He later pursued a western education. While working on his Masters in Philosophy at University of Rajasthan, he met American poet David Ray, who encouraged him to write and publish his poetry. He has published nine collections of poetry and his work has been widely translated. He recently published a book of nonfiction, *Annapurnas & Stains of Blood: Life, Travel and Writing a Page of Snow* (Nirala, 2010), edits *Pratik: A Magazine of Contemporary Writing*, and contributes literary columns to Nepal's leading daily, *The Himalayan Times*. ■ 'London Bombings' from *Space Cake, Amsterdam and Other Poems from Europe and America* (Howling Dog Press, Colorado, 2009), by permission of the author.

NETHERLANDS
ARJEN DUINKER

Arjen Duinker was born in Delft in 1956 and studied psychology and philosophy. He has published one novel, *Het moeras* (The Morass, 1992), and twelve volumes of poetry. In 2001 Duinker received the Jan Campert Prize for his volume *De geschiedenis van een opsomming* (The History of an Enumeration, 2000). His book *De zon en de wereld* (The Sun and The World, 2004) won the VSB Poetry Prize and has been published in English translation in Australia. Other books have been published in France, Portugal, Italy, Iran, Russia and the UK. One of Duinker's poems was translated into 220 different languages for a project called World Poem. ■ Part X from 'The Sublime Song of a Maybe' from *The Sublime Song of a Maybe: Selected Poems* (Arc Publications, 2005).

NEW ZEALAND
BILL MANHIRE

Bill Manhire was New Zealand's inaugural Poet Laureate and has won the New Zealand Book Award for Poetry five times. In 2007 he was honoured with the Prime Minister's Award for Literary Achievement. His poetry and fiction are published in New Zealand, the UK and USA; several of the anthologies he has coordinated have become bestsellers. He is Professor of English and Creative Writing at Victoria University of Wellington, where he is also the director of the International Institute of Modern Letters. Recently he has been writing songs with the jazz musician Norman Meehan, and his *Selected Poems* will be published in September 2012. ■ 'Entering America' from *Lifted* (Carcanet Press, 2007), © Bill Manhire 2005, 2007.

NICARAGUA
GIOCONDA BELLI

Born in 1948 in Managua, Gioconda Belli is a poet, writer and political activist. She took part in the Sandinista struggle against the Somoza dictatorship, and was forced into exile in Mexico in 1975. Returning in 1979 after the Sandinista victory, she worked for the new FSLN government, but left the party in 1993, and is now a major critic of the current government. She has written six novels, a memoir, six books of poetry and two children's books, as well as essays and political commentary. Her work has been translated into many languages and she has received several literary prizes, including the Casa de las Américas Prize in 1978 and Best Political Novel of the Year in Germany in 1989, and was a finalist for the *Los Angeles Times* Book Prize in 2003. She divides her time between Los Angeles and Managua. ■ 'Brief lessons in Eroticism I' from *Escándalo de Miel* (Seix Barral, Barcelona, 2011), by permission of the author.

NIGER
ADAMOU IDÉ

Born in 1951, Adamou Idé is a Nigerien poet and novelist. He studied in France, receiving degrees from the Sorbonne and the Institut international d'administration publique in Paris, and has served as an official in the Niger government and in the international organisation ACCT (now known as Organisation Internationale de la Francophonie). He published his first collection of poems, *Cri inachevé* (The Unfinished Cry), in 1984, and won the first Nigerien National Poetry Prize (Prix national de Poésie) in 1981, and the Grand Prix Littéraire Boubou Hama du Niger in 1996. ■ 'I'm Scared!' from Poetry International Web, by permission of the author.

NIGERIA
WOLE SOYINKA

Akinwande Oluwole 'Wole' Soyinka was awarded the 1986 Nobel Prize in Literature. He has published eight poetry collections and is also known for his political and human rights engagement. He has been arrested several times and imprisoned twice, one involving a long spell in solitary confinement. Soyinka was born into a Yoruba family in Abeokuta. He studied at the University College, Ibadan (1952-54), and then the University of Leeds (1954-57) from which he received a degree in English Literature. He became a Professor of Drama and Comparative Literature at the then University of Ife in 1975. He is currently an Emeritus Professor at the same university. Soyinka has played an active role in Nigeria's political history. ■ 'Her Joy is Wild' from *Selected Poems* (Methuen, 2001), by permission of the author.

NORWAY
ENDRE RUSET

Endre Ruset is a young Norwegian poet who currently lives in Oslo. Born in 1981, he published his first collection of poems in 2001. His poetry is known for its eroticism and its exploration of childhood interpersonal relationships. He was the artistic advisor for the Norwegian Festival of Literature in 2008-11, and was awarded the Bjornson Scholarship for his collection *Kims lek* (2005). Some of his poems have been translated into English for the *3:AM Maintenant* series by Marlene Veivåg. ■ 'Plum tree' from *The Plum Tree*, published in *ny poesi* for *Maintenant* series (3:AM).

OMAN
ZAHIR AL-GHAFRI

Zahir Al-Ghafri was born in Oman in 1956. His work is part of his country's avant-garde prose poetry movement. Following studies in Baghdad and Rabat, and a BA in Philosophy (1982), he published several books of poetry, including *Athlaf Baidaa* (White Hooves, Paris, 1985), *Assamtu Ya'tee lel-i'teraaf* (Silence Comes to Confess, 1991) and *Azhar fee bi'ar* (Flowers in a Well, 2000), the latter two published in Cologne. After living in Iraq, Morocco, France, the US and Sweden for extended periods, he returned to Oman and is now editor-in-chief of *Albermaz*, a visual arts quarterly. ■ 'A Room at the End of the World' from *Gathering the Tide: An Anthology of Contemporary Arabian Gulf Poetry*, ed. Patty Paine, Jeff Lodge & Samia Touati (Ithaca Press, 2011), by permission of the author.

PAKISTAN
IMTIAZ DHARKER

Born in Pakistan, Imtiaz Dharker grew up a Muslim Calvinist in a Lahori household in Glasgow and eloped with a Hindu Indian to live in Bombay. She now lives between India, London and Wales. She is an accomplished artist and documentary film-maker, and has published four books with Bloodaxe, *Postcards from god* (including *Purdah*) (1997), *I speak for the devil* (2001), *The terrorist at my table* (2006) and *Leaving Fingerprints* (2009), all including her own drawings. ■ 'Honour killing' from *I speak for the devil* (Bloodaxe Books, 2001).

PALAU
ANONYMOUS
■ 'The Bungle-man' from *The Song Atlas: a book of world poetry*, ed. John Gallas (Carcanet Press, 2002).

PALESTINE
RAFEEF ZIADAH
'Rafeef's poetry demands to be heard. She is powerful, emotional and political. Please read her work and see her perform. You cannot then be indifferent to the Palestinian cause,' says Ken Loach of Rafeef Ziadah's poetry. Rafeef is a Palestinian refugee, poet and human rights activist based in London. Her performances of poems like 'We Teach Life, Sir' and 'Shades of Anger' went viral online within days of their release. She received an Ontario Arts Council Grant from the Word of Mouth programme to create her debut spoken-word album *Hadeel*. Since releasing her album, she has toured many countries, performing poetry and conducting educational workshops. ■ 'We Teach Life, Sir' by permission of the author.

PANAMA
LUCY CRISTINA CHAU
Born in Panama in 1971, Lucy Cristina Chau has received several awards, including the Central America 2010 Literature Award, National Poetry Award 2008, and National Youth Poetry Prize 2006. As a singer she has performed with folk bands Clavo y Canela (2000) and Trópico de Cáncer (2004). She has published two collections of poetry, *La Casa Rota* and *La Virgen de la Cueva*, and a book of short stories, *De la puerta hacia adentro*. ■ 'The Night' by permission of the author.

PAPUA NEW GUINEA
STEVEN WINDUO
Steven Winduo is a Papua New Guinean poet and scholar who teaches at the University of Papua New Guinea. He writes poetry, short stories,

essays, and reviews books which are of interest to him. He graduated from the University of Minnesota, in the United States of America, with a PhD in English (1998), returning as a visiting Professor in English at the University of Minnesota in 2007-08. He has published three poetry collections, *Lomo'ha I am in Spirits' Voice I Call* (1991), *Hembemba: Rivers of the Forest* (2000), *A Rower's Song* (2009) and *Detwan How? Poems in Tok Pisin and English* (2012), and a short story collection, *The Unpainted Mask* (2010). He speaks several languages, including English, Tokpisin (PNG pidgin), Nagum Boiken (mother tongue), and some Japanese. ■ 'Lomo'ha I am, in Spirits' Voice I Call' by permission of the author.

PARAGUAY
LIA COLOMBINO

Lia Colombino is the founder and an active member of the cultural collective Ediciones de la Ura. She is a coordinator of two writing workshops in Paraguay, one of which is part of the National University's Instituto Superior de Arte official curriculum. Her books include *Las cavidades ausentes* (2000), *Tierra de Secano* (2001), *Proyecto Auricular* (audio book with musician Javier Palma, 2006) and *(lupa)* (2009). She has taken part in several festivals in Latin America, most recently in Nicaragua, Chile and Cuba. ■ Extract from 'The Side' by permission of the author.

PERU
VICTORIA GUERRERO PEIRANO

Born in Lima in 1971, Victoria Guerrero Peirano is a poet, teacher and researcher. She has a PhD in Hispanic Literature from Boston University and has published several books of poems, including *El mar ese oscuro porvenir* (2002), *Ya nadie incendia el mundo* (2005) and more recently *Berlin* (2011). She has taken part in poetry festivals in cities like Berlin, Boston, Providence, Buenos Aires, Quito, Santiago and Lima, and is the editor of *Intermezzo Tropical*, a magazine specialising in literature and politics. She is a professor at Pontificia Universidad Católica del Perú in Lima, and has one cat. ■ 'The Cyclist' from *Berlin* (Intermezzo Tropical, Lima, 2011), by permission of the author.

PHILIPPINES
MARJORIE EVASCO

Marjorie Evasco has three published collections of poetry: *Dreamweavers* (1986); *Ochre Tones* (1999) and *Skin of Water* (2009). The first two won National Book Awards from the Manila Critics Circle. Her poems have been translated into Cebuano, Tagalog, Waray, German, Spanish, Japanese, Russian, Chinese, Kannada, Malay, Vietnamese, Romanian and Estonian. Her other books include *Six Women Poets* (1996), *A Life Shaped by Music* (2001) and *Ani: The Life and Art of Hermogena Borja Lungay* (2006), which won National Book Awards for oral history, biography and art, respectively, from the Manila Critics Circle. She is a SEA Write (South East Asia) Laureate of 2010. ■ 'Despedida' by permission of the author and Aria Edition, Inc.

POLAND
JACEK DEHNEL

Jacek Dehnel was born in Gdansk in 1980. He graduated in Polish studies at Warsaw University and lives in Warsaw's Powisle district. He has published six collections of poetry, including *Parallel Lives* and *Journey South*. His two novels, *Lala* and *Saturn*, have been widely translated, and are due to be published in the UK in 2012. He has translated poetry by writers including Philip Larkin, W.H. Auden, Osip Mandelstam, George Szirtes and Karlis Verdins, as well as song lyrics. He has won many major literary prizes in Poland, including the Koscielski Foundation Prize (2005) and the Paszport Polityki (2006, for *Lala*). ■ 'The Death of Oscar Wilde' from *Six Polish Poets*, ed. Jacek Dehnel (Arc Publications, 2009), by permission of the author.

PORTUGAL
ROSA ALICE BRANCO

Rosa Alice Branco is a poet, essayist, and translator with a PhD in Philosophy. She has published eleven volumes of poetry, including *Cattle of the Lord*, which won the prestigious 2009 Espiral Maior de Poesía Award, and *The World Does Not End in the Cold of Your Bones*, as well as three volumes of essays on perception, the last of these published in Brazil. Books of her poetry have appeared in Tunisia, Spain, Switzerland, Luxembourg, France, Brazil, Venezuela and Francophone Canada. Her poetry has appeared in many anthologies, including books published in Russia, Latvia, Hungary, Macedonia, Germany, Corsica and the US. ■ 'No Complaint Book' by permission of the author.

PUERTO RICO
VANESSA DROSS

Vanessa Dross is a writer, journalist, graphic designer and public relations professional from Puerto Rico. During the 70s, she was a contributor to the leading Puerto Rican literary journals, and she has served as president of the PEN Club, Puerto Rico Chapter. In 2008, she received the San Sebastián Prize for Literature. She currently serves on the editorial advisory board of the publishing division of the Institute of Puerto Rican Culture. Her radio programme, *Esto es cultura*, has been broadcast by one of the island's most important radio stations since August 2011. ■ 'The Absent Warrior' by permission of the author.

QATAR
SOAD AL KUWARI

Soad Al Kuwari was born in Doha and studied at Qatar University, and now works for the Ministry of Culture, Arts and Heritage. She has published five collections of poetry: *Lam Takun Rouhi* (2000), *Wareethat al-Saharaa* (2001), Bahtan ani al-Omr (2001), *Bab Jadeed li-Dukhoul* (2001) and *Malikat al-Jibal* (2004). Her work has appeared in many Arabic and local newspapers, and in several anthologies, including the seminal *Language for a New Century: Contemporary Poetry from the Middle East, Asia, and Beyond* (ed. Tina Chang, Nathalie Handal & Ravi Shankar, Norton, 2008). She has taken part in Qatar's Doha Cultural Festival and the al-Begrawiya Festival in Sudan, and in poetry festivals in the UAE, France, Yemen, Switzerland and Colombia. ■ 'The Flood' from *Gathering the Tide: An Anthology of Contemporary Arabian Gulf Poetry*, ed. Patty Paine, Jeff Lodge & Samia Touati (Ithaca Press, 2011), by permission of the author.

ROMANIA
DOINA IOANID

Born in 1968, Doina Ioanid studied French language and literature at the University of Bucharest, where she became a member of Mircea Cartarescu's writers' workshop Litere. The collective released an anthology, *Ferestre* (Windows, 1998), all the poets from which later became identified with Romania's 'Generation 2000'. She has published five collections of poetry, including her debut, *Duduca de martipan* (The Marzipan Damsel, 2000), and most recently, *Ritmuri de îmblânzit aricioaica* (Chants for Taming the Hedgehog Sow, 2010). Since 2005 she has worked as senior editor for *The Cultural Observer*, a leading Romanian weekly. ■ 'The Yellow Dog' from *Ritmuri de îmblînzit aricioaica* (Cartea Româneasca, Bucharest, 2010).

RUSSIAN FEDERATION
ILYA KAMINSKY

Ilya Kaminsky was born in Odessa, former Soviet Union in 1977, and arrived in the United States in 1993, when his family was granted asylum by the US government. He now writes in English, and his collection. Dancing in Odessa (Tupelo Press, 2004), won numerous awards including the Whiting Writer's Award, and the American Academy of Arts and Letters' Metcalf Award. He is also the co-editor of *The Ecco Anthology of International Poetry* (Harper Collins, 2011). He is the editor of the annual poetry journal *Poetry International* (San Diego), poetry editor of *Words Without Borders*, and professor of Contemporary World Poetry in the Master of Fine Arts Program in Creative Writing at San Diego State University. ■ 'Author's Prayer' from *Dancing in Odessa* (Tupelo Press, 2004), by permission of the author.

RWANDA
EDOUARD BAMPORIKI

Edouard Bamporiki is an award-winning filmmaker, actor, poet and peacemaker. As a young Rwandan artist, he has received national and international attention for his stories of hope, unity and reconciliation. Born in a small village in the Western province, he was educated in Rwandan schools, and lives in the capital city of Kigali. His feature debut in Lee Isaac Chung's *Munyurangabo* yielded him a Best Actor nomination in Cannes. In 2008, he wrote, directed, starred in, and produced *Long Coat*, winner of first prize in African film at the Focus Future Film Festival in New York. In 2011, he appeared in *Kinyarwanda* (as Emmanuel) alongside Cassandra Freeman. He performs his poetry in the national football stadium each year for Genocide Memorial Day, and recently published his first book of poetry and memoir, *Icyaha Kuri Bo, Ikimwaro Kuri Jye*, drawing on his experience as a child during the Rwandese genocide. ■ Extract from 'A Cock Crows in Rwanda' by permission of the author.

SAINT KITTS AND NEVIS
ISHAQ IMRUH BAKARI

Ishaq Imruh Bakari is a writer and filmmaker born in St Kitts. He has published two poetry collection, *Sounds & Echoes* (Karnak House, 1980) and *Secret Lives* (Bogle-L'Ouverture, 1986). From 1999 to 2004 he was Festival Director of the Zanzibar International Film Festival. His films include *African Tales – Short Film Series* (2005/2008), *Blue Notes and*

Exiled Voices (1991), *The Mark of the Hand* (1986) and *Riots and Rumours of Riots* (1981). He lives and works between the UK and East Africa. He is a Senior Lecturer in Film and Media Studies at the University of Winchester. ■ 'Haiti is once again...' by permission of the author.

SAINT LUCIA
DEREK WALCOTT

Born in Saint Lucia in 1930, Derek Walcott is not only the foremost Caribbean poet writing today (as well as a dramatist and painter) but a major figure in world literature, recognised with the award of the Nobel Prize in Literature in 1992 'for a poetic *œuvre* of great luminosity, sustained by a historical vision, the outcome of a multicultural commitment'. Most of his work explores the Caribbean cultural experience, the history, landscape and lives of its multiracial people, fusing folk culture and oral tales with the classical, avant-garde and English literary tradition. He was awarded the Queen's Medal for Poetry in 1988, and now divides his time between homes in Saint Lucia and New York. ■ 'As John to Patmos' from *Collected Poems 1948-1984* (Faber & Faber, 1986), by permission of the publisher.

ST VINCENT & THE GRENADINES
PHILIP NANTON

Philip Nanton is a sociologist by training, but also works as a freelance writer, poet and producer of radio documentaries. He lectured at the University of Birmingham in the UK for many years before relocating to Barbados in 1999 where he held various positions at UWI and at St George's University, Grenada. As a critic he has published widely in journals on many aspects of Caribbean literature. His recent publications include editing a commemoration of the life and work of Frank Collymore, *Remembering the Sea*, and the spoken word CD *Island Voices from St Christopher & the Barracudas*, a sequence of dramatic monologues which he both wrote and performed. ■ 'Douglas' Dinky Death' from *Cave Hill Literary Journal*, 6 (December 2004), by permission of the author.

SAMOA
TUSIATA AVIA

Tusiata Avia is a poet, performer and children's writer. She has published two books of poetry, *Wild Dogs Under My Skirt* (2004) and *Bloodclot* (2009), and two children's books, *The Song* and *Mele and the fofo* (2001). Tusiata is well known for her dynamic performance poetry and has a one-woman poetry theatre show – also called *Wild Dogs Under My Skirt* – which has toured in Austria, Germany, Hawai'i, New Zealand, Australia, American Samoa, Bali and Russia. She has held a number of writing residencies, including the Fulbright Pacific Writers residency at the University of Hawai'i. At present she lives in New Zealand with her four-year-old daughter, Sepela. ■ 'Return to Paradise' from 'Wild Dogs Under My Skirt' (Victoria University Press, 2004).

AMERICAN SAMOA
SIA FIGIEL

Born in 1967 in Matautu Tai, Samoa, Sia Figiel is a novelist, poet, and painter. She grew up amidst the traditional Samoan singing and poetry which heavily influenced her writing. She has travelled in Europe and held writers' residencies at the University of the South Pacific, Suva, and University of Technology, Sydney. She won the Polynesian Literary Competition in 1994 and her novel *Where We Once Belonged* was awarded the 1997 Commonwealth Writers' Prize for fiction, South East Asia/South Pacific region. Her work has been translated into French, German, Catalan, Danish, Spanish, Swedish, Turkish and Portuguese. ■ 'The Daffodils from a Native's Perspective' by permission of the author.

SAN MARINO
MILENA ERCOLANI

Milena Ercolani was born in San Marino in 1963 and has written poetry since childhood. She co-founded the cultural and literary association, La Sammarina, in 2011, and is currently its president, and has been a member of the Sammarinese cultural academy, Le Tre Castella, since 2005. In 2010 she represented her country at the 20th International Festival of Poetry in Medellín and in 2012 she took part in the International Festival of Lima. ■ 'A Woman Is a Woman' by permission of the author.

SÃO TOMÉ AND PRÍNCIPE
CONCEIÇÃO LIMA

Born in 1961, Maria da Conceição de Deus Lima (known as Conceição Lima), is a Santomean poet from the town of Santana in São Tomé, one of two islands in the small nation of São Tomé and Príncipe in the Gulf of Guinea. Her poetry has been published in newspapers, magazines and anthologies in several countries. She is a postcolonial writer, one of the few poets who came of age after the independence of her country in 1975. She started writing poems as a teenager and, in 1979, at the age of 19, travelled to Angola where she took part in the Sixth Conference of Afro-Asian Writers. ■ 'Cataclysm and Songs' by permission of the Poetry Translation Centre.

SAUDI ARABIA
ASHJAN AL HENDI

Born in Jeddah, Ashjan Al Hendi gained her doctorate in the Department of Language and Arabic Literature at the School of Oriental and African Studies of the University of London. She has published three collections of poetry, *Dream Smell of Rain* (1996), *Rain Has a Taste of Lemon* (2007) and *Riq al-Ghaimat* (2010), as well as a book of literary criticism, *Engagement with Heritage in the Contemporary Poetry of Women in the Arabian Peninsula* (1996). Her poems have been translated into French, German, Spanish and Turkish. She is currently an assistant professor in the Arabic Department of the Faculty of Arts and Humanities in King Abdulaziz University, Jeddah. ■ 'In Search of the Other' from *Gathering the Tide: An Anthology of Contemporary Arabian Gulf Poetry*, ed. Patty Paine, Jeff Lodge & Samia Touati (Ithaca Press, 2011), by permission of the author.

SENEGAL
DIDIER AWADI

Didier Awadi is one of the most prominent figures in Francophone West African hip hop, and RFI World Music award winner in 2003. As a founding member of Positive Black Soul (PBS) with Duggy Tee, he toured the world contributing to the international popularity of Hip Hop Galsen. He is a pioneer and trailblazer of a music genre which has become hugely popular with the youth of Africa. As an artist and entrepreneur, his talents range from artistic production to radio and TV presenting. He also runs his own studio, label and rehearsal space, Studio Sankara. ■ 'In My Dream' by permission of the author.

SERBIA
ANA RISTOVIĆ

Ana Ristović was born in 1972 in Belgrade, and studied comparative literature at the philological faculty in Belgrade. She has published six books of poetry: *Snovidna voda* (Dreamwater, 1994, Branko Radicevic Prize), *Uže od peska* (Rope of Sand, 1997), *Zabava za dokone kceri*

(Party for Lazybones Daughters, 1999, Branko Miljkovic Prize), *Život na razglednici* (Life on the postcard, 2003), *Oko nule* (Round the Zero, 2006), and *P.S. – Selected Poems* (2009), winner of the Milica Stojadinovic Srpkinja Prize in 2010. She won the Hubert Burda Prize for young East European poets in 2005. She has translated 18 books of poetry and prose from Slovenian into Serbian, and her own poems have been translated into English, German, Slovak, Macedonian, Slovenian, Polish, Bulgarian, Swedish and Finnish, She lives in Belgrade. ■ 'Circling Zero' from *Zabava za dokone kceri* (Rad, Belgrade, 2000).

SEYCHELLES
ANTOINE ABEL

Antoine Abel was born in 1934 on Mahé, the main island of the Seychelles. He went to school there and studied at the universities of Reading and Bristol in Britain. He returned to teach in Victoria, the capital. He has written short stories and collected oral pieces for publication, and published his first poetry collection in 1969. ■ 'Your Country' from *Contes et Poemes de Seychelles* (Paris, 1977).

SIERRA LEONE
SYL CHENEY-COKER

Syl Cheney-Coker is a poet and novelist. He has published several volumes of poetry, including *Stone Child & Other Poems* (2008), and has just completed his latest collection, *Farewell to Dreams & Other Poems*. He won the Commonwealth Writer's Prize (Africa Region best book) in 1991 for his novel *The Last Harmattan of Alusine Dunbar*, which was also named as 'One of the 20th Century's 100 best Africa books' (in all categories) by an international panel of judges. In 2000 he was named the first International Parliament of Writers' writer-in-residence in the USA, under their cities of asylum programme, and has held other residencies and taught at universities in Africa, Asia and the USA. His poems have been translated into Dutch, French, Greek, Italian, Portuguese, Persian, Russian, Spanish and Tagalog. ■ 'On the 50th Anniversary of Amnesty International' from *Farewell to Dreams*, by permission of the author.

SINGAPORE
ALVIN PANG

Born in Singapore in 1972, Alvin Pang is a poet, writer and editor who has been featured in major festivals, anthologies and journals around the world, and translated into over fifteen languages. He was Singapore's

Young Artist of the Year for Literature in 2005 and received the Singapore Youth Award in 2007 for Arts and Culture. A founding director of The Literary Centre in Singapore, he is also managing editor of an internationally circulated public policy journal. His publications include *City of Rain* (2003), *Over There: Poems from Singapore and Australia* (co-edited with John Kinsella, 2008) and *Tumasik: Contemporary Writing from Singapore* (USA, 2009). His latest book is *When the Barbarians Arrive*, a volume of new and selected poems, from Arc in the UK. ■ 'When the Barbarians Arrive' from *When the Barbarians Arrive* (Arc Publications, 2012), by permission of the publisher.

SLOVAKIA
KATARINA KUCBELOVÁ

Born in 1979 in Banská Bystrica, Katarina Kucbelová is considered to be one of Slovakia's best young poets. She obtained an MA in screenwriting at the Academy of Dramatic Art, Bratislava, and works as a cultural manager. She has published two books of poetry, *Duals* (2003) and *Sport* (2006), and the long poem *Little Big City* (2008). In 2006 she founded – and is also director of – the prestigious Slovak literary award for fiction, Anasoft Litera. A selection of her work is included in the Arc anthology *A Fine Line: New Poetry from Eastern and Central Europe* (2004). She lives in Bratislava. ■ Extract from *Little Big City* by permission of the author.

SLOVENIA
TAJA KRAMBERGER

Taja Kramberger was born in Ljubljana, Slovenia in 1970. She is a poet, translator, essayist and historical anthropologist. She has a PhD in historical anthropology from the University of Primorska. She is Editor-in-Chief of *Monitor ISH-Review of Humanities and Social Sciences* (2001–03), in 2004 retitled *Monitor ZSA-Review for Historical, Social and Other Anthropologies* (2004–10). Her first book of poems, *Marzipan*, was released in 1997, and she has since published eight further collections: *The Sea Says* in 1999; the German-language *Counter-current* in a collectors' edition in 2002; in 2004, *Mobilisations*, in four languages; *The Velvet Indigo* in 2004; *Everyday talks* in 2006; *Opus quinque dierum* in 2009; a book of blackout poetry from the constitution of the Republic of Slovenia; and in 2011, *From the Edge of a Cliff*. Her work has been translated into several European languages. ■ 'Every dead one has a name' tr. Špela Drnovšek Zorko from *Z roba klifa* (CSK, Ljubljana, 2011), by permission of the author.

SOLOMON ISLANDS
JULLY MAKINI

Jully Makini was born in Gizo in the Western Province, Solomon Islands, and is a graduate of the University of the South Pacific. She began writing seriously in 1980 after attending the first Solomon Islands Women Writers' Workshop, and worked for a time with the USP Solomon Islands Centre as an editor, helping to produce the first collection of Solomon Islands women's writing, *Mi Mere*. Her books include the collections *Civilised Girl* (1981), *Praying Parents* (1986, whose title was adopted as the name of a women's association), and *Flotsam & Jetsam* (2007). Her poetry ranges widely, addressing issues such as the difficulty of balancing motherhood with other commitments, the dark side of human relationships, global and local challenges to peace and environmental sustainability, and the struggle of developing societies dealing with the impact of globalisation. ■ 'Praying Parents' from *Praying Parents* (Aruligo Book Centre, Honiara, 1986), by permission of the author.

SOMALIA
ABDULLAHI BOTAAN HASSAN

Abdullahi Botaan Hassan 'Kurweyne' was born in Somalia in 1969 and started composing poems as a teenager. He came to London in 1998 and has become well known for his poems based on his experiences there. In 2003 he founded Soohan Somali Arts which works with Somali children in primary schools in Camden. His work incorporates Somali language and traditions, educating the public in the rich creativity, arts and culture of Somalia. He has led inspirational workshops described by students as 'unforgettable' and 'supremely important'. ■ 'Central London' by permission of the author.

SOUTH AFRICA
KATHARINE KILALEA

Katharine Kilalea moved from South Africa to London in 2005 to study for an MA in Creative Writing at the University of East Anglia. Her first book, *One Eye'd Leigh*, was shortlisted for the Costa Poetry Award and longlisted for the Dylan Thomas Prize for writers under 30. She has received Arts Council Awards for poetry, and her poems have appeared in publications including *Carcanet's New Poetries V*, *Best British Poetry 2011* and the *The Forward Book of Poetry 2010*. ■ 'You were a bird' from *One Eye'd Leigh* (Carcanet Press, 2009), by permission of the publisher.

SPAIN
ELI TOLARETXIPI

Eli Tolaretxipi lives and works in San Sebastian, Spain. She is a poet, a poetry translator and a teacher at the Official Language School. Her debut poetry collection, *Amor Muerto – Naturaleza muerta* (1999), was followed by *Los lazos del número* (2002) and *El especulador* (2009), with *Edgar* forthcoming from Trea. Philip Jenkins' bilingual edition of a selection of her poems, *Still Life with Loops*, was published by Arc in 2008. The poets she has translated into Spanish include Sylvia Plath, Elizabeth Bishop, Patti Smith, Tess Gallagher and Menna Elfyn. She has taken part in poetry readings in Europe, the UK, Canada and South America. ■ Extract from 'Still Life with Loops' from *Still Life with Loops* (Arc Publications, 2008), by permission of the publisher.

SRI LANKA
MINOLI SALGADO

Minoli Salgado is a writer and Senior Lecturer in English at the University of Sussex. She is the author of *Writing Sri Lanka: Literature, Resistance and the Politics of Place* (Routledge, 2007). Her literary work has been published in journals such as *Wasafiri*, *Short Story* and *South Asian Review*, as well as in *Bridges: A Global Anthology of Short Stories* (2012). She serves on the editorial board of *Wasafiri*, the *Journal of Commonwealth Literature* and the *Journal of Caribbean Literature*. ■ 'Patriot Games' by permission of the author.

SUDAN
AL-SADDIQ AL-RADDI

Al-Saddiq Al-Raddi is a charismatic Sudanese poet who became the youngest member of the Sudanese Writers' Union in 1986, at the age of 17. His poetry is sensitive to the complexities of his position as an African poet writing in Arabic, and attempts to articulate these contradictions. He uses imagery in a way that inspires hope for his country. His first two books, *Ghina' al-'Uzlah* (Songs of Solitude), and *Matahat al-Sultan* (The Sultan's Labyrinth), were published simultaneously in 1996. His third collection, *Aqasi Shashat al-Isgha'* (The Limits of the Screen of Listening), appeared in 2000 and a volume of his collected poems was published in 2009. He has worked extensively with The Poetry Translation Centre who have translated, recorded and published a selection of his work (*Poems*, 2008). ■ 'Nothing' from *Poems*, tr. Sarah Maguire & Atef Alshaer (Poetry Translation Centre, 2008), reprinted by permission of the publisher.

SURINAME
JIT NARAIN

Born in Livorno in 1948, a village just south of Suriname's capital Paramaribo, Jit Narain grew up in a close-knit Hindustani family. He studied medicine in the Netherlands and established himself as a general practitioner in 1979, in The Hague. In 1991 he returned to Suriname, where he now runs a polyclinic in the Saramacca district, devoting his spare time to building a cultural centre at the back of his house. During his years in the Netherlands, Jit Narain came to be the godfather of literature in Sarnami, the language of the Hindustani Surinamese. In 1978 he published his first collection of poetry, titled *Dal bhat chatni* (Rice, yellow peas, chutney), the staple diet of peasant Hindustanis. In his most recent poems he reflects upon life as a limited lease on time, a sordid affair, but full of colour and hope, even in the face of hardship and death. ■ 'Working all day, dreaming at night' from *Agni ke yad yad ke rakhi: Ter herinnering aan Agni de as van de herinnering* (SSN, 1991), by permission of the author.

SWAZILAND
MSANDI KABABA

Msandi Kababa (Sandile Nxumalo) is a popular and much loved poet in Swaziland, also known as 'Imbongi'. His stage performances have been described as captivating and heart-wrenching. He recites poems about peace, suffering, hope, dreams, traditions and African heritage, with particular reference to urgent social, traditional and cultural issues. In the face of political turmoil and a horrific AIDS epidemic that has swept the African continent, Msandi's humour and optimism creates an appeal that crosses generations. He performs in the Siswati language of Swaziland as well as in English. ■ 'Nayibamba Bophezu Kwemkhono (Hard Working Women)' by permission of the author.

SWEDEN
LAURA WIHLBORG

Laura Wihlborg is a poet and slam artist from Sweden. Her poems are about everyday situations, worries and thoughts, always with a dark and comic twist. She won the Swedish national poetry slam championship of 2008, and the following year took part in the Poetry Slam World Cup in Paris and won the Slam!Revue competition at the Internationales Literaturfestival in Berlin. In 2010, together with eight other European poets and a musician, she toured in Europe with a poetry show called *Smoke and Mirrors*. She is currently studying radio production at Stockholm Academy of Dramatic Arts. ■ 'Google Search Results' by permission of the author.

SWITZERLAND
VALERIA MELCHIORETTO
Valeria Melchioretto is the author of *The End of Limbo* (Salt, 2007), and *Podding Peas* (Hearing Eye, 2004). In 2005 she won the New Writing Ventures Award for Poetry and the following year received a bursary from the Arts Council of England. Her poems have appeared in many magazines in the UK and Ireland as well as in anthologies such as *Women's Work* (Seren Books, 2008). She has also published short stories and reviews, and was a Hawthornden Fellow in 2007. She was born in Winterthur, Switzerland and now lives in London. ■ 'The Suitcase' from *The End of Limbo* (Salt Publishing, 2007), by permission of the author.

SYRIA
RASHA OMRAN
Rasha Omran was born in Tartus, Syria, in 1964. She has a degree in Arabic literature from Damascus University, and is the director of Al-Sindiyan festival of culture. Since 1997 she has published three collections of poetry. ■ 'Ophelia, As I Want To Be' from *The Wolf*, 22 (November 2009), by permission of the author.

TAJIKISTAN
FARZANEH KHOJANDI
Born in the remote Khojand province of Tajikistan in 1964, Farzaneh Khojandi is widely regarded as the most exciting woman poet writing in Persian (Farsi, Tajik) today. She has a huge following in Iran and Afghanistan as well as in Tajikistan. Her frequently playful and witty poetry draws on the rich tradition of Persian literature in an often subversive and humorous way. She has published many volumes of poetry, and her poems have been translated into English by Jo Shapcott and Narguess Farzad for The Poetry Translation Centre. ■ 'Behind the Mass of Green' from *Poems* (The Poetry Translation Centre, 2008).

TANZANIA
HAJI GORA HAJI
Haji Gora Haji is a poet, a writer and a minstrel whose art remained largely unknown to a wider Swahili public until the publication of his

book *Kimbunga* (The Hurricane) in 1994. Born in Zanzibar, on the island of Tumbatu, in 1933, he received an Islamic education from a Qur'an school, his family being too poor to pay for a public primary school. His uncles trained him to be a fisherman, and for many years he earned his living from the sea, as a sailor on small sail-driven cargo boats, as a clove shipper, and as a porter on the docks. Taught how to compose Taarab songs during the 1970s, he went on to write songs which have become famous in many African countries. He has worked in every genre of Swahili literature, from songs, stories and lengthy epics to three-line riddles, from folk tales handed down by oral tradition to a full-length novel, and has published a succession of children's books. He is currently working on the world's first Tumbatu dialects dictionary. ■ 'Wonders' by permission of the author.

THAILAND
CHIRANAN PITPREECHA

Chiranan Pitpreecha was born in Thailand in 1955. She was a well-known figure in the 1970s student movement in Thailand. Following the violent suppression in 1976, she, along with thousands of Thai students, fled to the jungle and joined the Communist insurrection. Almost immediately after she returned from the jungle in 1981 – under the protection of amnesty law – her poem, 'Cracked Pebble' was selected as 'The Best Poem of 1981' by P.E.N. International, Thailand. In 1989, her poetry book, *The Missing Leaf*, won the Southeast Asian Write Award. Chiranan Pitpreecha is one of Thailand's best known authors, and has produced a wide range of writings for Thai periodicals and newspapers, from poetry, history and travel articles to social comment-aries. Her works have been translated into English, French, German, Japanese and Malay. ■ 'The Defiance of a Flower' by permission of the author.

TIMOR-LESTE
XANANA GUSMÃO

Xanana Gusmão was the first President of the newly liberated Demo-cratic Republic of Timor-Leste (East Timor), from 2002 to 2007, and has been his country's fourth and current Prime Minister since 2007. Born in 1946 in what was then Portuguese Timor, he had to leave school at 15, working at various unskilled jobs while continuing his education at night school. During the 1970s he joined FRETILIN (Revolutionary Front for an Independent East Timor), and was im-prisoned by the rival UDT faction for a short time in 1975. He was briefly Press Secretary of FRETILIN when independence was declared some months later, immediately before the country was invaded by Indonesia. In 1986, he helped created the National Council of Maubere Resistance (CNRM), the umbrella organisation against Indonesian rule in East Timor, and was able to act as a resistance leader and spokesman for several years. Captured in 1992, he spent seven years in prison, where he was visited by UN representatives and dignatories including Nelson Mandela, and finally released when the international peace-keeping force interceded to end the Indonesian military's reign of terror. In 2008 he survived a possible assassination or coup attempt when his motorcade came under gunfire an hour after President José Ramos-Horta was shot in the stomach. Xanana Gusmão has written poetry since his youth, and continued to write through the years of resistance against Indonesian occupation and later while in prison in Indonesia. ■ 'Grandfather Crocodile' from *Mar Meu* (Granito, Oporto, 2002), by permission of the author.

TOGO
JÉMIMA FIADJOE-PRINCE AGBODJAN
Born in 1950 in Batié, Burkina Faso, Jémima Fiadjoe-Prince Agbodjan studied medicine at the University of Dakar and in France at the University of Lille. She works as a paediatrician in Lomé, Togo. ■ 'Thank You for Being a Woman' from *A Rain of Words: A Bilingual Anthology of Women's Poetry in Francophile Africa*, ed. Irène Assiba d'Almeida (University of Virginia Press, 2009), by permission of the author.

TONGA
KARLO MILA
Karlo Mila is a poet, mother, researcher, columnist and writer. Born in New Zealand to a Tongan father, she went to school and worked in Tonga for a number of years. Her collection *Dream Fish Floating* (Huia Publishers), won New Zealand's Best first book of poetry New Zealand literary award for 2006. *A Well Written Body* (2008) focused on the passing of Tonga's monarch, political upheaval and change. She is currently a Postdoctoral Fellow at the University of Otago. ■ 'Oceania' by permission of the author.

TRINIDAD & TOBAGO
ANTHONY JOSEPH
Anthony Joseph is a Trinidadian-born poet, novelist, musician and lecturer. He has published four poetry collections: *Desafinado* (1994),

Teragaton (1998), *Bird Head Son* (2009) and *Rubber Orchestras* (2011). His hybrid novel, *The African Origins of UFOs*, appeared in 2006. Joseph's written work and performance fuse his Caribbean background with an experimental aesthetic. He has been described as 'the leader of the black avant-garde in Britain' and cites his main influences as 'liminalism, surrealism, Jazz syncopation and the rhythms of Trinidadian speech and music'. He performs and tours internationally accompanied by his band The Spasm Band, and has released three critically acclaimed albums with them. He is also a lecturer in Creative Writing at Birkbeck College, University of London. ■ 'Buddha' from *The African Origins of UFOs* (Salt Publishing, 2006), by permission of the publisher.

TUNISIA
AMINA SAÏD
Amina Saïd was born in Tunis in 1953, and has lived in Paris for many years. As well as fourteen collections of poems, she has published two volumes of Tunisian folktales. Her literary imagination draws primarily from French and Arabic sources, and from Mediterranean landscapes. She has also translated seven novels and short stories by the major Filipino writer, Francisco Sionil José, from English into French. She has received several literary prizes in France, and her work has been the subject of critical studies, and translated widely, in particular into Spanish and English (*The Present Tense of the World: Poems 2000-2009*, tr. Marilyn Hacker, Black Widow Press, Boston, 2011). The Australian composer Richard Mills used her poetry for his work *Songlines of the Heart's Desire* (2007). ■ 'Each day...' from *L'absence l'inachievé* (Editions de la Différence, Paris, 2009) by permission of the author.

TURKEY
RONI MARGULIES
Roni Margulies was born in Istanbul in 1955, where he studied at the English High School for Boys and at Robert College. He moved to London in 1972 to study at university and has since split his time between the UK and Turkey. Although he has a PhD in Economics, he has never worked as an economist. He has published eight books of poetry as well as Turkish translations of selected poetry by Ted Hughes, Philip Larkin and Yehuda Amichai. ■ 'The Slipper' from Poetry International Web, first published in *Adam Sanat*, 223 (2004), by permission of the author.

TURKMENISTAN
AK WELSAPAR
Ak Welsapar was born in 1956 in the former Soviet Republic of Turkmenistan. After six years of membership, he was excluded from the Soviet Writers' Association in 1987 following his publication of investigative articles about major ecological problems in Turkmenistan. He left his home country in 1993 and now lives in Sweden, where he is a member of the Swedish Writers' Association. He has also been an honorary member of the International PEN-Club since 1993. He has published 18 books and received many national and international awards. He writes in Russian, Turkmen and Swedish. ■ 'The Night Stars Dropped from the Sky' by permission of the author.

TUVALU
SELINA TUSITALA MARSH
Selina Tusitala Marsh is a poet and scholar of Samoan, Tuvaluan, Scottish and French descent. Now a lecturer in Maori and Pacific literary studies, she is a strong advocate of Pacific poetry and literature, and is the force behind *Pasifika Poetry*, an online hub celebrating the poetry of the peoples of the Pacific. She published her first collection of poetry, *Fast Talking PI* (pronounced pee-eye), in 2009. The book won the 2010 NZSA Jessie Mackay Best First Book Award for Poetry, made the top 5 bestsellers list shortly after publication, and is published in the UK in 2012. It reflects her focus on issues affecting Pacific communities in New Zealand and indigenous peoples around the world, including the challenges and triumphs of being *afakasi* (mixed race). ■ 'Googling Tusitala' from *Fast Talking PI* (Arc Publications, 2012), by permission of the publisher.

UGANDA
NICK MAKOHA
Nick Makoha was born in Uganda, and fled the country with his mother during the Idi Amin dictatorship. He then lived in Kenya and Saudi Arabia before settling in London. His writing deals with displacement, loneliness and the impact of forced exile. His first pamphlet, *The Lost Collection of an Invisible Man*, was published by flipped eye. His one-man show, *My Father & Other Superheroes*, exploring how a man was raised by pop culture in the absence of his father, was showcased at Stratford Theatre East and toured to Olso with the British Council. He was one of ten UK poets selected for Spread the Word's Complete Works writer development programme,

and his poems are included in *Ten: new poets* (Bloodaxe Books/Spread the Word, 2010). ■ 'Who do they say I am' by permission of the author.

UKRAINE
SERHIY ZHADAN

Serhiy Zhadan is the most popular poet of the post-independence generation in Ukraine. He began writing during the era of political upheavals in the Soviet Union, using poetry as a way to capture the essence of a post-Socialist society. His awards include the Hubert Burda Prize for young East European poets. He works as a translator and has translated the works of such poets as Paul Celan and Charles Bukowski. Aside from his literary work, Serhiy is also an organiser of poetry and art festivals. He recites his poems with the band *Sobaki v Kosmosi* (Dogs in Space). ■ 'The Sell-Out Poets of the 60s' by permission of Folio.

UNITED ARAB EMIRATES
DHABIYA KHAMIS

Dhabiya Khamis is an author, translator and diplomat with over 45 published works, including 18 poetry collections and four works of fiction. She studied modern Arabic literature and anthropology at the University of London, where she also edited the literary magazine *Awarq*, and received her Master's degree in Arabic Literature from the American University in Cairo. She was a diplomat with the Arab League (1992-2009), and served as UAE Ambassador to India (2004-2005). Her poetry, prose, and literary criticism have been translated into German, Spanish, English and French. ■ 'The History of That Tree' from *Gathering the Tide: An Anthology of Contemporary Arabian Gulf Poetry*, ed. Patty Paine, Jeff Lodge & Samia Touati (Ithaca Press, 2011), by permission of the author and translators.

URUGUAY
MELISA MACHADO

Melisa Machado was born in Durazno, Uruguay, in 1966. She is a poet, performer, journalist, art consultant, dancer and a physical therapist. She has worked as an assistant editor and as an editor in several national publications. She has published five books of poetry, collected under the title *Rituals* (Montevideo, 2011). Her poems and short stories have been included in anthologies like *El Amplio Jardín* (published by the Colombian embassy and Ministry of Education,

2005) and *Nada es igual después de la poesía: cincuenta poetas uruguayos del medio siglo* (Ministry of Education and Archivo General de la Nación, 2005). She is now writing a book about Uruguayan artist, Marcelo Legrand, and writing articles for culture magazine *Dossier* on dance, literature and plastic arts. ■ 'Marjal' by permission of the author.

USA
KAY RYAN

Kay Ryan was born in California in 1945. She was the USA's 16th Poet Laureate from 2008 to 2010. Her work remained largely unrecognised until the 1990s, when some of her poems were anthologised and her first reviews in national journals were published. She received the Ruth Lilly Poetry Prize in 2004 and the Pulitzer Prize in 2011 for *The Best of It*, a collection of selected and new poems. She has published ten volumes of poetry, including the British volume, *Odd Blocks* (Carcanet Press, 2011). In 2011 she was named a MacArthur Fellow. She has long lived in Marin County, California. ■ 'Flamingo Watching' from *Flamingo Watching* (Copper Beech Press 1994) copyright © 1994 Kay Ryan, by permission of the author.

UZBEKISTAN
HAMID ISMAILOV

Born in Kyrgyzstan in 1954, Hamid Ismailov is an Uzbek journalist and writer. He was forced to flee Uzbekistan in 1992 and his works are banned there. He currently lives in the UK, where he has worked with the BBC World Service as writer-in-residence. His poetry collections include *Sad* (Garden, 1987) and *Pustynya* (Desert, 1988), and he has also published visual poetry. *Post Faustum* (1990), *Kniga Otsutstvi* (1992). His books have been published in several languages, including Uzbek, Russian, French, German and Turkish. ■ 'Garden' by permission of the author.

VANUATU
GRACE MERA MOLISA

Grace Mera Molisa (1946-2002) was a ni-Vanatu politician, poet, and campaigner for women's equality in politics. She was known as a 'a vanguard for Melanesian culture' and a voice of the ni-Vanuatu, especially women. She has also been described as one of the Pacific's 'leading public intellectuals and activists'. She was the first woman from her country to gain a university degree, a bachelor of arts degree at the University of the South Pacific in 1977. She was spokeswoman for Prime Minister Walter Lini from 1987 to 1991, and created Vanuatu's National Arts Festival. She spoke five languages. ■ 'Delightful Acquiescence' from *Black Stone* (South Pacific Creative Arts Society, 1983/1991), by permission of the publisher.

VENEZUELA
BEVERLY PÉREZ REGO

Beverly Pérez Rego is the author of five volumes of poetry, *Artes del vidrio* (1992), *Libro de cetrería* (1994), *Providencia* (1998), *Grimorio* (2002) and *Escurana* (2004), collected in 2006 as *Poesía reunida*. Her poems have appeared in numerous anthologies, and she has also translated works by Louise Glück and Mark Strand. She received the Rafael Bolívar Coronado Biennial Literary Prize in Poetry and the Elías David Curiel Poetry Award. Based in Caracas, she is currently living in Iowa City, attending the University of Iowa. ■ 'Escurana', originally published in Spanish in *Poesía reunida* (Monte Ávila Editores Latinoamericana, Caracas, 2006), by permission of the author.

VIETNAM
NGUYEN BAO CHAN

Nguyen Bao Chan was born in 1969. She is a member of the Vietnam Writers Association. Her book *Burned River* received a Vietnamese Literary and Arts Union award in 1994. Her other collections include *Barefoot in Winter* (Youth Publications, 1999) and *Thorns in Dreams* (Vietnamese-English bilingual edition, Gioi Publishers, 2010). Her work has been included in many anthologies, including *The Defiant Muse: Vietnamese Feminist Poems from Antiquity to the Present* (Women's Publishing House, Hanoi, 2007). She has read her poetry at literary festivals in Vietnam and abroad, most recently at the international poetry festival of Medellín in Colombia. She currently works for Vietnam Television as an editor in arts and culture. ■ 'Memory' from *Thorns in Dreams* (Gioi Publishers, 2010), by permission of the author.

BRITISH VIRGIN ISLANDS
OREN HODGE

Oren Hodge is a native of Tortola, the largest and most populated of the British Virgin Islands. He picked up the art of poetry and song writing while away at school because he found a sense of relief in writing. His writing was done in secret, until a friend and fellow poet encouraged him to publish a few of his poems in the local newspaper. His poetry has appeared in the Caribbean poetry anthology *Virgin*

Islands: Callaloo, a book celebrating the diverse writing styles of poets in the region. ■ 'Sharks in Sharp Suits' by permission of the author.

US VIRGIN ISLANDS
PATRICIA HARKINS-PIERRE
Patricia Harkins-Pierre is a Professor of English, and Chair of EHMLA (English, Humanities, Modern Languages and Philosophy) at the University of the Virgin Islands in the United States Virgin Islands. She gained her PhD in Creative Writing at the University of Southern Mississippi, where she studied with Derek Walcott, and spent a term working with Mervyn Morris at the University of West Indies campus in Jamaica. She has been teaching Creative Writing at UVI for over 20 years. Examples of her poems with Caribbean settings appear in *The Caribbean Writer* and in *Seasoning for the Mortar: Virgin Islanders Writing*. ■ 'Post-Hurricane Letter to the Author of "Easter Wings"' by permission of the author.

YEMEN
NABILA AZZUBAIR
Born in al-Hagara, Yemen, in 1964, Nabila Azzubair gained a BA in Psychology from the University of Sanaa. She has published five books of poetry and two novels, including *It's My Body* (2000), awarded the Naguib Mahfouz Medal for Literature in 2002. Her work has appears in the seminal anthology, *Language for a New Century*. ■ 'The Closed Game' from *Language for a New Century: Contemporary Poetry from the Middle East, Asia, and Beyond* (ed. Tina Chang, Nathalie Handal & Ravi Shankar, Norton, 2008).

ZAMBIA
KAYO CHINGONYI
Kayo Chingonyi was born in Zambia in 1987 and came to the UK in 1993. He studied English Literature at the University of Sheffield, completing an undergraduate dissertation on Saul Williams and co-founding a poetry night called *Word Life*. He is an emerging writer-in-residence at Kingston University, and works as a freelance writer, performer and creative writing tutor. His poems have appeared in such publications as *Verbalized* (British Council, 2010), *Paradise By Night* (Booth-Clibborn Editions, 2010), *Clinic II* (Clinic Presents & Egg Box Publishing, 2011), *The Best British Poetry 2011*, *The Salt Book of Younger Poets* (both Salt Publishing, 2011), *Bedford Square 5* (Ward Wood Publishing, 2011) and *Out of Bounds* (Bloodaxe Books,

2012). His debut pamphlet of poems, *Some Bright Elegance*, was published by Salt Publishing in 2012. ■ 'calling a spade a spade' from Poetry International Web (2011), by permission of the author.

ZIMBABWE
TOGARA MUZANENHAMO

Togara Muzanenhamo was born in 1975 in Lusaka, Zambia, to Zimbabwean parents. He grew up on his family's farm in Zimbabwe and studied Business Administration in France and The Netherlands. After his studies he returned to Zimbabwe and worked as a journalist, then moved to an organisation dedicated to developing African screenplays. He eventually came to England to pursue an MA in creative writing. His poems have appeared in magazines and anthologies in Europe, South Africa and Zimbabwe. His first collection, *Spirit Brides*, was published by Carcanet Press in 2006. He now divides his time between writing and farming. ■ 'Smoke' from *Spirit Brides* (Carcanet Press, 2006).

INDEX OF POETS